THE RUSSIAN TERRORISTS

The Story of the Narodniki

by

RONALD SETH

Also by Ronald Seth

Baltic Corner: Travel in Estonia
"A Spy Has No Friends"
The Art of Spying
Spies at Work
A New Prose Translation of Ovid's *Art of Love*
The Undaunted: The Story of Resistance in Western Europe
Lion With Blue Wings: The Story of the Glider Pilot Regiment
Secret Servants: The Story of Japanese Espionage
For My Name's Sake: Catholic Resistance to Nazis and Communists
Stalingrad—Point of Return: The Story of the Battle
Two Fleets Surprised: The Battle of Cape Matapan
The Fiercest Battle: The Story of Convoy ONS 5
The Specials: The Story of the Special Constabulary
Anatomy of Spying
Petiot—Victim of Chance
The Day War Broke Out
Operation Barbarossa: The Defence of Moscow
Caporetto—The Scapegoat Battle
Forty Years of Soviet Spying
The Spy Who Wasn't Caught

Fiction

The Patriot
Spy in the Nude

For Children

Operation Retriever
Operation Lama
Operation Ormer
The Spy and the Atom-gun
Rockets on Moon Island
Smoke Without Fire
How Spies Work
How the Resistance Worked
The True Book about The Secret Service
R. G. Menzies—a biography
Montgomery—a biography
Sir Archibald McIndoe—a biography
Trotsky—a biography
Four Greek Fairy Tales

1. Maria Spiridonova in prison. Spiridonova, on her own initiative,
    shot General Luzhenovsky on 16th January 1906, at Borisso-
    glebsk railway station. From 1906 until her death during World
    War II she had only 16 months' freedom, for in 1918 she fell
    foul of the Bolsheviks, who banished her to Siberia.

    Radio Times-Hulton Library

RONALD SETH

THE RUSSIAN TERRORISTS

*The Story of
the Narodniki*

Barrie and Rockliff

London

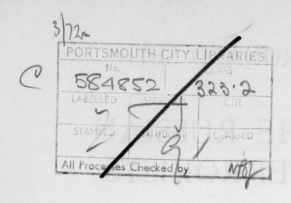
© 1966 by Ronald Seth
First Published 1966 by
Barrie & Rockliff (Barrie Books Ltd)
2 Clement's Inn, London WC2
Printed in Great Britain by
Western Printing Services Ltd, Bristol

With joyous and grateful memories of

SEPHA

who alone made it possible for me
to be a writer, such as I am

Da mi basia mille . . . .

CONTENTS

ILLUSTRATIONS

THE RUSSIAN TERRORISTS

The Story of the Narodniki

Chapter One

PROLOGUE TO REVOLT

On 1st March 1881, Tsar Alexander II of Russia was assassinated.

The event marked the end of one phase in a long struggle between autocrat and independently-spirited people, and the beginning of another. This new phase in its turn was to lead on until the culmination was achieved by the overthrow of the monarchy and the prima facie assumption of power by the people.

We English, compared with some of our European neighbours, find it difficult to apprehend the full meaning of autocracy, the wielding of all and absolute power by one man. For from the beginning of our recorded history whenever our rulers have looked like becoming too powerful, either aristocracy, or people, or both acting in unison, have rapidly and decisively taken steps to prevent the Throne from having the people obedient to its slightest whim. Even that great and wise monarch Elizabeth Tudor quickly discovered that no matter how beloved she might be by her subjects, those subjects soon inflicted sanctions when they believed she was wanting too much of them. They reduced her to a position which her Russian contemporary, Ivan the Terrible, could not understand, as he explained when he wrote to her in 1570, "We had thought that you were sovereign in your state and ruled yourself, and that you saw to your sovereign honour and to the interests of the country. But it turns out that in your land people rule besides you, and not only people but trading peasants. . . ." Similarly, when a King equally wilful

1

but not half so intelligent took it into his head to try conclusions with the people he soon found out that Divine Right was no protection against the will of subjects too proud to bow to petty human demands. The example of Charles I was sufficient to persuade all our future monarchs that they were the servants as well as the protectors of their subjects; and were rewarded by the unstinting protection and service of those subjects.

In other countries of Europe—in France, Spain and Prussia, for example—the people, by early missing the opportunity of controlling their rulers, were destined to be their victims for many years after the English had lopped off the first Charles Stuart's head. Deprived by autocrats of constitutions under which their rights could be safeguarded, the peoples of these nations advanced into modern times as chattels rather than human individuals. One such people were the Russians, and they were among the last to find freedom—even if their definition of this term differs from ours—by achieving a constitution in which a monarchy found no place.

But apart from her slow development in this direction, Russia was, and had always been, a rather special case. No other country, for instance, could boast so vast a territory, nor a people which was in effect an agglomeration of peoples each possessing distinct ambitions and characteristics. The Russian nation was a polyglot collection of ethnic groups which had the potentiality of being powerful if combined into one group, but which separately had practically no strength at all.

It was the intention of all the early rulers to consolidate this potential strength by subjecting the separate states to one overlordship. It took several hundred years to achieve this, for it was not until the second half of the fifteenth century that Ivan III the Great, governing all Russia from Moscow, could describe himself as the unchallenged overlord.

Before Ivan III the struggle was waged by the people to prevent the establishment of an overlordship. After Ivan it was the struggle of the rulers to maintain the overlordship.

Because there was this continuous undercurrent of opposition of people to ruler, the nationhood of Russia, it is suggested, could be protected only by a firm direction from the top. In other words, autocracy was the most effective form of government when the special circumstances obtaining in this part of Europe were taken into account.

It is true, of course, that autocracies elsewhere in Europe had occasionally to contend with popular uprisings, but not all the west European rulers put together were required to deal with the number of such revolts with which the successive tsars were confronted. When this fact is appreciated then, I believe, the repressive form of government which the tsars imposed at least becomes comprehensible.

Nor was it only its ethnic composition and territorial vastness which made Russia a "special case" in Europe. Because of internal upheavals and the attempted encroachments of foreigners, the rulers of Russia had little opportunity for making contact with their neighbours in Europe, and for this reason to other European peoples the Russians were always something of a mystery. Lumped together as Russians they tended to represent in western eyes a coarse, cruel, uncultured people who had nothing to contribute to western civilisation. Their Slav characteristics appeared to make them unstable and their view of the sanctity of human life seemed to reveal them as the most barbarous of barbarians, even in periods when the cruelty of western man to man, in twentieth-century eyes, represented the cardinal difference between our ancestors and our allegedly civilised selves.

The first Russian monarch to appreciate what his country was missing by this virtual isolation was Peter the Great (1672–1725) and he attempted to change it all by making his country a first-class sea-power. His plans bore fruit and from the early part of the eighteenth century Russia was a great power whose support and alliance were sought by leading European nations.

Despite this, however, in the following centuries there still remained a great fundamental difference between the role of the Russian masses and that of the majority of their western counterparts. For, for all his admiration of the Prussian system, Peter had not dared to adopt the Prussian brand of autocratic rule, and as a result the Russian peasant, representing the vast preponderance of the nation, had still to be controlled by a feudal system which had disappeared from western Europe during the Middle Ages.

Though in the latter half of the eighteenth century liberal ideas were already beginning to spark elsewhere in Europe and though Catherine the Great (1762–96), her son Paul I (1796–1801) and her grandson Alexander I (1801–25) all had good intentions towards their millions of serfs, for one reason or another they had to abandon their plans for reform. All this time, however, the ideas and ideals of the French Revolution had slowly been infiltrating Russia to the extent that when Alexander I died unexpectedly in 1825 the army, at least, contained within its ranks a number of elements intent upon forcing reform. But the plotters were such inept conspirators that when their vague plans were made even vaguer by the suddenness with which events overtook them, their attempts at revolt collapsed ignominiously under the firm handling of the new Tsar.

The very fact that the Decembrists, as these revolutionaries became known, could be guilty of plotting against the throne effectively stifled any leanings towards reform that Nicholas I may have had. He introduced a regime so oppressively autocratic and instituted an instrument for the suppression of resistence—the infamous Third Division of the Imperial Chancellery—which was so ruthless in its operation that he succeeded in curbing the activities of would-be revolutionaries. It was his blind refusal to move with the times that led to the emergence of the revolutionary movement which grew later into Nihilism and terrorism.

For by this time changes were taking place all over Europe. The industrial revolution, with all its attendant problems, was getting fully into swing, and the changes in their physical condition put new political ideas into the heads of the masses. Revolutionary movements broke out in various parts of Europe in 1820, 1830 and 1848, with the only constitutionally governed country so far on the European mainland, France, always involved. Behind these movements were the thinkers, the men who were putting into words the groping thoughts of their less articulate fellows, and now and again putting ideas into their heads. It is not an exaggeration to say that throughout the last two-thirds of the nineteenth century Europe was in a continuous state of flux.

It would have been strange indeed if the outer ripples of this movement had not reached Russia, where there were also people capable of assimilating the liberal ideas eddying about Europe. For at this point it must be stressed that the long-standing popular conception of Russia as a barbaric country peopled by coarse uncultured barbarians could not have been wider of the mark.

In the arts Russia has a history of long standing, but it was not until the eighteenth century that Russian writers, musicians and artists began to assume a stature which brought their work into comparable terms with the arts of other European countries. In literature it was a period of experimentation, which also produced Russia's greatest poet to date, Alexander Pushkin and that outstanding writer of prose-works and plays, Nikolai Gogol.

The period covered by *The Terrorists'* story—the middle and second half of the nineteenth century—was particularly rich in writers of all kinds. For the most part, their works were still too local in character to command much interest outside their own country, but three great novelists among them have achieved world fame and a lasting popularity inside and outside Russia—Turgenev, Dostoevsky and Leo Tolstoy; while Anton Chekhov, though belonging to a different generation, won a similar status with his plays.

The visual arts remained within somewhat more nationalistic bounds, though painting produced such world-famous names as Serov and Chagall. Music, on the other hand, which up to the seventeenth century had been represented entirely by settings of the church liturgy and folk-songs, now suddenly burgeoned into a phase of exceptional brilliance which was to last until the Revolution. The great names need only to be mentioned to be recognised the world over—Rubinstein, Tchaikovsky, Mussorgsky, Rimsky-Korsakov, Borodin, Glazunov, Scriabin, Rachmaninov.

It is quite clear that such a culture could not have developed had there not existed an educated layer of society capable not only of producing its exponents but of appreciating its products. It was Peter the Great who, by including education in his great reform programme, gave an impetus to learning that was to prove irresistible. Though in the reigns of his immediate successors the achievements won in this field during Peter's life-time were not sustained, with the accession of Catherine the Great education once again became one of the priorities. By the end of the eighteenth century 315 popular elementary and advanced schools, with 20,000 pupils, were functioning throughout Russia, while by the time of Alexander I's death in 1825 there were six universities, forty-eight state secondary schools and 337 improved state primary schools.

Unfortunately many of the plans of his successor, Nicholas I, proved harmful to the development of education. Between 1833 and 1849 the government attempted "to centralise and standardise education; to limit the individual's schooling to his social background, so that each person would remain in his assigned place in life; to foster the official ideology exclusively; and above all to eliminate every trace or possibility of intellectual opposition or subversion."[1]

Besides attempting to introduce absolute order and regularity into the state system the Ministry of Education extended its control to private schools and even to private tutors. The restrictions, of course, were based on class distinctions. To discourage the lower classes, tuition fees were raised and even primary school pupils wishing to go on to secondary schools had to acquire certificates of leave from the civic authorities of town or village. On the other hand the upper classes were encouraged by special inducements to provide higher education for their children, and many boarding schools were set up specifically for the sons of gentry.

Despite the restrictive nature of education during this period Russian scholarship made considerable strides, and the contributions of leading scholars in their various fields created a kind of *quid pro quo* for the influence of west European culture on the cultural development of Russia. Peter the Great and his more enlightened successors by their deliberate attraction of western ideas and systems, created a doorway through which the ideologies developing in the social and political thought of the west could penetrate and influence the political and social thinkers who were inevitably beginning to emerge in Russia.

Nicholas's reactions to the Decembrists' attempted revolt, while curbing the activities of would-be revolutionaries, had the effect of forcing the development of the philosophies of the socialist revolution which was to overtake Russia as inevitably as it was to overtake western Europe. So while the twenty years following the Decembrist uprising saw only individual acts of revolt and the machinations of small groups of courageous men and women who could only hope to lay the fuse for future actions, they were not sterile years.

[1] N. Riasanovsky, A *History of Russia* (New York: Oxford University Press, 1963), pp. 387–8.

Chapter Two

TWO BASIC RUSSIAN PECULIARITIES

For a proper understanding of the background against which so many of the events of the following narrative took place and to appreciate the motives of those who participated in these events, it is useful to have a broad idea of two characteristics of Russian society which differed in their nature from the same characteristics found elsewhere.

Even from the very brief account of Russian historical development in the preceding chapter, it will have become plain that compared with western Europe, Russia was backward in social and educational development; and the same is true of her economic development. By the end of the eighteenth century the economy of western Europe was already firmly based on capitalist principles which had evolved over the intervening centuries between the abolition of the feudal system in the Middle Ages and the initiation of the industrial revolution.

Because the industrial revolution came to a western Europe already provided with a capitalist form of economy, the future development of industry received a tremendous momentum which had the effect of entrenching this capitalist form of economy so firmly that today, more than a century later, it is still the main-spring of west European economic life. Russia on the other hand, when she eventually became caught up in the industrial revolution, had not evolved a capitalist economy and this was to have consequences for the industrial and economic development of the country not found elsewhere.

7

The main difference between Russia and the countries of western Europe at the beginning of the nineteenth century was that whereas they had already developed a free society, she was still a feudal state. Her population was basically peasant, and the vast majority of the peasants were actually slaves. Thus while western Europe was by now provided with the nucleus of a proletariat capable of rapid expansion, Russia possessed no such nucleus. As will become apparent later, the emancipation of the serfs was, in fact, not quite the outcome of moral pressures alone that on the face of it it appears to be; it was linked with the necessity to produce a proletariat almost at the drop of a hat.

As Theodore Dan points out in his *Origins of Bolshevism*, when capitalist industry came to Russia about the middle of the nineteenth century "it was 'implanted' in a ready and indeed for the times a quite perfect form—in the sense of the technical equipment of the enterprises as well as their size. In this respect the development of heavy industry in Russia bore some resemblance to its development in colonial and semi-colonial countries."[1]

Foreigners played a large part in this "implantation". "A foreign director speaking broken Russian—an Englishman, Belgian, German, more rarely a Frenchman—was a commonplace figure in those businesses formed entirely with Russian funds."[2] On the other hand, the foreigners could not supply the workers and the majority of these could only be drawn from the peasantry.

This sudden "implantation" of heavy industry in Russia also gave a tremendous impetus to the development of a bourgeoisie. This, too, was drawn from the peasantry, though not from the serfs. Some peasants had been able to acquire modest wealth and had used it to educate their sons. Thus, says Dan, when this big bourgeoisie did emerge, it was "in no way inferior culturally to its older European brethren."

Such is man's nature that when he raises himself socially he tends to cut himself off from his origins. This happened to the Russian bourgeoisie who from the start were culturally separated from the peasant masses, and, because of their interests, were to

---

[1] Theodore Dan (trans. Joel Carmichael), *The Origins of Bolshevism* (Secker and Warburg, 1964), p. 15.

[2] Dan, *op. cit.*, p. 15.

become separated politically as well. They were equally out of contact with the broad urban masses.

The same was not true, however, of the proletariat and peasantry. Here there were contacts brought about chiefly by the fact that the fiscal laws required a peasant who had emigrated to the towns to contribute to the taxes of his former village for a number of years after his emigration. This, too, had its consequences politically. The peasants, who had not been fairly treated in the matter of the allotment of land at the time of the emancipation, clung tenaciously to a dream in which they would expropriate all the land to themselves. Since "total reapportionment", that is, expropriation, was a long time coming and the dream persisted, the peasants had no understanding of the bourgeois principles of the "sacredness of private property", and since these same principles were rejected by exploited industrial workers, it was natural that the peasants should feel they had a political bond with the proletariat's revolutionary socialist tendencies.

The aristocracy was still a land-owning class, though becoming progressively impoverished. Since the emancipation it had feared a new peasant uprising in the furtherance of the peasants' dream of total reapportionment of the land, and it therefore supported all the autocrat's measure to keep the peasant masses under control. The bourgeoisie, on the other hand, had developed liberal-democratic ideas which isolated it from the tsar and the aristocracy, and as the same ideas cut it off from the support of the masses, it was totally isolated, and thus politically weak.

"The result of the socio-political feebleness of the bourgeoisie," Dan comments, "was that the liquidation of the autocracy was postponed until the working-class had become strong enough to turn into an independent force."[1] There was, in effect, no strong political movement in Russia based on liberal principles and it was for this reason that the political field lay wide open for socialism.

In Europe during this period of Russian bourgeois development, says Dan, socialism "had become a massive political force in practice, and the sole revolutionary doctrine in theory."[2] This became known in Russia as other ideas and influences filtered in, and served as a stimulus to Russian socialism. As a result, says

[1] Dan, *op. cit.*, p. 21.
[2] Dan, *op. cit.*, p. 23.

Dan, in Russia all democratic thought was a monopoly of the "radical socialist intelligentsia". And here we come to the second peculiarity.

"Intelligentsia" is a Russian word which is incapable of precise translation in any other language, for the English word "intellectual", and its equivalents in other tongues, does not, in its definition, mean a special social group having a common political unity—as does "intelligentsia"—but rather educated people who engage principally in work of an intellectual nature, or get their means of livelihood from such work.

Generally speaking all ideas are propagated and disseminated by educated people. Since the upper classes have the best means for educating themselves and subsequently the leisure to devote themselves to thought, between the producers of ideas and the upper classes there is usually a strong alliance. Where members of the lower classes have had access to higher education and have produced thinkers, these thinkers have been assimilated into the intellectual and ruling classes.

This social feature—the close relation of the intellectuals with the aristocracy—was also found in Russia up to the time when there occurred a crisis in aristocratic culture, which coincided with the crisis represented by the emergence of the social conscience in the matter of serfdom. One might have expected that with the establishment of a bourgeoisie in Russia, this bourgeoisie would more naturally have attracted to it the educated, politically thinking elements in the upper classes on account of the narrower social gap between them. But it did not. Instead, these elements attached themselves to the lower classes.

One would have thought, bearing in mind the democratic ideas which they were pioneering, that these upper class thinkers would have been welcomed by the masses whose lot they were hoping to improve. But again this did not happen. Instead, they found themselves isolated, for the lower classes could not rid their minds of the conception of them as "masters". In their isolation they formed a separate and special group—the intelligentsia. To underline the "special" character of the intelligentsia as a group, the thinkers of aristocratic origins were soon joined by educated thinkers from the lower classes, the so-called *raznochintsy* (plebeians), who quickly dominated the group.

The first of the *raznochintsy* was Vissarion Belinsky. Belinsky had no aristocratic origins; he was the son of a naval doctor, and had known poverty from early childhood. He had been a student at Moscow university, from which he emerged as a formidable literary critic, revealing himself in his articles in *Fatherland Notes*, and after 1846 in *The Contemporary*, as a liberal-democrat with a burning concern for man's well-being here and now. Within a short time this young man, born, as he put it, "to howl like a jackal", had become the champion of the Westernist school of political philosophy, whose adherents were committed to the proposition that Russia's progress must follow the general lines of European development.

In outlook and thought the Westernists were opposed by the Slavophils, a group with upper class origins and thinking to match. They believed that Russian culture was distinct from European culture and much superior to it; and that it was therefore destined to supercede it. For this reason, Russia ought to refuse to borrow from other nations, but develop her own resources and thereby achieve her own and the world's salvation.

From the beginning the Slavophils were the advocates of civil liberties, and thus supporters of emancipation for the serfs. Their ideal Russian was the peasant, because while the privileged classes had adopted foreign ideas in practically every field of social and cultural life, the peasants, by their strong adherence to the Orthodox religion, had kept inviolate the ideal of brotherhood and community, in contrast with the individualism that had overtaken western Europe.

The Marquis de Custine said of the Russia of the late 1830s that she "is a cauldron of boiling water, tightly closed and placed on a fire which is becoming hotter and hotter; I fear an explosion." Though his fear was exaggerated as regards the period about which he wrote, it was true that ideas were beginning to foment, especially in Moscow. This process necessarily meant an exchange of views via the spoken and written word, and the intellectual life of Moscow in the late 1830s and early 1840s revolved round the arguments and counter-arguments of the Slavophils and Westernists. In this war Vissarion Belinsky played a major role.

Though at the end of his short life—he died in 1848 aged 37— he had become liberal-democratic in outlook, Belinsky had started out as a conservative Hegelian. His repudiation of these doctrines arose from the development of his personal philosophy, the essence of which was a belief in the dignity of every human being; a belief which presupposed perfect freedom and equality for all under a rule of reason. In a letter to Gogol only a few months before he died he set out his views of Russia's greatest needs. If Russia were to achieve salvation, he declared, she must have laws based on commonsense and justice; the people must press immediately for the abolition of corporal punishment, the strict enforcement of existing laws, and the emancipation of the serfs.

This was, in effect, the essence of liberal Westernism at the time. But as time passed, ideas became qualified, then modified and eventually transformed. This was bound to happen in the atmosphere in which these men thought and pondered, when the circle of intelligentsia was continually acquiring new blood, when the basic principles of socialism were still to be hammered out. Had Belinsky lived a few years more he would undoubtedly have become one of the pillars of revolution. As it was, this role was to fall to others. In the initial stages of the development of theoretical socialism three contemporaries of Belinsky were to have an outstanding influence—Alexander Herzen, his friend Nikolai Ogarev, and Mikhail Bakunin.

Chapter Three

SOCIALISM REARS ITS HEAD

Alexander Herzen, born in 1812 to a wealthy nobleman and a German girl of sixteen, himself maintained that though he was only thirteen when the Decembrists revolted, the account of the rising, the trial of the leaders and the horrors of their execution were the main-spring of the political philosophy towards which he had begun to fumble while still in his teens. With his friend Ogarev he entered Moscow university in 1829 and there studied the natural sciences. Among the students the two young men found many who were beginning to think along the same lines as themselves, and within a very short time Herzen had become the acknowledged leader of a group of teenage youths who spent the greater part of their leisure discussing the socialist ideas now infiltrating from western Europe.

After Herzen left the university in 1833, the group continued to meet and discuss, until presently the attention of the authorities was drawn to it and a number of its members were arrested. The subsequent investigations led the authorities to Herzen and Ogarev, and they were also seized and deported to inaccessible places in the provinces.

This exile lasted until 1842. On his recall Herzen settled in Moscow where he quickly achieved an eminence among the liberal thinkers there, though his own philosophy of socialism which was later to be known historically as Populism, was still in a state of flux. He soon found the atmosphere of Moscow too restrictive, however, and in 1847 he decided to go abroad with his wife and children. By this time his father had died and bequeathed him a considerable fortune, sufficient not only to keep him and his family in comfort for the rest of their lives, but also to allow him to embark on those activities through which he could disseminate his ideas, the chief being the publication and distribution of pamphlets and newspapers.

With the passing of time and arising out of his contact with the West he was by 1849 able to define for himself the fundamentals of Russian Populism—a distrust of all democracy, a belief in the development of socialism in Russia, the need for revolutionaries dedicated to the people, and confidence in the socialist potentials of the *Obschchina*;[1] and from these principles he was never to deviate from now on. They were the ideals he bequeathed to the generations to come.

Mikhail Bakunin, born two years after Herzen, in 1814, also came of a wealthy aristocratic family. But whereas Herzen's family had taken no part in the Decembrist uprising, Bakunin's father, a Guards officer, had participated in it, had escaped the aftermath and had emerged a timid aristocrat incapable of imparting any inspiration to his son. For while he was opposed to despotism, he was content with the other aspects of Russian life, including serfdom, and was convinced that in the light of his past personal experiences, it was most undesirable to become involved in clandestine group activities and plots. He therefore kept himself to himself, managing his vast estates near Tver and trying to become the Little Father to his serfs.

It was in this sheltered atmosphere and cautious environment that the boy Mikhail passed his early years. As the oldest son of a family with military traditions he eventually entered the St Petersburg officer cadet school. But it soon became apparent that he could not adapt himself to the life and he presently determined to escape from it.

He did not find the means of escape, however, until he was twenty-two. He had formed a friendship with Stankevich, a typical Russian idealist of the 1830s, who had a superb natural gift for teaching himself philosophy. Under Stankevich's guidance Bakunin read Kant, Fichte and Hegel, and was particularly drawn to the latter.

---

[1] A peculiarly Russian institution, the *Obshchina* was a rural commune which had joint responsibility for the collection of the poll-tax and the fulfilment of the serf's obligations to his master.

For a long time he had been wanting to visit Germany, but had not the financial means to do so. But in 1842 Herzen came to his practical aid and within a short period, almost at one bound as it were, he discarded his purely theoretical political philosophy for practical action, condemning those who would compromise with revolution. From now on his ideal was to be the active revolutionary and though he did not take part in any conspiracy to raise a popular revolt, this was to be his ideal throughout his life.

His activities abroad eventually brought him to the notice of the Russian authorities who made repeated requests for his extradition. He avoided this by keeping continuously on the move, until in May 1849 he was arrested in Dresden and handed over to St Petersburg. After two years' confinement in the Peter-Paul fortress, he was deported to Siberia, and ten years were to elapse before he found the means to escape, and eventually joined Herzen and Ogarev in London.

Nikolai Ogarev had joined his friend of a life-time in London in 1856, when Herzen decided to launch one of the most famous and certainly influential Russian revolutionary organs *Kolokol*, *The Bell*. When the two friends were joined by Bakunin it was not long before the trio were generally recognised as the three giants of the revolutionary movement. With the exception of Bakunin, whose attachment to Anarchism alienated many former supporters, they remained a dominant influence on the revolutionary scene until Herzen's death in January 1870. Though they did not see their aims achieved during their life-time, the legacy of their thought was an inspiration to the revolutionaries of the future, the men who were to succeed where they had failed though not always with the aims they had advocated, men like Lenin and Trotsky, Martov and Plekhanov.

The twenty years and more after the December uprising of 1825 were above all else a period of reading and discussing, of formulating theories, provoking thought and presenting tentative aims; a period, too, in which propaganda was more highly regarded as a weapon than the sword by those who had the ultimate transformation of Russia at heart. By and large intercourse between thinker and thinker ranged freely, but there did come into existence a few exclusive groups which assumed the character of clandestine societies with subversion as their aim, though not necessarily to be promoted by the stirring up of open revolt. More often than not the life of such groups was short, for, untrained and inexperienced in the practical behaviour of secret activity, no matter how innocuous, they quickly came to the notice of the police who had no difficulty in wiping them out by arrest and imprisonment or exile.

Ever since he had come to the throne to the accompaniment of the December uprising, Nicholas I had shown himself to be a ruthless sadist. It is said that on the day he assumed power he said to his younger brother, "The revolution is at Russia's gates, but I swear to you that it shall never enter so long as there is breath in my body." Whether this is apocryphal or not, he certainly acted as though he had said it and meant it. The twenty years of talking and thinking provided him with a period of quiet in which he could have carried out reforms had he been so minded; but he chose not to, and instead imposed tyranny upon his people that was outside the experience of even the centenarians then living.

One of the instruments he fashioned to keep the revolution at bay was the Third Division of His Imperial Majesty's Chancellery, whose function was "to guard the foundations of the Russian state." Its description was merely a high-faluting euphemism for a political police with all the built-in characteristics for excess. The Third Division was also a special force, utterly divorced from all other instruments of state administration, with an unlimited jurisdiction and answerable to no one but the Tsar. Akin to similar French institutions which flourished under Richelieu, Louis XVI and Napoleon Bonaparte, it was to be the prototype for the Security Forces of the Soviet Union—no matter what those forces were called: Cheka, GPU, NKVD—and for those other infamous instruments of modern terror, the Gestapo and the OVRA.

Having established this barrier between himself and a violent end—he hoped—he instituted a regime of extraordinary severity even for Russia. A strict censorship of all newspapers, journals and books was maintained; the acquisition of knowledge was rigidly supervised, as has already been mentioned; and with a tightening of control of the Church a new wave of persecution of the dissenters from the Orthodox faith was embarked upon. And over and above and around the minds of all citizens hovered the presence of the secret police, in their plain clothes listening, looking, prying and provoking, ready to pounce long before any deviation from strict conformism became clearly visible.

But like many another tyrant detested by his subjects, Nicholas often found it difficult to control his fear, and when he was afraid he allowed himself to be betrayed into excesses of one kind or another. Thrown into a panic by the revolutions of 1848 he gave orders that the Russian proletariat were to be prevented from expanding by forbidding the erection of new factories; he clamped down still further on schools and universities; he urged the censorship to greater vigilance; and he abandoned for good and all any thoughts he might at one time or another have entertained regarding the alleviation of the serf's intolerable lot. For nearly thirty years he suppressed and oppressed ninety-five per cent of his subjects; for nearly thirty years he prevented all progress to the exclusion of reason, personal liberty and brotherly love. No wonder that Herzen and his friends celebrated the news of his death in champagne immediately it became known in London on 4th March 1855.

Chapter Four

ENTER THE LIBERATOR

Alexander II mounted the throne of his father with almost an embarrassment of opportunity. In the back-lash of his predecessor's oppression it was within his power to save the monarchy, if not for all time, at least for another hundred years. Had he been prepared to emancipate the serfs into conditions that would have made it possible for them to provide themselves with a reasonable subsistence; had he been prepared to sweep aside all the autocratic controls so beloved by his father; and had he been prepared to grant a constitution; he would have had the support of the great mass of the people, the weight of which would have been quite enough to make it possible for him to overcome the intransigent enemies of reform, the reactionary privileged classes.

Alexander was misunderstood by his contemporaries and has been widely misunderstood ever since. He was thirty-seven when he came to the throne and from boyhood had been deeply attached to his father. As a young man he had been provided with a tutor, a famous poet and translator, Vasilyi Zhukovsky, an admirer of the German romantic school, who, says Sir Bernard Pares, "was by instinct and temperament conservative, and a supporter of autocracy." Zhukovsky's task as imperial tutor, as he saw it, was to produce a more rounded individual than Alexander would have undoubtedly been had he undergone only the military-type education which his father obsessively admired.

With the Empress's encouragement he tried to promote in the young Grand Duke some appreciation of more intellectual attainments. By nature, however, Alexander shared Nicholas's military interests, and this formed the basis for the attachment which developed between father and son from the latter's early childhood. In later life the admiration Alexander had for his father's political views made him loyally support the autocratic regime which Nicholas imposed so ruthlessly on his subjects.

In some ways, indeed, Alexander was more extremist than Nicholas. The latter, determined not to repeat the mistake that his own father had committed, had Alexander introduced to the intricacies of government and to political affairs at an early age. As part of this aspect of his education the Tsarevich sat on the repressive committee set up under the chairmanship of Buturlin to inspect and control the censorship; he was a more fervent supporter of the rights of the gentry even than Nicholas; and he was definitely opposed to the so-called inventories of Minister of the Interior Bibikov by which the obligations of the peasants in the south-west were defined.

On the other hand, the teaching of Zhukovsky was not entirely without effect. It made it possible for the future tsar to recognise the situation in which Russia found herself when the ignominious failure of the Russian armies in the Crimean War, which Nicholas had deliberately provoked, brought about the collapse of Russia's position in Europe, which had been inaugurated by Peter the Great, built up by Catherine II and enhanced by Alexander I; a situation aggravated still further by Nicholas's death which fatally undermined the system he had built up for internal government. The logic of this situation demanded reforms, and, conservative though he was, Alexander realised that reforms there must be. He also saw that the *sine qua non* for the success of any reforms must be the emancipation of the serfs. Having accepted this he thenceforward devoted his energies to bringing it about, and he showed himself fully prepared to face up to all sacrifices which the process of reform involved.

His first concern was to end the humiliating Crimean War. Before his death Nicholas had already been negotiating a peace, and Alexander now began to press for the negotiations to be concluded. The peace was almost as humiliating for Russia as the war had been, but Alexander declared it was worth the terms which had to be conceded to gain it.

Even before the peace of Paris was signed on 30th March 1856, Alexander had begun to demonstrate the sincerity of his intentions to carry out reforms by lifting a number of Nicholas's more repressive restrictions, such as the ban on travel abroad and the limitations placed on the numbers of university students. Reactions to these concessions were formidable, and were encouraged by the easing of the censorship to the extent of allowing criticism to be made by the Press which at once used its new liberty to unveil and attack the incredible incompetence of the whole administrational system. Now and again the censorship acted against the more outrageous attacks, but even so its operations were very restricted, and as a result an atmosphere entirely novel to Russia began, with an amazing rapidity, to envelop the entire Russian scene. In this atmosphere public opinion began to emerge and develop, providing, in the view of many, the most important result of the first changes. Almost as important was the advantage that was taken of the lifting of the restrictions on university entrance, for this was to produce a new genus of students who saw an active intervention in politics as important a part of their student role as the acquisition of learning.

Important though these acts and their concomitant results were—and Pares says they "were enough to start a new epoch" —it was equally clear that fundamental reforms could not be carried out until the greatest reform of all, the emancipation of the serfs, had been realised. What made this so urgent was the irrefutable fact startlingly disclosed by the Crimean War: that the serfs represented an economic force without which the country of the new epoch could not exist. As Riasanovsky[1] puts it: "With the growth of a money economy and competition for markets, the deficiencies of low-grade serf-labour became ever more obvious."

But apart from the economic reason, there were others which made the rapid resolution of the problem equally demanding. Forced by the oppressive life in which the system involved them, to assert their instinctive manhood the serfs began to react against their masters with ever increasing frequency and violence. A Russian historian, Vasilyi Semevsky, who died in 1916, using official records as a basis, claimed that there were 550 peasant uprisings in the sixty years of the nineteenth century prior to

[1] Riasanovsky, *op. cit.*, p. 409.

liberation; while a later Soviet historian, Inna Ignatovich, insists, upon equally valid records, that there were in fact 1,467 such rebellions in this period. And in addition to these uprisings serfs deserted their masters in hundreds and thousands, sometimes in great mass movements, when rumours circulated that freedom could be found "somewhere in the Caucasus."

Besides all these practical considerations there was also a constantly growing ethically based desire for emancipation. This desire had its roots in the development of education and culture and expanded proportionately with the speed of this development. Pushkin and Turgenev exerted a particularly great influence through their writings which portrayed the serf as a human being not inferior to any of his fellow-countrymen.

On the other hand, the revelation made by the Crimean War that Russia was an economically and technologically backward country undoubtedly provided the strongest motive for the emancipation of the serfs. For since these weaknesses could only be removed by the creation of a proletariat, the potential for such a proletariat had to be provided from the only available source— the serfs. This is, of course, taking the long-term view.

Though the majority of the landlords were experiencing considerable hardship in maintaining their serfs, and though, except for a few die-hards, they were prepared to accept emancipation in principle, they were not prepared to take any initiative. This was not a wholly unnatural attitude when one considers that for the most part their serfs represented a large part of their wealth, and they were determined that emancipation should be granted only on terms most advantageous to themselves. These terms they believed they would achieve if the government showed its hand first.

Alexander was quite prepared to do this, and made the initial move at his coronation a little less than a year after his accession. He stated his intention quite clearly by telling the landlords that it would be better to begin to abolish serfdom from above than to wait until it began to abolish itself from below. But the landlords wanted more than this, and they got it when a *ukase* was presently published declaring that emancipation *with land* was the official policy.

The publication of the *ukase* was hailed by the radicals and liberals with great enthusiasm. "Thou hast conquered, O Galilean!" Herzen told Alexander in *Kolokol*. But even so the gentry were in no hurry to make a move until at last Alexander realised that if anything were to be accomplished he himself must take a definite initiative, though he found this distasteful. However, on 20th November 1857 he called on the landowners of the north-western provinces to set up committees to discuss the terms for emancipation which had been drawn up by the administration at the Tsar's command. These committees, together with a Main Committee of nine permanent members representing the administration, and an Editing Committee, were established early in the following year.

The work of the committees went forward very slowly, however, and not without reason, for the subject was a complex one. The landlords of the rich fertile south naturally wished to keep as much of their land as possible and preferred a financial indemnity to be paid to the emancipated serfs. Those of the poorer north, on the other hand, who looked upon serf-labour as their main asset, were prepared to part with land, but insisted that they must receive a high financial indemnity for the loss of serf-labour.

After twenty months the committees had still not reached a decision and eventually Alexander decided to force the pace. By the autumn of 1860 the drafting committee was able to forward a scheme to the Main Committee. The chairman of the latter being ill, Alexander replaced him with his liberal-minded brother Constantine, and under Constantine's guidance the Main Committee passed this scheme only very slightly amended to the Council of State. Since a high proportion of the members of the Council were strongly conservative and could be expected to draw out their deliberations, once again Alexander intervened and, fixing a time-limit, ordered an early decision, telling the Council, "This I desire, I demand, I command." Under this stimulus the Council produced an emancipating *ukase* which was signed on 3rd March 1861, read in the Senate on 14th March, and promulgated on 17th March.

The emancipating *ukase* gave their personal liberty to twenty-three million serfs, the property of about one hundred thousand landowners. It earned for Alexander the courtesy-title of The Liberator and was a mile-stone in Russian history despite its aftermath. It ought to have marked the dawn of a new era in the life of a great nation, one of unlimited promise. What it did actually mark will presently emerge; and this grew out of the arrangements which were made to solve one of the two important questions that always had to be considered whenever the problem was discussed: How were the freed men to support themselves and their families?

What the *ukase* granted to the twenty-three million serfs was the freedom of their persons, while the former serf-owner received no compensation for his loss of rights in this respect. The latter, however, did keep possession of the land that he was required to grant to each freed man—a plot for house and garden, a plot of arable land and a strip of pasture, with which went free access to limited supplies of wood. These, with his freedom, the former serf was obliged to accept and had to agree to keep them in his possession for nine years, during which time he was to redeem the value of the land by services or money. On the face of it the arrangement appeared reasonable enough; but whether deliberately introduced or not, several snags soon appeared in the scheme, all of which operated to the detriment of the new peasant.

The change-over was not to be made at the scratching of a nib across parchment. Two years were allotted from the promulgation of the *ukase* during which peasant and landowner were to agree among themselves upon the size of the plots the former was to be granted and the rent the latter was to be paid. If they failed to agree in that time they were both required to accept the conditions of somewhat vague regulations drawn up by the government. The effect of these conditions would, in the long run, render the freed man indefinitely obligated to his former master, instead of only temporarily. In certain circumstances the peasant might put an end to his "obligations" by buying his allotments outright and should he decide to do so, the government undertook to finance the transaction and get its money back in annual instalments from the peasants.

Not in every case was the transaction to be carried out between master and individual serf. In those places where an ancient *obshchina* existed the agreement was to be made with the community, and the members of the community were to be collectively responsible for meeting all obligations to former master and to the state. All the peasants were granted a measure of self-government, but as the institutions of this government were still to be in the control of the landowners the peasants could claim with some justification that this was not freedom.

It did not coincide with their conception of freedom which was, that ownership of the land worked by them and their fore-fathers for themselves and their masters, was inseparable from personal liberty.

As a result in many cases the peasants refused to accept the reforms. They refused to continue their services, or to make pay-ments to their former masters, and would not put their marks on the agreements with the landlords.

The Tsar and government could have avoided much of the trouble that arose if only they had taken steps to have the plans explained to the peasants in simple terms by emissaries qualified to do so. But they did not. So wild rumours began to circulate, one of which maintained that Alexander had been wounded by assassins hired by the landowners, and had had to go into hiding. Attempts by local literates to interpret the emancipation laws also added to the confusion, and as a result of some of these efforts to unravel the legal intricacies it became a widespread belief that the true freedom would be proclaimed at the end of the two-year initial period and that anyone who accepted the terms *now* would be deprived of freedom *then*.

If the government had made no arrangements to explain the law, they were not slow in making arrangements for dealing with trouble. Troops were rushed to trouble-areas where their presence merely exacerbated the situation; flogging was the most usual form of punishment, but not a few of the trouble-makers were deported to the Siberian wastes.

The spring and summer of 1861 were marked by disorders in the villages, violence breaking out in twelve hundred estates; and when by the autumn the peasants had calmed down, equally serious outbreaks occurred among the students of the univer-sities. These had their roots in that other reform which Alexan-der had introduced when he lifted restrictions on entry to the universities. The result of this reasonable measure had been a mad rush of young people to the universities, particularly those of Moscow and St Petersburg. Unfortunately many were ill-provided with means and were reduced to the starvation line, while typhus and tuberculosis added to the misery and took their toll of life.

The students had quickly developed a strong *esprit de corps* and had taken many liberties to themselves. If they disapproved of a professor, a lecturer or a disciplinary rule, they let their displeasure be known in no uncertain terms, and they were constantly involved in clashes with the authorities. The troubles reached such a pitch by the middle of 1861 that Alexander decided to close some of the universities and at others greatly to reduce the number of State scholarships available; measures which automatically reduced the number of students, while a newly-appointed Minister of Education introduced even stricter curbs.

At the very outset of the winter semester in St Petersburg a pamphlet was distributed calling upon the students to resist these measures. A protest meeting was held and on the following day all the students in a body demanded to see the Rector, and when he refused threatened to put their threats into force. Police and troops then swung into action, with the result that several hundred young men soon found themselves, bruised and sore, behind bars, where they remained for two months. The majority were then released, but some were exiled to the provinces and the university was closed for two years. The same pattern was followed in Moscow. When the two universities opened again in the autumn of 1863 the students found they had gained exactly nothing.

All in all, the year 1861 had been a year of disappointment to those progressives who had believed that it would mark the beginning of The Great Transformation. The peasants had not achieved true freedom, and had failed to produce a revolution; while on the other hand the failure of his emancipatory plans and the consequent outbreaks of peasant and student upheavals had put into Alexander's mind doubts as to the wisdom of introducing further reforms. Nevertheless he could not bring himself entirely to abandon his role of Liberator, and over the next decade and a half he promulgated a series of measures which taken in the context of Russia's historical development were certainly not unimportant. There was for instance the institution of the *Zemstva* (local government councils) in 1864, and a measure designed to liberalise and expand education, while two considerable reforms were legislated for in 1870 and 1874 respectively—Municipal Self-Government and Army Reform.

These two, however, were to be the last great reforms of Alexander's reign, for the events of the previous decade had by slow degrees set in motion a stream of reaction whose impetus was eventually to prove unstemmable. First there had been a great fire of mysterious origin at the Apraksin Dvor in St Petersburg which was ascribed—without a shred of evidence—to revolutionaries. This was closely followed by an attempt to assassinate the Grand Duke Constantine, now Regent of Poland, when in January 1863 the Poles rose in ill-fated revolt.

This revolt was a particular blow to the revolutionary movement. Based more on the enthusiasm of individuals than on concerted commonsense planning, it failed from the very first moment of manifestation. It had been hoped by the plotters that the Russian garrison would join them at the first signal; instead the garrison remained firmly loyal to the Tsar. There had also been some wishful thinking that their example would fire a simultaneous peasant revolt in Russia itself, but there was not even a rebellious grumble. Briefly, the Polish revolt consisted of spasmodic outbreaks of guerilla fighting in widely separated parts of the country, and even these had petered out by May.

The attempted uprising, however, can be designated as the second important factor—the first being the failure of his emancipation measures—in the conversion of Alexander into his final role of unbending autocrat. Angered by the ingratitude of his Polish subjects Alexander was quite prepared to let the staunchest reactionaries at his Court take charge of punishment, and the Third Division moved into action with devastating results. Attempts were made to use the atrocities committed in Poland to stir up popular sympathy in Russia, but there had never been, and now was not, any deep-rooted fellow-feeling between Polish and Russian peasant, and the latter refused to be moved by grievances they considered purely Polish.

The Polish uprising, however, was not entirely without repercussions within Russia; and one series of violent outbreaks known since as the Kazan Conspiracy, and its aftermath, were to play a dominant role in revolutionary development.

Kazan is a provincial city some five hundred miles *east* of Moscow. For many years previous to 1863 Kazan university had been the scene of student disturbances more violent than any which occurred or were to occur anywhere else in Russia. The demonstrations in these early days were superficially directed against the administration of the university, from which, later, it was to be but a short step to resistance to the administration of the state.

The disorders which broke out in St Petersburg in 1861 had

their repercussions in Kazan, for among the prominent St Petersburg leaders was a group of students who had formed themselves into a compact society known as the Circle of Kazan Students, which had allied itself to the revolutionary movement *Land and Liberty*. (This *Land and Liberty* should not be confused with the *Zemlya i Volya* which achieved great fame in the late 1870s.)

It was to the parent organisation of *Land and Liberty*, the St Petersburg branch, to which the leaders of the Polish insurrection applied for help, and when *Land and Liberty* rejected the Polish requests, it was not surprising that the Warsaw National Committee should turn to the people who had preeminently demonstrated their willingness to act, and to the place where these people were for the most part concentrated, namely, Kazan university.

The Kazan students agreed to co-operate, but the consequent planning was so preposterously handled that before long the authorities were in full possession of what was being plotted. Under the direction of Third Division agents specially sent to Kazan by the Tsar, all the ringleaders of the Conspiracy were arrested, and a Commission of Inquiry was set up to investigate the whole affair. As a result of the Commission's findings, all the accused were found guilty, and five death sentences, and long terms of imprisonment and hard labour were imposed. The death sentences were carried out with particular brutality and marked the resurgence of terror as a weapon of repression.

The Kazan failure had far-reaching results. *Land and Liberty* ceased to exist; the London veterans, Herzen, Ogarev and Bakunin, lost most of their followers; the circulation of the famous *Kolokol* dropped from 2,500 to 500, and in a year or two disappeared altogether. For a time it looked as if all clandestine groups of whatever nature had also ceased to exist; for the next three years the Tsar and his government enjoyed comparative peace.

But the revolutionary spirit was merely quiescent, and very soon there emerged a group which was to produce one or two of the more bizarre figures of revolutionary history, whose doctrines were to introduce a new factor into the struggle for freedom, and who, for a brief moment, were to burst, like one of the bombs whose use they advocated, upon the Russian scene.

The first of these extraordinary young men was Nikolai

Ishutin. Now in his middle twenties, he was the son of a merchant and of a mother who came of a noble family. When he
was two both his parents died, and he was brought up until he
was eleven by relatives of his father. In 1863 he entered Moscow
university where he quickly gathered round him a group of
young men upon whom he was soon exerting a quite extraordinary influence.

Ishutin was not an intellectual, and though his scorn of learning might have been a pose, he had not been long at the university when he decided to give up his studies in order to devote all
his time to The Cause. Many of his followers imitated their
leader in this.

The group quickly became strong and active, and determined,
as they phrased it, "to go to the people", they sacrificed not only
careers but all personal belongings. As a practical step in making
contact with the people they set up co-operative and friendly
societies for the workmen, artisans and students.

All Ishutin's efforts and multifarious schemes were directed
to one sole end—the creation of a revolutionary force. To achieve
this he tossed all scruples out of the window, and introduced a
new approach to the means by which the end might be attained
—naked terrorism.

The group believed that a peasant revolution would take place
within five years. Their conception of this revolution differed
from any previous conception of popular revolt; it was to be
radical and "economic" and nothing must be allowed to prevent
its happening.

The ruthless extremist policy preached by Ishutin did not
appeal to all the members of the group, and as a result, between
1865 and 1866, there came into being a smaller group-within-
the-group who were prepared to transmute into activity the
extreme ideas of their leader. Named by Ishutin The Organisation, this smaller group consisted mostly of extremely poor
young men, many of whom were the sons of country priests
whose *modus vivendi* differed little from that of the peasants.
A few came from peasant families.

Even this small and select band, however, did not entirely
respond to all the aims of its founder. Extremist propaganda and
agitation, yes—but not out and out terrorism; and this last was
dear to Ishutin's heart. So within The Organisation there also
developed another group, a secret cell, even more select, com-

posed of students who lived together "in common". They gave themselves the name *Hell*.

The existence of *Hell* was to be kept secret even from the members of The Organisation. Dedicated to terrorism they decided at the outset not to embark on their special activities until they had increased their membership to thirty. While they were waiting for this to happen, they were to gain membership of other secret societies and take over control of them. If anyone made a mistake, he was to pay for it with his life.

The objects of their terrorism were to be the particularly hated members of the government and nobility, with the Tsar as the target-in-chief. The assassins would draw lots to decide who should carry out a particular assignment. The successful man was immediately to cease all contact with the other members of *Hell* and adopt a way of life that would make all think that the last thing he was was a revolutionary. To achieve this he was to become a drunkard, to consort only with the most doubtful characters, and even to act the informer. After the revolution *Hell* was to continue its functions, liquidating leaders who might appear dangerous, and secretly directing the political elements taking part in the struggle.

In order to impress his select followers with an even greater sense of self-importance—probably hoping to bind them to him more closely thereby—Ishutin gave it out that *Hell* was only one small section of a European Revolutionary Committee whose aim was to kill all crowned rulers wherever they might be found. The Committee did not exist outside Ishutin's imagination, but its supposed existence had great advantages for him in that if his followers believed he received his instructions from international leaders they would never question his aims or his methods; while on the other hand, by their acts committed in accordance with these beliefs, *Hell* would not only terrorise the enemy but inspire respect and fear; and respected and feared they stood a better chance of achieving all he planned.

The assassination of the Tsar, we have already noted, was to be the climax of *Hell*'s liquidating programme. Presently, however, there joined the group a distant relative of Ishutin's called Dmitry Karakozov, who was almost as strange. He was an introspective, egoistic youth in his early twenties, whose family, though gentry, were so poor that his whole life had been a struggle for existence. In 1861 he had been sent down from

Kazan university for taking part in the disturbances there, and three years later had entered Moscow university where he had not been long when he was dismissed for failing to pay his dues. He had then thrown himself into revolutionary activities, had come into contact with Ishutin and embraced his relation's extreme views.

His most passionate wish was "to do something for the people" before he died, and it was to this end that he informed *Hell* that he had decided to kill the Tsar. The rest of the group, including Ishutin, were of the opinion, however, that the time was not yet ripe for this crowning act, and all tried to persuade him to abandon his project. But their efforts were in vain, for he now uncovered qualities of character that no one before had suspected he possessed: exceptional obstinacy and powers of concentration.

On 4th April the Tsar took a walk in the Summer Garden, a public park, and as he was leaving the Garden to return to his carriage Karakozov fired at him, the shots going magnificently wide. Seeing that he had missed his target the failed assassin attempted to run, but was surrounded by the police and members of the public, to whom he shouted, "Fools, I have done this for you!" On Alexander's orders he was taken at once to the Tsar who questioned him on the spot.

"Are you a Pole?" Alexander asked.

"No," replied Karakozov. "Pure Russian."

"Why did you do this?"

"Look at the freedom you have given to the peasants!" Karakozov told him.

At police headquarters despite very rough handling he maintained for several days that he was a peasant called Alexey Petrov. His true identity was uncovered by chance when the police searched the room of a young man reported missing by a lodging-house keeper. In the room there were indications that the missing man was Karakozov. Far worse, however, was the additional discovery of some papers which contained Ishutin's address. Within a short time Ishutin and all the members of the Moscow group were arrested and transferred to St Petersburg.

At their subsequent trial Ishutin and Karakozov were sentenced to death. Karakozov was hanged, but when the executioner was already placing the mask over Ishutin's face he was told that Alexander had commuted his sentence to hard labour for life He died of tuberculosis in the prison hospital at Novaya

Kara, in Siberia, on 5th January 1874, having for the last eleven years been insane.

This attempt on the Tsar's life heralded in a period of intensified political reaction. The Liberator had had enough of emancipating an ungrateful people. Soon there were some who began to speak of the White Terror with which the authorities suppressed any sign of revolutionary activity. But the movement towards revolution had gone too far to be entirely checked, and all that these reactionaries were doing was stirring up for themselves even greater trouble for the future.

The measure of the attempts to impose reactionary discipline may be taken from the fact that during the winter of 1868–69 the students of St Petersburg and Moscow were again in a state of unrest serious enough to warrant the attention of the Third Division, who were soon to discover that another young man as strange as Nikolai Ishutin was at the bottom of it all. Meetings, often attended by two hundred students, were held almost daily, votes were taken and signatures to petitions collected.

It early became obvious that these demonstrations were not run of the mill student protests—which occurred by a kind of spontaneous combustion—but were being carefully organised. To find out who the organisers were police agents infiltrated the public meetings with the aim of discovering the identities of those who attended the secret meetings at which the demonstrations were planned.

On 30th January 1869 the police received information that a secret meeting had been held the previous day in the rooms of a certain Sergey Nechaev, a teacher of religion in the Parish School. Besides his teaching Nechaev also attended lectures at the university, and had, in fact, been identified by several police agents as having been a speaker at various student meetings. In the discussions which invariably formed part of these meetings, it had also been noted that he was consistently arguing in favour of the most radical views expressed.

It has never been established with any degree of certainty whether Nechaev was arrested or not, but he did disappear as soon as it became known that the police were on his track. A day or two later Vera Zasulich, then a girl of seventeen but who was later to become one of Lenin's most prominent colleagues on the editorial board of *Iskra* (*The Spark*) received a letter containing two slips of paper.

On one slip in a handwriting she did not know was written: "As I was walking over the bridge a police van passed me. A hand appeared through the bars of the window and threw out a scrap of paper, while a voice called out, 'If you are a student send this on to the address written on it.' I am a student and consider it my duty to carry out this request. Please destroy my letter immediately so that I cannot be betrayed by my handwriting." Unfortunately Vera Zasulich did as requested, otherwise closer examination of the handwriting might have produced some very interesting revelations.

The second note was from Nechaev. "They are taking me to a fortress. I do not know which. Inform our comrades. Do what you can for me. Do not lose courage and continue our work. God willing we shall see each other again."

This incident naturally led to much speculation among the students of the group which had formed round Nechaev. It was undeniable that he had always proposed the most radical action; he spoke always, too, of the coming revolution, and of the individual's duty to decide whether or not he could give it active support. But his words were so vague and so full of empty rhetoric that there were not many who heard him who had any belief in his revolutionary connections. Still, if he had now been shut up in a fortress, clearly they had misjudged him.

While they were still speculating, another surprise was sprung on them. News came that Nechaev had escaped from the fortress and had fled the country. At first this news led to even greater speculation, because though men might and did escape from Siberia, *they did not escape from fortresses.* Presently, however, it became quite clear that Nechaev was abroad, for he was issuing from that safety a spate of declarations.

Sergey Nechaev was the son of a serf from Ivanovo, some two hundred miles north-east of Moscow. His mother was a seamstress. When the Emancipation *ukase* was promulgated he was thirteen and working in an office. He had acquired the most rudimentary education and was sixteen before he could read or write with fluency. But he had a quick intelligence and by the time he was nineteen he had passed an examination qualifying him to teach religion in primary schools. His first post was at the St Petersburg Parish School where he was employed at the time of his disappearance two years later.

Arrived in St Petersburg he had begun to attend lectures at the university. From the outset he made contact with revolutionary-minded students, at whose disposal he placed his rooms in the school as a meeting-place.

His aim was to unite all the various groups and circles that existed in the universities and colleges into one organisation, and he was firmly convinced that he could achieve this aim if only he could find the right people and involve them in situations where they had to obey him. Then he would immerse them in real revolutionary activity, turn them into good revolutionary material and send them out to bring in more recruits. The trouble was that he did not possess the authority to impress people, to make it impossible for them not to follow him, and it was to gain this authority that he designed as the first step in his personal master-plan his going abroad and establishing contact with the veteran exiles.

Evidence brought to light since the 1917 Revolution has proved that though he may have been taken in for questioning, Nechaev was not thrown into a fortress. The note to Vera Zasulich was a deception which had two aims: his claim to have escaped from a fortress would at once establish him as a bona fide revolutionary, while the same story would be an infallible entrée into exile circles.

Nechaev went first to Geneva where he contacted old Bakunin who held the fort there of the Central Committee of the International Social-Democratic Alliance, a body almost, but not quite, as mythical as Nechaev's fortress. Cut off from direct contact with Russia since the Polish uprising the veteran was overjoyed to be appealed to for help by a young revolutionary of the new generation, and he was completely taken in by Nechaev's claims and stories, which were aimed at obtaining from Bakunin a document which would clothe him in a certain authority among his followers in Russia. This aim he quickly achieved when on 12th May 1869 Bakunin handed him a certificate of membership of the Alliance Révolutionnaire Européenne, Comité Général.

To organise revolution one must have money, and Nechaev now turned to his second aim—the acquisition of funds. Herzen and Ogarev were the trustees of a fund set up by a Russian nobleman ten years earlier for the support of "revolutionary purposes in Russia." Bakunin put Nechaev in touch with

Herzen and Ogarev, and while Herzen refused to part with his
share of the fund, Ogarev willingly handed over his.

Early in September 1869 Nechaev secretly arrived back in
Russia. He was no longer a nobody but recognised as an important revolutionary and as the accredited delegate—with a
document to prove it—of an huge (imaginary) international
organisation.

Nechaev returned to Russia with giant-sized intentions: to
destroy the Empire and found a new social order on its ruins.
He at once set to work to build up an organisation which he
named *The People's Vengeance* with the achievement of these
aims as its programme.

Among his first recruits were a number of young men who
had already formed themselves into a group under the leadership of Nikolai Dolgov, a student at the Moscow Academy of
Agriculture. The group was introduced to Nechaev by one of
the most desperate of revolutionary characters, Peter Uspensky,
who had belonged to Ishutin's *Hell* but had escaped the catastrophe which had overtaken it. He became Nechaev's right-hand
man in *The People's Vengeance*, and remained so until catastrophe overtook this organisation, too.

This catastrophe was brought about by a combination of
Nechaev's obsession with personal power and the stubbornness
of Ivan Ivanovich Ivanov.

Even Uspensky was scarcely a more enthusiastic supporter
of Nechaev than Ivanov, who produced tremendous feats in the
field of recruitment, work which placed him high in the hier-
archy. His position and outspokenness often made him criticise
Nechaev, though up to now he had always obeyed the rules and
submitted to "higher authority", namely Nechaev.

There came a day, however, when he overstepped the mark.
Nechaev instructed him to arrange for a manifesto to be
scattered in the students' kitchens. Ivanov refused point blank,
arguing with complete justification that such an act would
inevitably lead to the kitchens being closed, which would cause
a great deal of suffering among the students.

"I will not do it!" he told Nechaev firmly. "Even if the Committee order me to, I will not do it!"

Nechaev had had enough of Ivanov, and this point-blank
infraction of the rule demanding unquestioning obedience to
orders increased his personal jealousy of this young man.

It was also Nechaev's first real test as a leader, and he decided that if he let Ivanov get away with it, it might lead to widespread reaction against his authority, and the organisation would be weakened. Ivanov must be liquidated to furnish an example.

According to Nechaev as he told it to his accomplices, the Committee had passed sentence of death on Ivanov, and had appointed himself, Pryzhov, Kuznetsov and Nikolaev to be his executioners. Pretending that his disobedience had been overlooked, Nechaev told Ivanov that he had been given another assignment. In a cave in the Petrovsk Academy Park, Nechaev said, a small printing machine had been hidden. It was now urgently needed and Ivanov was to go to the cave and bring it back to Moscow. Ivanov accepted the new assignment without question. But when he arrived at the cave he found the four executioners already there. Pryzhov, Kuznetsov and Nikolaev had protested that they had no desire to become murderers, and had been told by Nechaev that if they refused to carry out the order to kill Ivanov they would be liquidated themselves for their disobedience.

Unfortunately for the executioners Ivanov fought desperately for his life, and though the intention had been to strangle him Nechaev seems to have lost his head, for he produced a revolver which he fired at point blank range into the back of his victim's skull. He then ordered the body to be weighted with bricks and thrown into a nearby pond. They botched this too, for three days later a passing workman discovered the corpse floating on the surface.

The police were puzzled at the lack of motive for the killing and also by the fact that the victim was an innocuous student. Very soon, however, they were to have their mystery solved by a stroke of chance similar to that which had put them on the track of Ishutin's *Hell*.

On 19th November 1869, while engaged in mopping up operations following recent disturbances, the Third Division searched a certain bookshop and the manager's flat above, and in doing so came upon evidence which seemed to reveal the existence in Russia of a widespread terrorist organisation called *The People's Vengeance*, with a whole network of cells, about which they had no inkling. Not only that but the organisation appeared to be only one section of a continent-wide revolutionary alliance whose aim was to raise rebellion throughout Europe, placing in jeopardy the lives of all Europe's most prominent men. Fortunately for them they also found a note-book containing names and addresses, including those of the murdered student. Now the motive existed.

The Third Division moved quickly. Searches, arrests and interrogations came in rapid succession. As the information was sifted one name and one name alone emerged as that of the man who drew up the programme, was self-appointed guardian of morale and issuer of orders—Sergey Nechaev.

An immediate intensive search for him was ordered, but he had disappeared as effectively as though he had dissolved into thin air. He had, in fact, fled to Switzerland, and in Geneva in January 1870 appeared first to Ogarev who at once contacted Bakunin in Locarno. The old man urged Nechaev to join him there, since he had the means of hiding him.

For more than a year and a half Nechaev was kept on the run trying to avoid the agents of the Third Division. Eventually he was trapped and arrested by the Swiss police. The Swiss government would agree to his extradition only on condition that the Russians would try him solely for the murder of Ivanov. To this the Russians agreed.

Nechaev's accomplices had already been found guilty on this charge and had been sentenced to from seven to fifteen years hard labour in the Siberian mines. When Nechaev was brought to trial in Moscow on 8th January 1873 he was inevitably found guilty also and sentenced to life-long exile in Siberia. Because of his subsequent behaviour instead of being sent to Siberia he was confined in one of the most notorious prisons in Russia, the Alexey-Ravelin dungeons of the Peter-Paul fortress. Eleven years later he was to appear once more on the revolutionary scene.

As for *The People's Vengeance* it was utterly smashed. One hundred and fifty-two had been arrested, of whom seventy-nine were arraigned, and upon being found guilty of revolutionary activities received comparatively light sentences.

The story of Sergey Nechaev from the moment he set out to win the support of the veterans in exile until his arrest and trial covers the period January 1869 to January 1873. During this time there were other individuals, other groups who, hoping to achieve the same aim by other methods, were beginning to dominate the Russian revolutionary scene. Indeed, these very years during which Nechaev was organising his group on the principle of the strictest subordination of self to The Cause saw the root-striking of a philosophy of revolution which was to influence revolutionary thought for the remainder of the century, until it came up against a formidable rival, Marxism.

Known as *narodnichestvo* (populism), this philosophy, which was to gain widespread currency in the seventies, had several of the great names of Russian revolutionary history among its apostles and disciples. The word *narodnichestvo* is derived from *narod*, the people—the broad social base which comprised the manual worker and the peasant. Specifically its main concern was for the material welfare of the masses, but it had in reality a much deeper significance. By some the People were considered a potential or actual historical force which could not be resisted; while others regarded it as the one and only source of spiritual energy, and as the one hope for the world. It projected a vision of the poor rising up against their oppressors and eventually possessing the earth, based on a sincere belief that, of all peoples, the Russians were ideally fitted by temperament, history and folkways to bring into actuality the Socialist ideals.

The peasant, so the thinkers held, did not understand or appreciate the splendid role which he had to play whether he liked it or not, and had to have it explained to him by those who did understand it. In the motivation of the intelligentsia there was, however, not merely the working of a desire to raise the peasant from the depths of material and spiritual squalor into which centuries of suppression had ground him, but a deep sense of guilt, for the most part subconscious, but nonetheless effectual for that. This, too, must be understood if there is to be a proper apprehension of Populism.

It was this reaction of conscience which moved those who worked for The Cause to humble themselves before the people. But this humility carried with it also a sense of pride; those devoted to The Cause came to look upon themselves as The Chosen, elected by Providence to lead The People out of their bondage. The absolute consecration of self to The Cause, the willingness to sacrifice all, even life itself, can only be explained by these reactions of guilty conscience and pride in the role of liberator. Understanding of this makes it much easier to understand the rashness, which at times seems foolish to the point of unadorned stupidity, that is only too apparent in the acts and deeds of many of those whose stories illuminate revolutionary history.

It is against the back-cloth of Populist philosophy that the bulk of our story from now on must be set. Only by bearing in mind the psychological factors involved and the intellectual viewpoint from which the liberation of the masses was seen, is it possible to make sense of so much that happened in Russia from 1870 onwards.

The disclosures made at the trial of the Nechaevists had a tremendous impact on the whole revolutionary movement, and particularly upon those sections of it which, like the Nechaevists, had been dedicated more to action than to preparation. Nechaev had always had many opponents who saw only danger in such fanaticism because of its potentiality to destroy reason; and now it was widely believed that the whole concept of a centralised secret society had not only been discredited but had proved fatal to all proper progress. The immediate reaction of the revolutionary movement was to form informal "circles for self-education" and "brotherhoods" in which men and women lived on a community basis. Many of these "communes" sprang up in the early 1870s, but as a rule did not last long.

There was one "circle", however, which not only lasted some years but formed a link in a series of revolutionary associations. It was founded by Mark Natanson, a student of the St Petersburg School of Medicine, who, unfortunately, within two years fell foul of the Third Division and was banished to Archangel. The "Circle" did not disintegrate at the loss of its founder, for the leadership was taken over by one of its most capable members, Nikolai Chaikovsky, a senior student at St Petersburg university, whose name it now took.

The Chaikovsky Circle was the absolute antithesis of Nechaev's organisation and was in fact an informal association of men and women bound together in friendship, mutual trust and unanimity of views. Decisions were taken by unanimous consent.

The parent-body in St Petersburg had fifty members, provincial branches another fifty; and in this hundred were some of the greatest names in Russian revolutionary history. There were, for example, Sergey Kravchinsky, Leonid Shisko, Prince Peter Kropotkin, Nikolai Morosov and Lev Tikhomirov, while the most prominent woman was Sofia Perovskaya, daughter of General Perovsky, sometime Governor-General of St Petersburg.

As adherents of Populism, it was incumbent upon the members of the Circle to make contact with the masses in order to educate them. Numbers of them "went to the people", as the phrase was, and prominent among those who enlisted in this practical expression of their aims were Perovskaya, Kravchinsky and his friend Dmitry Rogachev.

By 1872 a change gradually began to overtake the Circle. Many began to lean more to the Left, and it was being suggested that a more rigid organisation was necessary. These views did not meet with Chaikovsky's approval and he decided to withdraw from the Circle, though it continued to bear his name. At about the same time Kropotkin, Perovskaya and several other of the most active members were arrested.

The loss of their leaders seems to have acted as a spur to the majority of the remainder, who, encouraged by the uncertainty of their own continuing freedom, either prepared to or did "go to the people". By the spring of 1874 this movement had reached the proportions almost of a mass movement.

All set out under the motivation of a boundless enthusiasm and an unshakable faith in The People. Before long, however, they were brought up with a jolt by realities. The peasants displayed an almost complete lack of interest in what the "educators" had to teach, and proved, by and large, young and old alike, unresponsive to socialist ideas.

Left alone, by the summer the "educators" would have realised the hopelessness of their mission; by the autumn they would have been back in their classrooms, disillusioned and chastened. But the authorities decided to intervene, and with such ruthlessness that before long the Chaikovsky Circle had ceased to exist.

Even so, the enthusiasm was not entirely killed and at least one new circle came into being. Known as the Moscow Circle, among its members was Vera Figner who will figure conspicuously later in our story.

Originally conceived, like the Chaikovsky Circle, as an informal group, within a short time the ambitions of its members made it apparent that at least a form of constitution would be needed. This remodelling took place in February 1875, and the circle was renamed The All-Russian Social-Revolutionary Organisation.

The Organisation evolved no set of doctrines, but steered a middle course between the two main schools of revolutionary thinking. It did, however, include one novelty. Though it had a great reluctance to sanction the use of force to attain its ends, it did allow for the introduction of small bands whose double task was to rouse the people and to terrorise the government and the nobility. It also planned to set free its comrades in prison or exile. It was in favour of "education" and to this end formed small groups to infiltrate small works and a selected score of large mills.

But the security of its members was poor. By March 1875 the police already had the names and addresses of most of them. In April the authorities pounced and arrested a third of them. By the end of another four months the All-Russian Social-Revolutionary Organisation was no more.

The majority of those arrested had to wait two years in prison before they were tried. They were then arraigned before the Senate in two great trials; the first, known as the Trial of the Fifty, occupied three weeks of March 1877; the second, the Great Trial, also known as The Trial of the 193 and also held before the Senate, began on 18th October 1877 and was concluded on 23rd January 1878. The public were admitted to both, although numbers were limited and all applicants for tickets were carefully screened.

The defendants in the Trial of the Fifty were for the most part members of the Moscow Circle, all without exception young men in their early twenties. Their sentences were severe, ranging from prison to hard labour and banishment to Siberia.

Most of the 193 had been a number of years in prison, a good proportion of them being those who had "gone to the people". Not a few of them had no connection whatsoever with the revolutionary movement, but as a result of their experiences became firm adherents thereafter.

The Great Trial lasted nearly four months, and ended with roughly half the prisoners being acquitted. The remaining ninety or so received sentences ranging from five days imprisonment to ten years hard labour. Because sixty-two of the condemned had already been in prison for periods far longer than their sentences the Senate recommended to the Tsar that they should be released at once. The Tsar chose to ignore this recommendation and in some cases increased the sentences. The majority of those acquitted were banished by administrative process to the remote provinces.

Chapter Five

ENTER ANDREY ZHELYABOV

Among those acquitted at the Great Trial was Andrey Zhelyabov. His involvement had come about in this way.

Born in 1850 in the Crimea, he was the son of a house serf. By the time he was five, other children had made their appearance, and to ease things for them he was sent to live with his maternal grandparents, the Frolovs, at Kashki-Chekrak, where he was to stay for four years.

Grandfather Frolov had been given his freedom as a reward for his long service to the family of a gentleman called Stein. He had married a free Cossack girl and until her death Grandmother Frolov was proud of her Cossack blood, a pride which she passed on to her grandson Andrey.

When the boy was seven, an incident happened which was to have a lasting effect on him. One of his younger aunts, Lyuba Frolov, who was a sewing-maid in the big house, arrived distressed at her parents' cottage and told of being raped by her master Lovrontsov. Her father, acting with great courage, had at once gone to Feodosia to lay a complaint with the police. No action was taken, and the boy, so he has recorded, burned for the next five years with an intense hatred for Lovrontsov, becoming obsessed with the desire to grow up quickly so that he might return and kill the man.

A year or so later Andrey returned to his parents' home. Their master, a former Army officer called Nelidov, was a good master, and now in retirement, devoted much of his time to the welfare of his serfs. While staying with his grandparents, Andrey had been taught by his grandfather to read the church script. This was an accomplishment which excited his parents' friends, and Nelidov got to hear of it. One day he sent for the boy, and discovering that he was unable to read ordinary print, set about teaching him. Every day the boy went to the big house, and in a very short time was reading with ease. This encouraged Nelidov to help him further, and when he was ten Andrey was sent to the Junior School in Kerch as a boarder.

Andrey was a sensitive boy, tall for his age, and as "thin as a post". He was not a model pupil by any means; there are records that described him as being constantly in trouble with his masters as the ringleader and provocateur of kindred spirits among his school-fellows. In the summer holidays he returned to his parents' house, and there helped in the fields.

By the time he was sixteen he had become the enemy of the Tsar, and the attempt on Alexander's life by Karakozov in 1866 deeply moved him. In those days secret political societies were often formed by schoolboys and "illegal" literature was circulated, read and discussed. Though there is no evidence of this having happened at the Kerch school, there were long and serious discussions of revolutionary ideas among the older pupils.

He sustained his early academic promise, and had it not been for a strong predilection for practical jokes he would have left school the recipient of the Gold Medal instead of the Silver one which was awarded him. Even the award of the Silver Medal carried with it certain perquisites, among them automatic entry to the Civil Service.

Zhelyabov's ambitions, however, lay in another direction. He decided that he must study at the Novorossisk university at Odessa, and this he achieved with the help of a grant of thirty roubles a month from a fund set up by Lududaki, a local merchant. His stipend worked out at about two shillings a day, but it was enough for a student to live on, who had been exempted from paying the university fees by reason of "his poverty and his disposition towards study," an exemption which had been granted Zhelyabov. At the university he studied Law.

He was popular among his fellow students, one of whom has left a description of him. During the two years he remained at the university, this man has written, he wore the same suit, a second-hand one bought off a stall in the Greek bazaar. It was too small for him, the jacket short in the arms, the trousers tight in the leg. He always seemed to be bursting out of it. He was full of great vitality, never content with half-measures.

Often his stipend would be late in arriving. In any case, almost as soon as he received it he gave the greater part of it away, so for the larger part of the month, and particularly during the last few days, he lived on one bowl of soup a day from the students' canteen, or *Kukhmisterska*. The *Kukhmisterska*, of which there was one in every university, was supported by private donations for the most part, with occasional help from official funds. Its chief aim was to provide poor students with cheap meals, but many, like the one at Odessa, became more like a junior common room than a canteen, the centre of student life, where newspapers could be read and books borrowed, and where discussions were the order of the day and half the night.

Zhelyabov spent most of his free time in the *Kukhmisterska* arguing with his fellow students about the social theories of Fourier and Saint-Simon, while drinking endless glasses of tea. At this time Odessa was just developing into a boom town, as a result of the arrival of the railway, and as the police were also sharing in the new prosperity they seemed to have little interest in running to earth those who propagated and disseminated revolutionary theories.

Apart from these few general facts, little is known about Zhelyabov's life at the university, until in 1870 he obtained the post of tutor, in the long vacation, to the children of a rich family at their *datcha* near Simbirsk. The master of the house was an autocrat of the old school, and was horrified when Zhelyabov repeated at the dinner-table the ideas he had argued about in the *Kukhmisterska*. The first few days were difficult, and he was almost sent packing; but his considerable gift for making people like him came to his aid and he worked out his engagement though his employer often called him "a Jacobin and a gallows-bird."

In 1871, Odessa was hit by a slump as a consequence of American competition in the grain trade. Workers were dismissed, wages cut and disorders broke out. If Zhelyabov took part in these disorders he did not attract the notice of the university authorities. However, in the early summer a personal misfortune did overtake him. His stipend had always been irregular, but now it stopped altogether. Zhelyabov appealed to the authorities, and because he was of "excellent behaviour and studious disposition" they made him a grant of twenty roubles a month.

At about this time a new curriculum for schools came into force. It had been devised by the Minister of Education, Count Tolstoy, in an attempt to counter the liberalising influence of the new social ideas now becoming increasingly current among Russian students. Though the liberal-minded students were enraged by the new programme, it was not possible to do anything to compel a return to the old one, which had been drawn up under Alexander's direction when his desire for reform was at its strongest. So a number of Odessa students arranged to give secret lessons in French, German, Physics, Algebra, Geometry, History and Geography—all of which had been cut out of the new curriculum—to all young people who cared to attend.

Zhelyabov made himself responsible for classes in Russian, and very soon was having difficulty in coping with the large numbers who flocked to him. Tall, powerfully built, handsome and of a forceful personality, he was at the same time, simple and friendly. The effect he had on his class, and especially on the girls, was overwhelming.

The classes had not been going long, however, when Zhelyabov was expelled from the university as the result of a basically trivial incident. A Czech professor, Bogishich, while lecturing on 16th October 1871, saw a student called Baer lounging in his seat. Bogishich had been brought up in the German tradition of discipline and his understanding of the Russian temperament was negligible. Pausing in his lecture, he screamed at Baer at the top of his voice, ordering him to leave the room.

Bogishich was scheduled to lecture again four days later. When he arrived at his lecture room, there was not a single student there. As he left the room, however, he found the corridor outside suddenly full of young men who hissed him as he passed through them.

The matter was reported to the Rector who arranged to meet the students on the following day, 21st October. Though Zhelyabov did not attend Bogishich's lectures he was appointed one of the four spokesmen who were to discuss the affair with the Rector. As a result of their interview, the delegates went to

call on the professor. Bogishich was concilatory. He explained
that his poor understanding of Russian had made him use words
to Baer which he would not have used had he known their
associations. He was prepared to explain this and to say that he
had had no intention of hurting anyone's susceptibilities, when
he next lectured, on 23rd October. The delegates were satisfied
with this reasonableness and it seemed that the whole unfortunate business was now resolved.

On the 23rd, Bogishich's lecture-room was filled to overflow-
ing; but the professor did not arrive. When the students had
left him, it had occurred to him that they were expecting him
to make a public apology. In his view this would cause him to
lose face, so he sent a message that he was ill.

The students were furious, and accused Bogishich of breaking
his promise. They adjourned to the university hall where they
were joined by large numbers of their fellow-students and were
addressed by Zhelyabov who told them that as a matter of
principle they must have an apology from the professor.
Zhelyabov was still speaking when the Vice-Rector arrived.

The Vice-Rector called for silence, and when this was not
accorded him, he nervously threatened to send for the police.
At this, the uproar increased, until at last the students left the
hall and collecting in groups in the university square and the
town, chanted "Bogishich must go!"

The university authorities could still have restored order.
But the Tsar was shortly to pass through Odessa and this seems
to have affected their judgment, for a meeting of the University
Council resolved to ask the Governor-General for police protection. They also decided to hold a University Court to try the
ringleaders and to make a formal apology to Bogishich.

All these goings-on were, perhaps, somewhat naturally reported to the Minister of Education, who approved the Council's
measures. On 25th October Count Tolstoy telegraphed the
Governor-General:

> Holding of court and execution of its decisions to be carried out
> immediately. Students, however great their number, who are
> expelled from the university to be banished from Odessa. No
> lectures to be held till this is done.

The Court sat from 25th October until 5th November. On
the latter date it reported its decision to the Council, who con-

firmed it on the 9th. It was milder than had been expected. Having allocated certain minor punishments they expelled one student for a year "with the right to attend educational establishments elsewhere", and two to a year's expulsion but without this right. Zhelyabov was one of these. The three were automatically expelled from Odessa.

On 11th November the three were arrested and put on a steamer for Kerch. Large numbers of sympathisers went to the harbour to see them off, but owing to fog, the sailing was postponed until next day. A rich man of some position in the town, who was a friend of Zhelyabov, offered to stand bail for him so that he might spend the night at his house. Though the authorities agreed they posted a police guard at the house and limited the number of callers to half a dozen or so. Next day Zhelyabov was taken back to the ship and sailed into banishment.

He went to his village, Sultanovka, but within a fortnight of arriving there he petitioned the authorities to be allowed to live in Feodosia. He gave as his reason for the request that his family was too poor to support him; in Feodosia he could support himself by giving private lessons. His petition was approved.

Before he left Odessa the Vice-Rector, on behalf of the university authorities, had told him that the university would welcome him back when his period of banishment expired. So when in early August 1872 he applied for readmission at the beginning of the next academic year—October—they sent him the necessary certificates and supported his application. On 21st August the papers were forwarded by the university Council to the Odessa Director of Education for endorsement. The latter in turn sent the papers to St Petersburg, and late in September the Ministry gave its ruling. It pointed out that the expulsion had been for one year, and that this period had not yet expired. In view of this and because it was essential to protect the university from undesirable influences, the application could not be approved.

Somewhat chagrined by the rejection of their own recommendation the university Council applied to the Ministry for permission to reinstate Zhelyabov on 8th November, the day after the expulsion order expired. But again the Ministry demonstrated its disapproval of Zhelyabov by adhering to the letter of the university regulations, which laid down that students could only be admitted at the beginning of the academic year and not after the year had started.

There was nothing more Zhelyabov could do. In July of the following year he asked the university to return his papers to him. How he passed the next year or so it is not possible to say in detail, for the records are very scanty. It is known, however, that when his banishment had finished he returned to Odessa where he made a living by giving private lessons. He also joined, though he never became a prominent member, one of the most advanced groups in Odessa, the Volkhovsky Circle.

He did not stay long in Odessa, for he obtained a post as tutor in the family of a wealthy merchant named Yakhnenko, who had a country house and a sugar factory near Kiev, where Zhelyabov joined the family. Within a short time he had fallen in love with his employer's daughter, Olga Semenovna, and despite the fact that Zhelyabov was a peasant, Yakhnenko, who prided himself on his liberal ideas, gave his permission for them to marry, which they did in the summer of 1873.

It is quite clear that Olga was deeply in love with her husband, and it is highly probable that this, together with her inexperience—she was not quite twenty—blinded her to what the future might hold for them. She was not long, however, in finding out.

In the autumn Olga and Zhelyabov returned to Odessa, where he had obtained a teaching post at the Odessa Municipal Poor House. The salary was very small, but he insisted that they should live on it, and not accept any assistance from his father-in-law. He also told Olga that they must so order their lives as to be of assistance to the poorer people; and to play her part in this, Olga took a course of instruction in midwifery. One of his contributions was to hold secret evening classes for working men.

In the first weeks of 1874 he joined a new group lately formed in Odessa, whose moving spirit was Makarevich. The group's main objective was to smuggle in banned literature from abroad and distribute it. Their security, however, was poor. Within a short time the police were on to them and Makarevich was arrested and imprisoned. A few days later Zhelyabov was also arrested, but the police could find nothing against him and had to let him go. He had not been long at liberty when the police intercepted a coded message from him to Madame Makarevich, which owing to the primitiveness of the cipher, they read with ease. In the letter Zhelyabov had told Madame Makarevich that if she were arrested she must persuade her parents to go bail for her. He also asked her to send him some money and gave directions for sending it. It seems that he had a plan for bribing her husband's warders.

Naturally Zhelyabov was immediately re-arrested, but under interrogation he gave such a plausible explanation of what he had said in the letter that the chief of the Odessa Third Division was satisfied, and once more let him go, but only after he had put up bail of two thousand roubles. In his report to St Petersburg, Colonel Knoop pointed out that on the evidence Zhelyabov could not be convicted of belonging to the Makarevich circle, and in any case, his social position as the son-in-law of a wealthy merchant and municipal councillor made it very unlikely that he would want to run the risk of joining such a group.

St Petersburg were not impressed and ordered Zhelyabov's immediate seizure. This took place on 11th November. "On that day," Zhelyabov said later, "I became a revolutionary."

After four months in prison, however, he was again released for lack of evidence, this time on bail of three thousand roubles. He was to remain on bail and under constant police supervision for the next two and a half years.

During this time he took no active part in the revolutionary movement, though he did collect funds to support the Slav uprisings in Bosnia and Herzegovina against the Turks. He would have liked to go and fight with them, but was prevented by his being on bail. He interested himself in chemistry, and though one of his friends, Semenyuta, advised him against doing so, he took a course in explosives. He also acquired a large circle of acquaintances which included local fishermen and young naval and army officers.

Though on bail it was possible for Zhelyabov to leave Odessa. Twice he visited the sugar factory at Kerch, where his only child was born; while in the summer months he went to his parents' home where he worked in the fields. Here his vitality and energy impressed even the sturdy peasants.

He was happy both in his teaching and his labouring. Olga, on the other hand, though she made great efforts to adapt herself to this entirely new way of life, was very unhappy. "Sometimes," she said later, "I would think of my grand piano at home, and go and hide in the bushes and cry."

Zhelyabov had never taken part in the great "going to the people" movement, which, as we have seen, collapsed in 1875. Shortly afterwards Mark Natanson—who, it will be recalled, had founded the Chaikovsky Circle, left it, been arrested and exiled—returned from his exile. He was now more convinced than ever that only organisation could save the revolutionary movement, and he began to devote all his energies to this end.

His idea was for there to be one great centralised organisation, and in order to gain recruits he visited almost every known radical centre in Russia. He then switched his attention abroad, and went to London and Switzerland where he was successful in persuading a number of self-imposed exiles to return home.

By the end of 1876, so successful had his efforts been that for the first time in the revolutionary history of Russia there had been established on Russian soil a substantial organisation which had been given the name of *Zemlya i Volya*, the *Society of Land and Liberty*, after the society of the same name which had existed in the 1860s.

The new *Land and Liberty* was not so much a compact organisation as an umbrella sheltering all those associations whose members were fully committed militants. Natanson's wish was to co-ordinate aims and activities under a centralised leadership which would produce a comprehensive programme, while, at the same time it made no attempt to influence the individual structure or specific doctrines of any of its associate members. Later, this league of revolutionaries became known as the Social Revolutionary Party, a description which provided a label for all those who were sympathetic in any way and to all degrees with its radical ideology.

Unfortunately before the work of consolidation could be completed Natanson was arrested again. This was a blow to *Land and Liberty*, for Natanson was a great organiser, but it was not a fatal one, for among those who had rallied to Natanson were several very able men among whom were Alexander Mikhailov, who had formerly been an engineering student, and Aron Zundelevich, whose skill as a smuggler both of men and illegal literature has rarely been equalled. These two men, together with Plekhanov, who was to become later an international figure, and others, continued the drive.

The statutes of the Party provided for a General Council, the supreme authority, and a small Administrative Centre, the executive. Under the Centre came the various sections, one of which has a special significance in revolutionary history. This was the Disorganisation Section, whose function was to rescue comrades from prison, to liquidate spies and traitors, and to provide protection against the arbitrary conduct of officials. Its significance lay in the fact that this was the first time in the movement's history that any organisation or group had formally given approval to the use of violence in combatting police activities and policy.

Though it is unlikely that Zhelyabov had not heard of *Land and Liberty*, he had not joined it, or even contacted it, when in September 1877 he was ordered to surrender to his bail, and he discovered that he was to be arraigned in the Great Trial. He was eventually acquitted and had been free only a few hours when a most sensational event occurred.

Chapter Six

THE VENGEANCE OF VERA ZASULICH

Vera Zasulich, it will be recalled, was the seventeen year old girl to whom Nechaev had sent the letter claiming that he had been arrested and was being taken to a fortress, when he was attempting to provide for himself a reputation of revolutionary one-upmanship. She had been arrested with the other Nechaevists in 1869, sentenced to two years' imprisonment, and on her release in 1871 had been banished to Kharkov, where she was placed under police supervision.

In 1875, her banishment terminated, she went to Kiev, where she joined the revolutionaries. Here she heard of *Land and Liberty*, and in 1877 moved to St Petersburg where she offered her services to the Centre and was taken on as a typesetter on the Party's clandestine Press.

She was, if the phrase is permissible, a true-blue revolutionary. She had a singleness of purpose which marked her down as dedicated, reliable, safe. Taking no thought for her personal appearance, she presented a picture of extreme dowdiness and unkemptness, which did nothing to enhance her somewhat mongoloid features. In 1878 she was approaching thirty, but looked much older. And so far, apart from her full commitment to The Cause, she gave no indication of the promise which was to make her one of the great names of Russian Socialism, a member of the editorial board of Lenin's *Iskra*, though the deed she was about to commit would have assured her a place in revolutionary history had she thereafter decided to rest on her laurels.

The first demonstration organised by *Land and Liberty* had been in the cathedral square in that cradle of demonstrators, Kazan. It had not been a very effective affair, partly due to the prompt and extremely suppressive response of the police.

Among those arrested was a former student, a young man of twenty-four, Alexey Stepanovich Emelyanov, who gave his name to the police as Bogolyubov, by which he has ever since been more generally identified. He was not a member of *Land and Liberty*, nor was he one of the workers on whose original plea the Centre had decided to hold the demonstration. He had merely heard that something was in the wind and had gone to see what it was.

The police, however, believed that they recognised in him a student who had particularly distinguished himself in the fight that had broken out at the end of the demonstration. Of this he was found guilty and sentenced to the excessively harsh term of fifteen years imprisonment. Even in the light of the sentences imposed upon revolutionaries at this time, this was a particularly vicious one, as were those inflicted on his comrades, two of whom received ten years, one eight and another six.

After sentence, according to custom, Bogolyubov was put in the St Petersburg House of Detention to await transfer to the prison where he would serve his sentence. This was in July 1877, when there were also in the House of Detention the 193 defendants who were to figure in the Great Trial.

On 25th July General Trepov, the Governor-General of St Petersburg and chief of the police, visited the prison. Trepov already had to his credit a career marked by exceptional brutality. As chief of police in Warsaw he had ordered his men to open fire on Polish demonstrators, and the repressive measures which he had habitually enforced in Poland had led to attempts to assassinate him. After Karakozov's attempted regicide he had been transferred to St Petersburg.

Now, as he paced before the prisoners drawn up in the prison yard, he noticed that one of them was not showing him the respect he demanded. The man had actually omitted to doff his cap. In a typical access of frenzy, he rushed at the prisoner and tried to strike him. The man, who happened to be Bogolyubov, struck back. Brought up by this audacity, Trepov paused for a moment, and then strode across to Pahlen, the Minister of Justice, who had accompanied him, and asked permission to have the prisoner flogged. Pahlen gave permission and Bogolyubov was so brutally beaten that he went mad, lingered for a year or two, and died.

The 193 had been watching from the windows of their cells, and had seen what had happened. They had heard the punishment Bogolyubov had received, and they, as well as Trepov and Pahlen, knew that it was an illegal punishment. The incident made them seethe with anger, and for weeks the atmosphere in the prison was tense.

Nor were the prisoners the only ones to be so affected. The news had quickly reached the outside world by the "grapevine" and a meeting of *Land and Liberty* was called in St Petersburg at which Alexander Mikhailov, the Party leader, arrived pale and stammering. He announced simply that "the requisite measures have been put in hand," and even when pressed would say no more. Actually he had just returned from Kiev where he had contacted Valerian Osinski, who was the leader of the Disorganisation Section. Osinski had unhesitatingly agreed to take the necessary steps to "punish" Trepov. It had also been agreed between the two men that any action taken by the Disorganisation Section should be postponed until after the Great Trial, lest the chances of the defendants should be prejudiced.

It was a pity in a way that Mikhailov had been so evasive when asked what he meant. At least one misunderstood him. Vera Zasulich believed that the Party had decided to do nothing and made up her mind to act herself. She would kill Trepov, and she persuaded the girl who was staying with her to assassinate the prosecutor at the Great Trial at the same time. (This latter attempt failed as the intended victim was not receiving visitors on that day.)

It was Trepov's custom to give public audiences each morning to receive petitions and hear complaints. On the morning after the conclusion of the Great Trial, Vera Zasulich joined the crowd at Trepov's offices, and when her turn came she drew a revolver and shot him point-blank, though only wounding him. After she had fired, she dropped her revolver and stood where she was awaiting arrest.

Trepov was an extremely unpopular man, and the bulk of

the general public, wherever their political sympathies might lie, were of the opinion that he had received his deserts. Somewhat strangely Zasulich was not considered by the authorities to have committed a political crime, but was regarded merely as a common criminal. This was odd, because had the attempt been designated a political crime, Zasulich would have been tried without a jury, and would have been subject only to the verdict of prejudiced judges; whereas, as a common criminal, she was entitled to, and was given, a jury trial.

She was defended by a brilliant lawyer, and had the added good fortune that the judge was a man of liberal sympathies. Nevertheless no one could conceive that the verdict would be any other than guilty; so the surprise was all the more great when the jury pronounced her Not Guilty.

The spectators in court cheered, and the news travelled so quickly that when she emerged from the court-house a large crowd was waiting to greet and congratulate her. It accompanied her to the prison where she went to collect her belongings.

But the Tsar had also quickly heard the news and had ordered her immediate re-arrest. Again fortune favoured her. The order was slow in reaching the prison, and she was already greeting the crowd when the police arrived to execute it. They managed to seize her, however, and put her in a carriage; but they failed to disperse the crowd, who, learning what was afoot, attacked the police and a scuffle ensued in which a youth of nineteen was shot.

In the confusion Vera Zasulich was spirited away. A day or two later she was on her way to Switzerland.

The result of the trial and its aftermath excited not only the Russians, but the people in most countries of Europe. The *Revue des Deux Mondes* called her the Muscovite Charlotte Corday; while another writer proclaimed that a new era had been opened by the verdict.

In a sense, this was true; it did initiate a new era, but one in which a series of acts of violence was committed by the revolutionaries. In fact, the assassinations had begun before Zasulich was brought to trial. On 1st February 1878 Akim Nikonov, an exposed police spy who had infiltrated the Social Revolutionary ranks, was killed by Osinski's men. A day or so later, an attempt was made on the life of the assistant public prosecutor in Kiev. In May the chief of the Kiev Third Division was killed. In

August, Sergey Kravchinsky, a prominent member of the defunct Chaikovsky Circle, returned from fighting with the Slavs in the Balkans to help edit the organ of *Land and Liberty*. On 4th August he stabbed to death in broad daylight in the heart of the city, Mezentsev, chief of the St Petersburg Third Division, and made good his escape.

The authorities refused to be intimidated by these acts of violence and retaliated with even more vicious repressive measures than ever before.

Chapter Seven

ZHELYABOV AND LAND AND LIBERTY

After his acquittal at the Great Trial, Zhelyabov returned to Odessa. Since a friend had taken a farm at Kamenets-Podolsk he decided to rent a nearby market garden. His wife and son were still with him, and as he employed no labourer, he, Olga and the boy did all the work between them, the bulk falling on him. His habitual working day was one of sixteen hours.

This was a period of frustration for Zhelyabov. He had seen the failure of the "going to the people" movement, and the virtual failure of every other attempt since then. Despite all the good intentions of *Land and Liberty*, the Party itself had not become the cohesive and realistic force it had set out to be, and this lack of cohesion and sense of realities was reflected in the people. This, in turn, meant that there was lacking, too, an effective weapon against the ruthlessness of the police.

The mood of the people he knew at first hand. After a long day's toil in the garden, he would try to talk to the peasants. But he was too tired to be effective in argument, and they too tired to listen to him. He realised his failure. "As long as the peasant has to work as he does," he said, "to get himself a crust of bread, you will never turn him into a good political animal."

In the summer of 1878, Osinski's Disorganising Section was the only revolutionary group of importance in southern Russia. Zhelyabov had met them frequently when they lived in Odessa, but two things held him back from joining them: he had not yet decided in his own mind the efficacy of terrorist tactics, and, with peasant obstinacy, he formed a personal dislike for Osinski, the aristocrat.

Zhelyabov was not alone in his doubts about terrorism. Many in *Land and Liberty* were as hesitant as he, while many others flatly rejected it. Alexander Mikhailov, the leader, was not one of these. He had become more and more convinced that terrorism would pay high dividends. In this he was supported, among others, by Morozov, one of the editors of the Party's clandestine newspaper. When he began to print articles in support of terrorism, Plekhanov, who was against, declared himself outraged. To avoid the fierce quarrel which seemed imminent Mikhailov found the money to start another paper, the *Listok Zemli i Voli*, of which he made Morozov sole editor, with carte blanche to develop his views. Within a very short time Mikhailov and Morozov had gathered round them a select band of supporters who called themselves the *Death or Freedom* Group, or the Troglodites.

From the formation of the group, terrorist action increased. Early in 1879 news reached the revolutionaries that a number of students in Kharkov gaol had been flogged. The incident made a deep impression on a little Ukrainian Jew called Goldenberg, a sincere and courageous man but with several flaws in his character which made him unsuitable "revolutionary material"; he was muddle-headed, extremely excitable and excessively vain.

Goldenberg made up his mind that he would avenge the students of Kharkov by killing Prince Dmitry Kropotkin, the Governor-General of Kharkov, and he went to Kiev to obtain the support of Osinski. Osinski did not think much of his chances of success, but nevertheless gave Goldenberg a revolver and some money.

From Kiev, Goldenberg went directly to Kharkov where, having set up a temporary headquarters, he kept a watch on Prince Kropotkin. It was some time, however, before he got the chance to shoot. If all the other conditions were favourable either it was too dark to see properly, or the range was too long.

However, on 9th February 1879 the Prince attended a reception at the opening of a new school. There Goldenberg followed him, but, unable to see a favourable opportunity in the building, he left and installed himself in the frosty night air on a bench in a public park not far from the Prince's home.

His wait was not long. Heralded by the sharp clop of the horses' hooves on the hard ground, the carriage came in sight. Goldenberg dashed towards it, and seizing the shaft with one hand, he fired through the window. The noise of the shot frightened the horses and they bolted before he could fire further shots. He hurried back to his temporary headquarters, changed his clothes and left Kharkov. Not until next day did he learn of his success. Kropotkin had died of his wounds within a few hours.

Elated by his success, Goldenberg moved to St Petersburg, where he declared his intention to kill the Tsar. The Troglodites, however, were already considering two similar offers, one from a man called Kobilianski, a Pole, the other from a Russian, a Goldenberg-like character called Solovyev.

At that time Mikhailov himself was involved in preparations for the assassination of Drenteln, Mezentsov's successor as chief of the Third Division, and told the three men that they must wait until this assignment had been carried out. The attempt failed, and the would-be assassin, Mirski, was arrested.

Wasting no time, Mikhailov appointed two of his colleagues, Kviatovski and Zundelevich, to consider and report on the proposals to kill the Tsar. Kviatkovsky and Zundelevich, after due consideration, said that in their view the attempt ought to be made by one of pure Russian blood, and that in any case, of the three men Solovyev seemed the best choice for the job.

Throughout the following weeks meetings were held to plan the attempt. It was decided that Solovyev must act on his own, but his friends would provide him with the revolver and a getaway cart. Next it was necessary to decide whether it should be regarded as a private act or performed in the name of *Land and Liberty*. Mikhailov and his Troglodites were in favour of the Party being committed, but strong opposition came from Plekhanov and M. R. Popov, another prominent member of the movement, and a number of their friends, who opposed the idea of killing the Tsar. Popov even went so far as to say that if the preparations were not cancelled, he would inform the Tsar, a threat which threw the meeting into uproar. Eventually, the Party did not give the attempt its blessing, and the preparations went forward.

On 2nd April as Alexander came out of the palace for his regular morning walk, Solovyev ran up to him and fired his revolver. The official report states that "His Imperial Majesty proceeded in a zig-zag manner, moving now to the right, now to the left." This evasive action undoubtedly saved his life.

Solovyev was seized. Tried by court-martial in May, he was hanged on the 28th of the same month.

The official reaction to the attempt was the division of Russia into six districts, each in the charge of a Governor-General wielding full power. Many of the members of *Land and Liberty*, led by Plekhanov, believed this to be a grave set-back for their organisation of the revolution. They laid the blame on the terrorists and required them to desist, arguing that violence would only in the end alienate many men of liberal views from The Cause.

Mikhailov, however, refused to give way. Terrorism was the only means of arousing the masses, of dispelling the inertia which was a much greater enemy even than the Third Division. It was a positive act which would show that the revolutionaries meant business; it would inspire faith; and in the long run, the government would bow before it.

The whole argument threatened to split the Party from top to bottom. Intransigent though he was in his views on terrorism, Mikhailov did not wish this to happen, so he suggested that all the leaders should meet in conference at Voronezh at the end of June. This, however, was merely a time-saver, because he realised that at such a conference the Troglodites could be out-voted, and to ensure against this he planned to hold a prelimin-ary meeting of those who shared his views so that they might decide how best to present a solid united front, capable of over-coming any opposition at Voronezh.

Mikhail Frolenko, formerly of Osinski's Kiev group, had now joined him. (There had been heavy casualties there; two were already dead, and Osinski was awaiting execution.) So Mik-hailov sent Frolenko on a mission to the south to win recruits to their support. In Odessa he met Zhelyabov.

No one had ever suggested Zhelyabov as a possible member of *Land and Liberty*. Though known as a talker, he had no reputation in the revolutionary movement. He had cold-shouldered Osinski and had argued against terrorism.

Frolenko, however, was very impressed when they met, and when Mikhailov, who was also on a recruiting mission, passed through Odessa, he arranged for him to meet Zhelyabov. Mik-

hailov was as impressed as Frolenko had been, and on his return
to St Petersburg suggested to his colleagues there that Zhelyabov
should be invited to join them. They were taken aback and at
first were inclined to think that Mikhailov was joking. But when
they discovered that he was speaking in all seriousness, they
put forward all possible reasons why the invitation should not
be extended. Eventually, however, Mikhailov brought them
round, and it was agreed that Zhelyabov should be asked to
join them on condition that he would take a personal part in
the assassination of the Tsar. When Frolenko put the proposal
to him, Zhelyabov said that he would take part in one attempt,
but then must be considered free to decide whether he should
carry on or not. This condition was accepted, and he was invited
to the preliminary conference.

It was quite clear to Zhelyabov that this was a climacteric in
his life. From the moment he joined *Land and Liberty* he knew
that the whole course of his life would be changed. He would
have to cut himself from all his past so as not to be held back
by ties of any kind. This meant family; Olga must divorce him.
When he next saw her, he told her this. Somewhat naturally,
she refused, even after the most earnest entreaties. So Zhelyabov
left home, and never saw his wife and son again.

Chapter Eight

THE CONFERENCES

Lipetsk was a spa. Once it had been one of the most fashionable watering-places in the Empire; but now its glory had deteriorated. Nowadays only minor gentry and merchants came to drink the waters.

Under false names and armed with false passports, Mikhailov and Zhelyabov arrived in Lipetsk on 13th June and rented a furnished flat together. Two days later the others began to arrive. There were ten of them altogether, and because there was danger in so many of them collecting in so small a town, they arranged their meetings with great care.

At the first meeting it was decided to devote all the time to the formulation of policy. In the discussions that took place Zhelyabov, to the surprise of the others except Mikhailov and Frolenko, played a prominent role. By the end of the first day he had won for himself a place in the Russian revolutionary movement.

Though the original constitution of *Land and Liberty* had provided for the setting up of an Executive Committee which was to be responsible for organising the group's action, such a Committee had never in fact been set up. At the meeting on the second day it was voted that all those present should constitute themselves as the Executive Committee, and co-opt Vera Figner, Anna Yakimova, Andrey Presnyakov and Sofia Ivanovna Perovskaya. In addition Mikhailov, Frolenko and Tikhomirov were elected to a small Directive Committee, which was to be responsible for policy. It so happened that the Directive Committee never functioned.

On the final day of the conference it was decided in principle that the Tsar must die; but not until two months later was formal sentence of death passed on him on the basis of an indictment drawn up by Mikhailov.

From Lipetsk most of those who had attended went on to the full conference at Voronezh. At the first session of this conference, Zhelyabov, Kolotkevich and Shiraev were elected to membership of *Land and Liberty*. Plekhanov's tactics were to launch a direct attack on the terrorists at once. He read aloud one of Morozov's most violent articles and at the end asked the conference if a single one of them agreed with it. Instead of the cries of dissent he expected, he was met with a bleak silence. When he repeated the question, still no one spoke. Telling the conference that he had nothing more to say he withdrew and returned at once to St Petersburg.

The argument was carried on, however, after Plekhanov's departure. The views put forward disgusted Zhelyabov, and he did not hesitate to say so. A part of his speech, though, introduced a new controversy. Having said that he knew a number of peasants who would never come out into the open for the sake of a dream, practical men as they were, he went on, "A constitution would give them a chance to come out in the open, and they would take it."

Constitutionalism, though once favoured by a significant section of the revolutionary movement, was now considered reactionary. A fairly typical point of view was that held by Sofia Perovskaya. In everything else, terrorism included, she could support Zhelyabov, but she believed that a Constituent Assembly would place the power in the hands of conniving politicians, whereas her aim was a free federation of peasant communes, an aim achievable only by a national uprising.

This speech of Zhelyabov's temporarily took precedence over all other matters and the debate which followed made it seem as if the delegates would be split in two equal halves, producing deadlock. When the session adjourned Zhelyabov's friends took him on one side and pleaded with him to go slowly. He promised to do so, and spoke no more in public, but devoted himself to lobbying, paying particular attention to Perovskaya, with whom he could make no headway at all.

The Voronezh conference ended with a kind of compromise whose sole aim was to prevent a split in the Party. On their return to St Petersburg, Mikhailov and his friends found that Plekhanov had rallied to his support Vera Zasulich, who had recently returned from abroad, and two other leaders, Deutsch and Stefanovich, and that he intended to do all he could to prevent terrorism from becoming official Party policy. For the next two months there were constant debates in which there was a fruitless search for a formula which would satisfy both factions. Realising that valuable time was being wasted, the Lipetsk group met in a forest near Lesna on 26th August and there formally passed sentence of death on the Tsar. At Zhelyabov's suggestion it was also decided that an attempt should be made to carry out the sentence by blowing up the imperial train as it carried the Tsar back from his summer holiday at Livadia, in the Crimea.

This decision had the effect of hardening opinion on both sides, and as it was clear that no compromise which would bring about unanimity would ever be devised, it was agreed that those who supported terrorism should form themselves into a new Party, to which they gave the name *Narodnaya Volya*, the *Will of the People*.

Chapter Nine

THE FIRST ATTEMPTS

Only a few weeks remained before the Tsar returned to St
Petersburg and preparations for the attempt to blow up the train
were now put feverishly in hand. Zhelyabov was designated to
carry out a reconnaissance of the railway line, and on the basis
of his report, the Executive Committee decided to make three
separate attacks—at Odessa, Alexandrovsk and Moscow. Frolenko, Lebedeva and Kolotkevich were made responsible for the
Odessa attack, Zhelyabov for that at Alexandrovsk and Mikhailov for the Moscow attempt.

At Odessa it was decided that the best plan would be for one
of the party to obtain a job as a watchman on the line some way
out of Odessa and to dig a tunnel from the watchman's hut
under the line, and there place the explosive. Frolenko elected
himself for this role, and Vera Figner was given the task of
getting him the post of watchman.

Her first plan was to ask some of her family's friends to
approach the railway administration on Frolenko's behalf. "But
I realised," she wrote later, "that I could not tell them my real
motive, and if I did not tell them it would be an abuse of
confidence. So I decided to go myself and ask." She chose Baron
Ungern-Sternberg, the future son-in-law of the Governor-
General of Odessa, to whom she explained that as the wife of
her house-porter had lung trouble she was trying to obtain for
the husband a post out of town, and thought a watchman's job

on the railway would be most suitable. Ungern-Sternberg was sympathetic and gave her a letter of recommendation to the Traffic Manager. The latter granted her request at once.

All was going well when news reached the little party that the Tsar would not be travelling by Odessa after all. The original arrangement had been for him to travel from the Crimea by ship, but the weather was bad and as he was not a good sailor Alexander decided to go all the way by train from Simferopol. This decision put Frolenko out of business.

Zhelyabov, who had been allocated Presnyakov, Yakimova and Barannikov as helpers, found that he would need the services of two more men, and on his own responsibility he engaged two workmen, Okladski and Tikhonov from Kharkov. (After the Lesna Conference he had gone to Kharkov on a recruiting campaign for *Narodnaya Volya*.) On 1st October he left Kharkov for Alexandrovsk carrying a false passport in the name of Cheremisov, a merchant from Yaroslav. His cover story was that he was interested in setting up a factory at Alexandrovsk.

Alexandrovsk was a small town of about six thousand inhabitants, and naturally the arrival of a wealthy merchant with such a proposal created quite a stir. Playing his role with gusto, he called on everybody, and made a particular friend of one of the town councillors, a man called Sagaidak, who told him that he did not think the proposal to build a macaroni or soap factory would be so successful as a tannery. Zhelyabov accepted this advice and applied to the town authorities for the lease of a site.

He then went to fetch Yakimova, who was to pose as his wife, and returned a few days later with her, their furniture and two of his workmen, Okladski and Tikhonov. Very quickly they set up their new home.

The town council rejected Cheremisov's application for the site he had chosen. This suited him very well for it enabled him to embark upon endless negotiations.

While he was acting the part of merchant, Zhelyabov and his collaborators were also working hard at their vastly more important project. They chose for the spot where they would plant their mine a place where the railway ran along an embankment seventy-five feet high. A road ran parallel with the embankment about a hundred yards from it, and between the embankment and road there was a deep depression.

Two brass cylinders, each containing forty pounds of dynamite primed with electric detonators were to be placed under the rails fifty yards apart. Leads from the cylinders were to run to a spot on the road where, at the crucial moment they would be connected to the battery. They believed that if the mine were exploded as the royal coach passed over it, there was sufficient force in the charge to send the train hurtling down the embankment, thus providing an extra chance of success.

Normally the royal party travelled in three trains, and for security the Tsar's coach could be attached to any of the three. The task of finding out the particular train on this occasion was given to Presnyakov, who went to Simferopol to watch in the first week of October.

Zhelyabov himself was responsible for laying the mines. He was helped by Tikhonov and Okladski. When Alexandrovsk had gone to sleep the three men would go out to the embankment. Zhelyabov did all the digging, the other two men were posted on either side of him to watch out for patrols. If a patrol came along, they took what cover they could, lying flat on the ground. Zhelyabov had to work at speed, for by the time dawn came all had to be made to look as though it had been undisturbed.

The weather was very bad; it rained without ceasing and so heavily that within a short time the men were wet through. Zhelyabov's night-vision was practically nil; so bad that one of his assistants had to lead him by the hand to the work site. Fortunately he had decided to lay the wires first; fortunately, because he had only just got them in place when the rain caused mud and debris to clog the culvert under the embankment, so that the dip between the road and the embankment became a lake.

Their one fear was that the rain would change to snow, which would reveal their tracks. Zhelyabov got little sleep, for during the day he had to engage in the business of the tannery. Soon he was ill and running a high temperature, but there was no time for him to rest.

The laying of the cylinders was the most difficult part of the operation, on account of the patrols. They had acquired a horse and cart, which they used to transport the mines to the embankment. On several nights they had to bring them home again because the patrols were so frequent. When Presnyakov arrived in Alexandrovsk on 16th November bringing the news that the

Tsar was setting out for home on the 18th, travelling in the fourth coach of the second train, Zhelyabov had only one of the cylinders in position.

On 17th November, Yakimova left Alexandrovsk with her luggage. Zhelyabov told his acquaintances that his wife had had to leave on family business and that he might have to follow her.

That night he made a desperate attempt to get the second mine in place. As he was dragging it up the side of the embankment he slipped and the cylinder slithered down to the flooded pit. Somehow he managed to get it out and at last successfully planted it.

Presnyakov had said that if there were any change in the imperial arrangements he would telegraph. As there was no word from him by the morning of 18th November, the three would-be assassins loaded the battery and an induction coil into the cart and drove to the embankment. It was still pouring with rain, and Zhelyabov was by this time very ill. By an effort of will he went to work, fixing the wires to the coil and battery.

At ten o'clock the first imperial train came in sight. A little later the second train appeared, and as the fourth coach passed over the first cyclinder Zhelyabov threw the switch.

Nothing happened.

When the third train had passed, Zhelyabov inspected the battery and wires. Though not a skilled technician, he knew enough to tell him that wherever the fault lay, it was not here.

They returned to Alexandrovsk, where Zhelyabov became even more ill. The great disappointment and the reaction to the strain of the past weeks increased his fever. But the material had to be salvaged and that night he insisted on going to the railway with his two companions. It was quite impossible for them to lift the cylinders, so Zhelyabov decided to leave them where they were. They might come in useful should the Tsar survive long enough to come this way again.

Presently news came that the Moscow attempt had also failed. There was nothing now to keep him in Alexandrovsk, so Zhelyabov said goodbye to his acquaintances, sold the horse and cart and put the furniture into store. On 23rd November he departed, never again to return.

The Moscow attempt had been organised by eight members of the Executive Committee under the leadership of Mikhailov, who had carried out the preliminary reconnaissance himself. He had then sent a comparative newcomer to the Executive Committee, Lev Hartmann, to buy a small house in the Preobrazhenskoye suburb near the mainline railway from the south. As "wife" to Hartmann he had suggested Sofia Perovskaya, who eagerly agreed though she was fully alive to the dangers to which this role would expose her. As soon as the present tenants had been evicted the couple settled down in the house, taking the name of Sokhorukov. Aronchik and Chernyskaya likewise installed themselves in a flat as man and wife. The rest of the conspirators took rooms in cheap hotels.

The Hartmann house was near enough to the railway, so Mikhailov thought, to enable a tunnel to be burrowed from the house right under the track. This was agreed by his colleagues and the work began.

Only Hartmann among them was a skilled manual worker, and he knew nothing about the art of tunnelling. The tools they had were also primitive; a short "English" spade and a couple of shovels.

The entrance to the tunnel—it was 3½ feet high and 2½ feet wide—was in the wall of the basement. It was kept securely boarded up to protect it against discovery by any stranger who might wander down there. To guard against surprise by the police, the conspirators kept a bottle of nitro-glycerine, enough to blow up the house, down in the basement. If they were discovered at work Perovskaya was to detonate the bottle with a pistol shot.

Their greatest problem was the disposal of the earth. One man worked with the spade at the tunnel head, a second shovelled the earth removed by the first into a little trolley which ran on wooden rails across the floor of the tunnel, and a third pulled the loaded trolley to the mouth and disposed of the earth. They piled as much of it as they could into the basement, and when it would take no more, lifted the floorboards of the sitting-room and packed it under them. When the floorboards would take no more they had to run the risk of taking it outside and dumping it on nearby rubbish tips.

Those who lived in rooms in the city would arrive at the house while it was still dark. They worked from six to eight, then had a tea-break, carried on till dinner time at two, then after a short rest went on until ten o'clock in the evenings. If

they were not held up by alarms—and these were frequent—
they could dig out a foot of tunnel every hour.

Time and time again it was Perovskaya who saved them from
discovery. On one occasion the former tenant called and said
she had left some jam in the cellar. The cellar was full of earth
and timber for shoring up the roof and walls of the tunnel, so
the woman could not be allowed down there. Perovskaya said
she had lost the key, and later took the jam round herself.
Neighbours called for a chat, and often asked awkward questions
to which Perovskaya had to produce satisfactory answers, in
which she never once failed.

As for the work itself, it was by no means straightforward.
They ran into the base of a telegraph pole and had to work
round it. The rain, as incessant here as in Alexandrovsk, seeped
into the tunnel and had to be baled out, which slowed up the
work and further exhausted the workers. Then the roof of the
tunnel fell in because it was not properly shored up, and, what
was even more dangerous, produced a deep depression in the
road above. Fortunately it was not noticed by passers-by, and
they were able to fill it in that night.

When they reached the embankment they ran into still more
trouble. It was full of large stones and they feared that if they
removed them the embankment might collapse. So they decided
to buy a drill. Since they had no money left, the only way they
could think of raising some was by obtaining a mortgage on the
house. This was extremely dangerous, as the moneylender and
an official from the Housing Department would have to inspect
the place. However, no suspicions were roused and Perovskaya
bargained with the moneylender until he agreed to let her have
six hundred roubles, the price of the drill.

They now began to have doubts about the amount of explosive they had for the mine, and reached the conclusion that it
was not enough. As they had learned by this time that the
Odessa attempt was off, they decided to use Frolenko's dynamite
as well as their own. They had recently been joined by the little
Jew, Goldenberg, who had assassinated Prince Dmitri Kropotkin,
and he agreed to go to Odessa to fetch the explosive. He set out
from Odessa carrying a small heavy portmanteau on the evening
of 12th November. A few hours later he was arrested on the
station at Elizavetgrad in possession of the dynamite.

On the 17th November the Moscow group received the information from Odessa that the Tsar would be travelling in the fourth carriage of the second train. At a final meeting they voted that Hartmann, the official tenant of the house, should fire the mine and that his "wife" Perovskaya should have the honour of watching from a window and giving the signal. The rest would stay in their Moscow rooms.

Throughout the afternoon and evening of the following day they waited for news from Alexandrovsk. They had already come to the conclusion that Zhelyabov had failed when confirmation of the fact reached them with word of the Tsar's safe arrival at Kharkov. Now all depended on them.

At eleven o'clock that evening, as the imperial trains approached Moscow the second train was suddenly derailed. Though it was in a pretty poor state, no one was hurt, for there were few people on it. It was in fact the baggage train, which on leaving Odessa had been in the lead. Along the route, however, extra wagons had been attached to it and it was unable to keep to schedule. The Tsar had, therefore, given orders that his train should lead the procession. Hartmann and Perovskaya did not know of this change, of course. But even if the derailed train had been the Tsar's it is unlikely that he would have been killed. The conspirators had been right; their charge was not heavy enough.

Chapter Ten

ANOTHER FAILURE

Stepan Khalturin had been born in 1857, the son of a peasant from near Viatka. He had learned the trade of joiner and from 1875 had worked in various factories in St Petersburg. In this year, too, he had begun to engage in subversive activities and three years later had organised the *Northern Workers' Union*. When this group was betrayed in 1879, he escaped arrest.

The experience of the crushing of his organisation had convinced him of the futility of the use of peaceful means to effect revolution and he made up his mind that the Tsar must be killed. By this time he had made the acquaintance of Alexander Kviatkovski, who was considered by the leaders of *Narodnaya Volya* as one of their best political brains and practical organisers. To Kviatkovski he put a plan for blowing up the Winter Palace with the Tsar in it.

When considered dispassionately, Khalturin's plan seems to have more than a touch of fantasy. To the eager and desperate young people of *Narodnaya Volya*, however, it sounded feasible enough to be given their blessing. Khalturin was co-opted on to the Executive Committee and Kviatkovski was detailed to stay in St Petersburg and give him any assistance and advice of which he might feel the need.

Khalturin was a first class worker, and when he applied for a job as carpenter on the imperial yacht, he was taken on. His behaviour was excellent, his work more than satisfactory, and when the renovating of the yacht was completed he was transferred to the staff of the Winter Palace. The Tsar was still holidaying in the Crimea, and there were strange paradoxes in the discipline of the Palace. While guards watched over the main entrance so strictly that members of the imperial family had difficulty in getting into the Palace, the back, tradesmen's and servants' entrances were completely unguarded and anyone could walk in unchallenged.

The false papers which Khalturin carried gave his name as Batiskov, and described him as a peasant from Olonetz. He gave an impressive performance of peasant simplicity and was soon regarded by his fellow servants as the staff jester. He was very popular and in every department he made friends whom he frequently visited and so learned the lay-out of the Palace. In this way he made the discovery that the room in which he and two others worked, lived and slept was directly under the guardroom, which in turn was directly below the Tsar's private dining-room. It seemed almost too good to be true.

The failures of the attempts to wreck the imperial train now made Khalturin's plan of first importance. Kviatkovski at once began to supply him with explosive. They would meet in the town and Kviatkovski would slip him a small packet which it was easy enough to smuggle into the Palace, where he hid it in his pillow.

Now, on 24th November, less than a week after the attack on the train, Kviatkovski was arrested. This event was not only serious for *Narodnaya Volya*, to whom the loss of so capable a man was a great blow, but threatened to compromise Khalturin, for plans of the Palace were found on the arrested man.

That night, when all the Palace servants were in bed, soldiers began to search. They came into the cellar and turned everything upside-down, but they did not look in Khalturin's pillow. From this moment discipline became much more rigid and a gendarmerie post was set up in the cellar, identity tags were issued which had to be produced on entering and leaving the Palace, while snap checks were often carried out on those coming in.

Zhelyabov, just returned from Alexandrovsk, took over Kviatkovski's role vis-à-vis Khalturin and continued to supply him with explosives. The packages, however, now had to be so small that Khalturin could hide them in his boots or stockings, or the lining of his coat. This greatly slowed up the supply operation, but there was nothing else to be done.

For his part, Khalturin carried on as before, playing the fool and ingratiating himself with the gendarmerie guards. He was so successful in this that the sergeant of the guard, Petrovski, introduced his daughter to Khalturin. Before long he suggested that they ought to get married. Khalturin would not commit himself, but he was very gratified to have this sign that this part of his plan was succeeding.

Soon, however, his health began to suffer. He was already in the first stages of tuberculosis, and now he began to have terrible headaches which would not abate. It took him some time to realise that the cause of his headaches was the gas given off by the dynamite in his pillow. Little by little, when no one was about, he moved the explosive to the box in which he kept his spare shirt and other odds and ends. It was very risky if the gendarmerie ever decided to carry out another search, but there was nowhere else to keep it.

By mid-January 1880, Khalturin had collected in his box one hundred pounds of dynamite, and the explosive expert, Kibalchich, assured the Executive Committee that this amount if exploded in Khalturin's box, which would have a considerable tamping effect, was sufficient to wreck the cellar, the guard-room and the private dining-room. On hearing this Zhelyabov demanded immediate action, on the grounds that the risk of discovery grew daily as did the possibility of Khalturin's physical collapse.

Khalturin objected. He wanted to be certain of success, and was not convinced by Kibalchich's calculations. For some days the two sides argued until Zhelyabov produced a rumour that all the Palace carpenters were to be moved to quarters outside the Palace. This forced Khalturin's hand, but he still had to wait for favourable conditions, namely, that the Tsar was in his private dining-room at the same time that Khalturin was alone in the cellar.

The official hour for the Tsar to sit down to dinner was half-past five, but he was not a punctual man and often did not begin until six o'clock. This condition therefore presented no difficulty, but the other did. Whether the workmen were in the cellar or not depended on what job they were doing; besides, Petrovski, the gendarmerie sergeant, had no set hours, and might be in the cellar at any time. However, Khalturin undertook to act at the first available opportunity.

This did not arrive until 5th February. At five o'clock in the afternoon on that day, Khalturin and two of his fellow workers, Razymovski and Bogdanov, were sitting in the cellar drinking tea, with the lamp unlit. Bogdanov finished his tea first and returned to his work. Almost immediately another workman came to the cellar doorway and asked if they knew where the gendarmerie sergeant was. They told him that they did not, and he went away. Razymovski now finished his tea, and as he needed some of his tools which were in the cellar, he went to the lamp and made as if to light it. Khalturin stopped him saying that he had spilt paraffin over it as he was filling it. As he spoke he lit a candle, which, when Razymovski had found his tools, he extinguished again at once. When Razymovski left the cellar, Khalturin was sitting in the dark. Another workman passing the cellar door at quarter-past five, had seen Khalturin there alone. He was holding a lighted stub of candle and crouching over something at the far end of the cellar, but as he had his back to the door, it was impossible to say what.

Now, every day for the past fortnight Zhelyabov had been going to the Admiralty Square. There Khalturin had met him and told him that conditions were unfavourable. Today, however, at about six o'clock Khalturin told him, "It's ready." Chatting as acquaintances do who have just met, but keeping the Winter Palace on the other side of the wintry dreary square in view, they waited. At twenty-past six there was a great explosion and all the lights in the Palace went out. People came running from the Palace exits followed presently by stretcher-bearers carrying out the wounded and dead. The two men stayed as long as they dared, hoping to have news of the Tsar's fate, but when police began to search the streets, they left, Zhelyabov taking Khalturin to the Executive Committee's headquarters.

Almost immediately they arrived Khalturin fainted. On coming round he inquired about the Tsar. When they were unable to tell him he began to shout light-headedly, insisting that the police were after him and that they must give him a pistol so that he might kill himself. They calmed him down eventually, but some time passed before he fully recovered.

Next day they heard that the Tsar was unhurt. On the day of the attempt Prince Alexander of Hesse had arrived in the capital and had been granted an audience. The audience had lasted longer than usual making the Tsar late for dinner. He was walking down the corridor towards the dining-room when the bomb went off. Though innocent persons were killed, and thirty-three soldiers and twenty-three civilians wounded, Alexander had received not a single scratch.

When he heard this news Khalturin wildly accused Zhelyabov of being responsible for the failure. Had it not been for his goading, his insistence on action, he, Khalturin, would have waited until there could have been no doubt of the outcome. The Executive Committee supported Zhelyabov, with the result that Khalturin withdrew his support of it and returned to St Petersburg. Not until Zhelyabov had been dead a year did Khalturin rejoin *Narodnaya Volya*.

The attack on the Palace had, as it was bound to have, wide repercussions. The Crown Prince, the leader of those who advocated no concessions to terrorism, having given his view that the root of the trouble lay in the lack of cohesion among government organs rather than in the failure of police methods, proposed the setting up of a Supreme Commission devoted entirely to the re-establishment of order. The proposal received the Tsar's blessing, and the Governor-General of Kharkov, Count Loris-Melikov, was appointed chairman.

Two weeks later an attempt was made on Loris-Melikov's life by a student called Mlodetski. At once the Executive Committee, which had openly proclaimed its responsibility for the attacks on the train and the Palace, issued a denial of all responsibility for Mlodetski's act.

Chapter Eleven

GOLDENBERG DECEIVED

Goldenberg, who had been arrested with his portmanteau of dynamite on 14th November, had not yet been brought to trial. There is no evidence that any member of *Narodnaya Volya* had feared that Goldenberg would betray his friends or give away any information regarding the Party and its activities.

Now, it so happened that the Party, taking a leaf out of the book of police methods, had been able to infiltrate an agent into the very headquarters of the Third Division. It had happened like this.

Nikolai Kletochnikov, a minor government official in Penza, having become disgusted by the life he and other officials of his rank were living in the provinces, threw up his job at the age of thirty and moved to St Petersburg, hoping to find higher general standards of morality in the capital. He was quickly disillusioned, however, and in his disillusionment had turned to the revolutionary movement.

There he made the acquaintance of Mikhailov and asked him what he could do to help The Cause. At this time Mikhailov suspected that the widow of a certain colonel was a Third Division agent. She ran a boarding-house and what made Mikhailov suspicious was the fact that she seemed to go out of her way to attract young lodgers. Within a short time of their going there all those lodgers who had any connection with the revolutionary movement were arrested.

77

Mikhailov told Kletochnikov to take a room with the widow and to keep his ears and eyes open. Kletochnikov did as he was bidden, and presently he discovered that his landlady had a strong addiction to cards. He offered to play with her, and by judicious use of his skill he pandered to her fondness for winning. Every night he made a point of losing two or three roubles to her.

Very soon she had become very attached to him, and when he complained that if he did not find work soon he would have to go home to the provinces, she did not dissemble her distress. Then one evening, when he told her that his money had almost run out, she asked him if he knew any young people who had subversive ideas, because if he did she had some friends who might be interested in him.

For the time being Kletochnikov temporised. He wanted to consult Mikhailov. The Executive Committee knew that one of *Narodnaya Volya's* young members was being watched by the police, and that Kletochnikov could do him no more harm than he had already done himself if he submitted a report on him to the widow's friends. The widow was delighted and arranged for the friend to meet Kletochnikov. The friend, who was a Third Division agent, was also impressed, and after questioning Kletochnikov closely offered him a job as an outside agent on probation at thirty roubles a month.

At the end of his probationary month Kletochnikov realised that he had not impressed his contact with the harmless reports that he had made, and felt certain that his engagement would be terminated. The whole operation had been a failure because he had learned nothing from the police.

But it so happened that the Third Division had a vacancy for a junior confidential clerk; and it also happened that Kletochnikov's neat handwriting had made an impression. So he was offered the post and presently found himself in the Investigations Department of the secret police.

It is unnecessary to expatiate on the value to *Narodnaya Volya* of having one of their number so placed. Not only did Kletochnikov supply Mikhailov with a list of all the secret agents in the capital, but gave the revolutionaries frequent forewarnings of intended police action.

It was Kletochnikov who was able to warn Mikhailov in April 1880 that Goldenberg had begun to talk.

The credit for getting the excitable but sincere young man to talk must be given to Captain Dobrinski of the Third Division, a really first-class police-agent, who had studied the psychology of political prisoners and used this knowledge to achieve his great reputation as interrogator. In his first encounter with Goldenberg shortly after the arrest, when Goldenberg refused to answer questions about the movement, Dobrinski did not press him. Instead he gave orders for Goldenberg to be put in a cell with another political prisoner, one Kuritsin. What Goldenberg did not know when he talked freely to his cell companion was that Kuritsin had turned traitor and was passing on all he said to Dobrinski.

This gave Dobrinski a tremendous advantage when he began to interrogate Goldenberg again. He was able to convince his victim that the police knew so much about the Party that the latter could never be successful. He also managed to persuade Goldenberg that he, Dobrinski, was a man of very liberal ideas, and when he suggested that Goldenberg should act as intermediary between the police and the terrorists Goldenberg agreed, on condition that none of his fellow revolutionaries should be harmed in any way. From then on the two men discussed, day after day, how the cause of mediation could best be served, and during these discussions Goldenberg innocently betrayed all he knew of the *Narodnaya Volya* and its activities.

In course of time another Jewish member of *Narodnaya Volya*, Aron Zundelevich, who had been arrested in the St Petersberg public library in 1879, was transferred to Goldenberg's prison. The two men made contact in the prison, and when he heard from Goldenberg what had taken place, Zundelevich was appalled. For some time Goldenberg refused to believe that he had been deceived by Dobrinski, and when it was at last borne in on him he made a rope of his towel, attached one end to a bar of the window and the other to his neck and hanged himself.

This act of self-sacrifice could not practically atone for the damage he had done to his friends. Exactly what he had told Dobrinski eventually came into Kletochnikov's hands in the Investigations Department of the Third Division. He passed all on to Mikhailov, and it was a formidable list. Not only had Goldenberg described past activities—the attempts at Alexandrovsk and Moscow, the assassination of Kropotkin, what had taken place at Lipetsk and Voronezh—but he had given away names, pseudonyms and deeds, and described the Party's organisation, its method of working and the identity of its leaders.

One important result of Goldenberg's revelations was that *Narodnaya Volya's* plans had to be changed or modified. There was no suggestion, however, that terrorist activities should be abandoned; the assassination of the Tsar was still its number one project.

Zhelyabov's plan to use the Alexandrovsk mines had to be abandoned because acting on Goldenberg's information the police dug them up. Vera Figner was sent to organise an attempt in Odessa, but this was foiled by the Tsar's decision not to pass through the place. Attention was then switched to the Governor-General of Odessa, General Todtleben, but the general left Odessa before any plan for his demise could be formulated.

One more attempt on the Tsar's life was made in St Petersburg during this first phase of *Narodnaya Volya's* terrorist activity. The plan, concocted and organised by Zhelyabov, was to blow up the Kamennyi bridge over the Ekaterinski canal as the Tsar's train passed over it. The bridge was successfully mined, but the plan failed because one of the would-be assassins had no watch and arrived too late. By the time he got to the rendezvous the imperial train had passed over the bridge.

Chapter Twelve

A LULL AND A GREAT BLOW

After the Kamennyi bridge fiasco there was a lull in *Narodnaya Volya's* terrorist activities; a lull that has never been explained, and which appears inexplicable. On the other hand, the Party was not entirely idle, for much was done during that summer and autumn to reorganise resources and gain recruits. Of the latter activity, the most important was undoubtedly the creation of a new section of the organisation, the Fighting Services' Section.

Nikolai Sukhanov was a young naval lieutenant who, in 1878, took the marine mines course at Kronstadt. When he had finished the course, he was put in charge of the Naval Electrical Institute in St Petersburg. Within a few months he made the acquaintance of Mikhailov, though it is not known in what circumstances. During the summer of 1879, Mikhailov introduced him to Zhelyabov and Nikolai Kolotkevich. It is quite clear that he was what was known as a "revolutionary spirit". He saw eye to eye with his new friends' views and could accept even the killing of the Tsar, despite his oath of allegiance.

He made one attempt to bring several like-minded brother officers into touch with the revolutionaries, and arranged a meeting of some of them with Zhelyabov. But Zhelyabov was off form that evening, and the encounter was a total failure. A second attempt was made after the Kamennyi bridge incident. This time Zhelyabov was inspired and on that evening the Fighting Services' Section came into being.

In October there took place what has become known in revolutionary history as the Trial of the Sixteen. Among the defendants were several of the Executive Committee. There was Alexander Kviatkovski, who had been wanted for the Trial of the 193, but had avoided arrest at the time; Aron Zundelevich, who had opened Goldenberg's eyes; Stepan Shiraev and Andrey Presnyakov, who had taken part in the Moscow train attempt; Jacob Tikhonov and Ivan Okladski, who had helped Zhelyabov at Alexandrovsk; and finally Sofia Perovskaya, who had been in charge of *Narodnaya Volya*'s printing press. With the exception of Zundelevich all these had been arrested as the result of Goldenberg's revelations.

When the trial ended on 30th October, Kviatkovski and Presnyakov received death sentences, the rest long terms of imprisonment and banishment. Presnyakov and Kviatkovski were hanged on 4th November. They were the first members of *Narodnaya Volya* to meet this fate, and their executions made a deep impression on the members of the Executive Committee, who also saw in them a sign of how far the Supreme Commission under Loris-Melikov was prepared to go.

Once more an attempt against the life of the Tsar became a burning question. A full meeting of the Executive Committee was called at which there was much argument about restarting terrorist activities. The point was that the carrying out of a programme of terrorism tended to impede the progress of the other work of the Party. Both Mikhailov and Zhelyabov stressed the importance of this other work—preparation for the revolution—but the two leading women, Perovskaya and Yakimova, "were all out for terrorism, whatever the cost," and they carried the majority with them.

The execution of Presnyakov also struck a great, if indirect, blow at *Narodnaya Volya*. It happened like this.

Mikhailov had a photograph of his friend which he wished to have copied. Unfortunately there was no one in the Party expert enough to do this for him, so he had to go to a professional photographer. For some reason or other not at all clear, the police had been expecting him to do just that, and they warned all the St Petersburg photographers to keep a look out for him, while an agent was set to watch every photographer's shop in the capital.

When Mikhailov visited the photographer he had an intuition that something was not quite right. Nevertheless when the photographer asked him to leave the photograph and come back in three days' time he agreed. On leaving the shop his suspicions were confirmed; he saw that he was being followed. But he was expert at throwing off shadows and quickly lost the man.

When he told his friends what had happened they begged him not to return to the shop on any account. He laughed and told them that he was not so stupid. Yet strangely he did just that and walked straight into the arms of the police.

Chapter Thirteen

ZHELYABOV TAKES CHARGE

The loss of Mikhailov was a blow to the Party from which it
never completely recovered. Together he and Zhelyabov had
presented a leadership which was inspiring as no other leadership had been up to this time. The wisdom of Mikhailov and the
drive of Zhelyabov combined to make them a formidable power
on the revolutionary scene.

Zhelyabov made one attempt to postpone the assassination of
the Tsar but was not supported by any other member of the
Executive Committee. His reason for asking for the postponement was the failure of the 1880 harvest, which had reduced
the peasants to the point of starvation and, so Zhelyabov
believed, had engendered in them a frame of mind in which
they might be encouraged to rise up in revolt. The other members of the Committee knew that the Party lacked the resources
to organise a peasant revolution and an attack on the Emperor,
and though Zhelyabov stressed that he was only asking for a
postponement and not a cancellation, they felt that if they did
not act against the Tsar now, they never would; and to this they
were publicly committed. Despite deep disappointment at having
his request turned down, Zhelyabov immediately began to draw
up plans for the assassination of Alexander.

One of the handicaps under which the conspirators laboured
was that they had no intelligence service in the Palace. Sofia
Perovskaya was therefore put in charge of organising a recon-

2. (*Above*) Vera Zasulich became notorious in 1878, when, at the age of 26, she tried to kill General Trepov (*left*), the unpopular Governor-General and chief of the St Petersburg police. She wounded him, but he recovered. She was acquitted owing to the general detestation felt for Trepov.

Paul Popper Ltd.

3. Vera Figner. (*Left*) Before her imprisonment by the Tsarist regime for 22 years in the notorious Schlüsselburg prison.

Radio Times-Hulton Library

(*Below*) After the Revolution she lived in retirement in Moscow, greatly respected. She died in 1942 aged 90.

Paul Popper Ltd.

naissance. She chose Natalia Olovennikova and a student called
Tyrkov, and three others, to help her. In pairs they kept watch
on the Palace, noted the times when the Tsar emerged and the
routes he followed.

While Perovskaya and her team were engaged in this essential
work, the Committee discussed the form the attack should take.
Kibalchich, the Party's explosives expert, it will be remembered,
had been experimenting with a new explosive material which
had recently begun to attract attention—nitro-glycerine—and
had come to the conclusion that with it bombs small enough to
conceal, light enough to throw and yet be fully effective, could
be made. Zhelyabov liked the idea of the hand-grenade, but again
was out-voted by the Committee, who preferred mines.

In the first weeks of December Perovskaya reported that
almost every time he went out, the Tsar passed down the Malaya
Sadovaya. Thorough in her reconnaissance this indomitable
young woman was also able to supply the information that in
that street there was a basement to let.

Zhelyabov went personally to inspect the basement. Unfortunately the head concierge was away and his assistant did not
know where the keys were, so he could only inspect the premises
from the outside. He reported to the Committee that the basement was not suitable in his opinion. Once more he was over-
ruled. The basement would be rented, a cheese shop would be
set up in it and from it a tunnel would be excavated to the
middle of the Malaya Sadovaya. Yuri Bogdanovich was cast for
the role of cheese merchant and Anna Yakimova was to pose as
his wife. They were to take the name of Kobozev, and were
supplied with suitable passports.

The Kobozevs negotiated with the landlord and eventually
agreed to lease the basement at a rental of 1200 roubles a year.
They signed the agreement and paid a deposit of fifty roubles as
an advance on the first quarter's rent, payable when they moved
in. As two of the rooms were still being plastered it was agreed
that they should take possession on 1st January (1881). In the
meantime they bought stock for their shop to the value of 150
roubles.

As a matter of fact the 200 roubles for the deposit and stock
had placed a severe strain on the Party's finances. Indeed there
was scarcely a rouble left. How the balance of the first quarter's
rent—250 roubles—was to be found taxed even Zhelyabov's

resources; taxed them so much in fact that he even approached a very poor boy of nineteen called Nikolai Rysakov. Rysakov somehow obtained a three-month advance of his allowance, some ninety roubles, fifty of which he gave to Zhelyabov. The boy's generosity and Zhelyabov's great need were to prove disastrous, as we shall presently see.

The Kobozevs moved into their cheese shop on 1st January as planned, and tunnelling operations began at once.

The basement premises consisted of three rooms. Steps going down from outside led one into the first room, which was the shop. The second room, which led out of the first, was the storeroom, while the room beyond that was the Kobozevs' bed-sitter.

The mouth of the tunnel opened into the bed-sitter. The tunnellers worked at night. They boarded up the window of the room so that not a chink of light could be seen from the outside. The window of the shop had no blind, however, and passers-by, glancing through, could see the little oil-lamp burning before the ikon of St George. Working in shifts, Zhelyabov, Kolotkevich, Frolenko—of Kiev fame—Langans, Sukhanov, Barannikov, Isaev, Merkulov, Sablin and Dignev carried out the excavating. The first six were members of the Executive Committee.

While they were engaged on the work there came to them, as it seemed, "a voice from the dead". The notorious Nechaev was now in his ninth year of imprisonment in the infamous Raveline dungeons of the Peter-Paul fortress. Somehow during that time, so he claimed, he had been able to convert several of his guards to The Cause.

Quite recently Stepan Shiraev, who had been a defendant with Kviatkovski and Presnyakov in the Trial of the Sixteen, had been transferred to the Raveline and the two men had been able to make contact. Shiraev told Nechaev how he could get in touch with the Executive Committee and the letter he had now sent them was a plea for them to rescue him. It was unfortunate for Nechaev that the Committee should at this moment be immersed in their preparations for killing the Tsar. For though Nechaev's deceptions and methods of working had been disclosed since his trial, to many of the older revolutionaries he had been their inspiration when they were in their early teens. They told him that as soon as their present task was accomplished they would concentrate all their attention on his liberation.

Even as the Kobozevs were negotiating for the basement

something else was happening that was to bring disaster to the
Party. Okladski, Zhelyabov's former colleague at Alexandrovsk,
had begun to talk, and had revealed the addresses of two flats.
In the ordinary course of events, Kletochnikov, safe in the
Investigation Department of the Third Division, would have
heard what was happening and warned the Party. Owing to the
reorganisation of the security forces by Loris-Melikov, however,
the City Police were also empowered to take action in political
cases independently of the Third Division. It was to the City
Police that Okladski was talking.

One of the flats betrayed by Okladski had been rented by
Mikhailov for his meetings with Kletochnikov. He had installed
Natalia Olovennikova there, but after his arrest the Party had
transferred Natalia to Moscow and surrendered the tenancy of
the flat. At the same time they appointed Kolotkevich to be
Kletochnikov's contact and the two men used to meet in the
former's room.

While the police watch on Mikhailov's former flat proved
fruitless, the watch on the other flat was more successful.
Barannikov was the tenant, and on 25th January 1881, they lay
in wait for him there and seized him. On the following day
Kolotkevich called to see Barannikov and walked into the arms
of the waiting police. From his passport they discovered where
Kolotkevich lived, and set watch there too.

These arrests were kept very quiet by the police, and it was
not until 28th January that Anna Korba heard of them, and at
once hurried to warn Kletochnikov. When she arrived he was
not in his office. In fact at that very moment he was being
arrested in Kolotkevich's lodgings. He had heard that very
morning of Barannikov's arrest, but not Kolotkevich's, and he
had hurried to warn his contact, and had walked into the police
ambush.

Barannikov, Kolotkevich and Kletochnikov! Three members
of the Executive Committee, and three of its most intelligent
members, too! It was a catastrophe of the first magnitude, the
more so because the arrest of Kletochnikov deprived *Narodnaya
Volya* of all intelligence. Besides, of the six men who had formed
the brains and driving force of the fighting section of the Party
—Mikhailov, Zhelyabov, Barannikov, Frolenko, Kolotkevich
and Kviatkovski—only two were still alive or at liberty, Zhelyabov and Frolenko.

Many another in Zhelyabov's shoes at this moment would have advised giving up the preparations for the Tsar's assassination and lying low for a time. Zhelyabov, on the contrary, urged that they should press on all the more resolutely.

Nor was everything connected with that project going according to plan. Neither Bogdanovich nor Yakimova had had any experience in running a shop and they were quickly in difficulties from which only further expenditure could extricate them, and there was no money left. Vera Figner, who visited the shop one day, was shocked by the meagreness of their stock, for she felt that anyone who had any experience of shop-keeping would see quickly enough that it was not a *bona fide* business. So she made a collection among her friends, raised 300 roubles and bought more cheese.

The tunnelling also produced problems. First, the concrete wall of the basement made drilling of the mouth of the tunnel a noisy business, and they were afraid that neighbours would hear and complain to the police. Then when they had begun to tunnel under the pavement they struck an iron watermain, and almost as soon as they had worked their way over it, found another obstruction in the shape of a large wooden pipe. They could not work over it because it was too near the road surface; they dared not work under it lest they struck the marsh on which the city was built, in which case the tunnel and basement would fill with water.

There appeared to be only one solution to the problem, and that was to cut away the top section of the pipe. But this would only be successful if the pipe were only half full and since there was no way of finding out, they had to take a chance. Luckily the pipe was only half full, but it proved to be a sewer and the stench from it filled the basement and was so overpowering that the men could not work in it. For a time they considered abandoning the project altogether, but eventually they devised a means of covering the pipe and at the same time leaving enough space for a man to crawl over it. Even so the men could only work half-shifts, and that only by wearing a primitive gas-mask which someone produced.

All this slowed down the work considerably, and when the Tsar next passed down the street—on Sunday 15th February—they were nothing like ready for him.

During the winter Loris-Melikov had been searching for a

formula which would allow for a degree of constitutional development and at the same time not seriously curtail the Tsar's autocratic powers. The chairman of the Supreme Commission hoped that the production of such proposals would be accepted by the revolutionaries as a sign of good faith on the part of the government and they would desist from their terrorist activities, at least for the time being. But it was not an easy task, and only after protracted secret discussions with the Tsar and his advisers, did Loris-Melikov put forward a draft Law of his own for increasing the membership of the Imperial Council by delegates from the *Zemstva*, the local councils, and the setting up of two commissions, one to consider financial, the other economic reforms.

Loris-Melikov presented this draft to the Tsar on 18th February. The conspirators in the Malaya Sadovaya knew nothing about it, of course, and at this time had finalised their plans. They were to make their attack as the Tsar passed down the street on Sunday 1st March.

Zhelyabov was still opposed to relying upon the mine alone, though he had taken his full share of the tunnelling work, and once more he raised the question of using hand-grenades. After the explosive expert, Kibalchich, had said that he did not think hand-grenades would be effective, Zhelyabov was supported by only one other member of the Executive Committee, his friend of long-standing from Odessa, Mikhail Trigony.

In the past, Zhelyabov had always bowed to the will of the majority. This time, however, he proved obstinately insistent, and eventually a compromise was reached. Zhelyabov could prepare two grenades which were to be thrown if the mine failed to work or did not do its job. Trigony also suggested that if the Tsar should escape death from both mine and grenades a dagger attack should be made. He offered to make the attack, but said he would need thirty men to support him. The Committee could not call on thirty men, so Zhelyabov proposed that he should make the dagger attack himself, unsupported.

Final preparations were now put in hand with some urgency. As it would be impossible to continue the usual activities of the Workers' Section of *Narodnaya Volya* while the attempt was in its last stages, the flat where the printing press was installed was given up, and the furniture put into store, the press itself being moved to the flat of Vera Figner, who was living there with Isaev. As headquarters for the conspirators a new flat was rented, and a Jewish girl, Hessia Helfmann, and Nikolay Sablin moved into it on the same day that they left their old flat.

Zhelyabov selected his grenade-throwers on 20th February, and they met in Helfmann's flat, where Kibalchich showed them models of the grenades—five-pound bombs shaped like rugby football balls—and explained how they worked. The four men chosen were Timofey Mikhailov, aged 21, a factory worker and no relation of Alexander Mikhailov; Ivan Emilianov, aged 18, a student; Nikolai Rysakov, aged 18, the student who had given Zhelyabov fifty roubles, and who had recently become a full-time worker in the Workers' Section; and Ignatyi Grinevitski, aged 24, also a full-time worker for the Party. Only Grinevitski and Timofey Mikhailov had previously known each other, and the meeting was primarily designed so that they could all become acquainted. They had a further meeting next day at which Zhelyabov explained what they were to do, and on 22nd February they practised bomb-throwing with dummies under Zhelyabov's supervision in a deserted part of the Pargolovo Park.

Chapter Fourteen

PERSISTENCE IN ADVERSITY

Perhaps they were too preoccupied with their schemes to have any thought for anything else; perhaps no one, no matter how security-minded he was, could have foreseen what would happen. Certainly Kletochnikov, in his job of clerk in the Third Division, could not have been more useful than at this time.

Somehow the police had discovered that a prominent revolutionary, known as "My Lord", had arrived in St Petersburg; somehow, probably through Okladski, who was still talking, they suspected that "My Lord" was Mikhail Trigony. At all events, acting on their suspicions they put a tail on Trigony, who, one night, tracked him down to the flat where Zhelyabov and Sofia Perovskaya were living. As Trigony was what was known in revolutionary parlance a "legal"—that is, he had no official police record, and so had no need to live under a false name with forged papers—he had registered in his own name, which made it a simple matter for the police to discover that he was living at a certain lodging house. It was even simpler for them to plant an agent as a fellow lodger. Before Trigony realised that he was under police surveillance—which he did on 25th February—he had been traced also to the cheese shop in the Malaya Sadovaya.

Trigony was a sufficiently experienced conspirator to have realised the jeopardy in which he was placing all his friends by continuing to meet them after he had satisfied himself that the police were very interested in him. Nevertheless, on the evening of 25th February he went to the cheese shop to do his stint of tunnelling.

The following day, Vasilyi Merkulov, the Odessa carpenter, called at Zhelyabov's flat and was given a number of empty sandbags to take to the cheese shop. They were to be used for tamping the mine. Merkulov delivered the sandbags and returned to Zhelyabov, who now gave him the explosive—a heavy bottle—also to take to the Malaya Sadovaya. That evening the bomb-throwers met Zhelyabov and Perovskaya in Grinevitski's room, and when the meeting ended, Zhelyabov went to work on the tunnel.

On the morning of 27th February, the police agent in Trigony's lodgings told his superiors that Trigony was expecting a visitor that evening. There was an empty flat on the same landing, and there the police installed themselves.

At four o'clock that afternoon Zhelyabov and Sofia Perovskaya left their flat and took a cab to the Public Library in the Bolshaya Sadovaya, where they parted company, Perovskaya going into the library and Zhelyabov setting out to walk. Zhelyabov soon discovered that he was being followed. He managed to elude his shadow, but the process made him late for two or three appointments and he did not arrive at his final destination, Trigony's flat, until seven o'clock.

When Zhelyabov went into Trigony's room, he said, "I think you have the police here." Trigony went out into the passage to look. There was no one about, and he called out to the servant to bring the samovar. He had scarcely done so when the police in the empty flat leapt on him and dragged him in with them. Zhelyabov heard nothing of this quick scuffle but when twenty minutes had passed and Trigony had not returned, he decided not to wait any longer. To his surprise, the main door of the block was locked. As he was fumbling with the catch, police pounced on him and disarmed him; then he and Trigony were taken to police headquarters, where they were put in separate cells.

Though one of the police officers, who had been involved in the Trial of the 193 claimed that he recognised Zhelyabov, Loris-Melikov was not certain that he had captured the man whom Goldenberg claimed to be the chief organiser of the terrorist attacks. He prayed that he was the man, for the arrest would do much to relieve the almost indescribable tension in which the Tsar, the members of his government, and the men detailed to protect them, lived. To make sure, he had Okladski brought from the Peter-Paul fortress to identify Zhelyabov. When this had been done, Zhelyabov still refused to say anything beyond what Loris-Melikov reported to the Tsar, "But the criminal had added that in spite of his arrest the attacks on His Imperial Majesty would be continued relentlessly." Nevertheless despite this threat there was general relief that this leading terrorist was behind bars. Perhaps the Tsar was most relieved of all. At all events, on 28th February he was in a particularly good mood.

The news of the arrests had not yet reached the conspirators when at nine o'clock in the morning of 28th February the four bomb-throwers met Kibalchich for a final briefing and practice. Zhelyabov was scheduled to attend this meeting, but when he had not arrived by ten o'clock, the five men imagining him to be busy with other affairs, went to the practice ground without him. There, in the grounds of the Smolni monastery, they threw their dummies and Timofey Mikhailov one small live bomb, which, beyond exploding, did not give a very impressive exhibition. When the practice was over, they were told to go their own ways and to report at Helfmann's flat, the conspiracy headquarters, very early next morning.

While Kibalchich and the young men had been rehearsing, the cheese shop in the Malaya Sadovaya had received a visit from the police. It would appear that this search had been carried out merely because it was known that Trigone had been there.

General Mrovinski of the Corps of Engineers was requested by the police to carry out the inspection, and accompanied by two plain-clothes men he had introduced himself to Bogdanovich as a municipal surveyor. He went into all three rooms. In the shop there was nothing out of the ordinary, but in the storeroom there was a heap of coke and a quantity of straw. Prodding the coke with a boot, he asked what the straw was for, and was told that it was packing for the cheese. Apparently satisfied, he passed into the bed-sitting-room. At once his attention was attracted to the boards covering the mouth of the tunnel. Bogdanovich explained that he had fixed them there to cover the damp which oozed from the wall. Mrovinski pulled at the boards, but they were fast, and he made no comment.

Returning to the store-room, Mrovinski noticed water oozing from one of the barrels. Bogdanovich quickly explained that the barrel had been dropped and had sprung a leak, and that the water was the cheese sweating. He made no attempt to prove Bogdanovich's veracity, yet he would not go away. He seemed to Yakimova to be trying to make up his mind what to do next. She was becoming increasingly apprehensive, because if he embarked upon a thorough search he could not fail to find the earth stowed under the bed, under the coke and the straw, and in the sacks and barrels.

As he stood there looking about him, the cat came in and rubbed itself against his legs. Mrovinski bent down and stroked it, and Yakimova launched into an account of its behaviour. The general, it seems, was a cat-lover, for the atmosphere became relaxed, and presently he bade them good morning and went away with his two policemen.

While Bogdanovich and Yakimova had been undergoing this ordeal, Nikolai Sukhanov of the Fighting Services' Section, had wanted to have a word with Trigony and had called at his lodgings. There he learned the awful truth. He hurried away to tell everyone he could find, and at three o'clock he, Frolenko, Perovskaya, Korba, Grachevski, Langans, Tikhomirov, and Lebedeva met together in Vera Figner's flat. The shop was clearly suspected and neither the mine nor the bombs were made yet. Above all, they had lost their leader. Nevertheless, they decided unanimously that the attempt must be made at least with the mine, and when Perovskaya proposed that she should take over Zhelyabov's role as leader of the grenade-throwers, this, too, was approved.

When they had reached these decisions, they split up. Isaev went to the Malaya Sadovaya to prepare the mine, while Sukhanov went to Zhelyabov's and Perovskaya's flat to remove anything that might be incriminating. He had just left the flat when the concierge was telephoned by the police who ordered him to let them know when the "male tenant" came home. Zhelyabov had been able to keep from the police where he was living, but, as in the case of the cheese shop, because Trigony had been to the flat, they decided to keep watch on it.

A little later Perovskaya came in to the flat to make sure that Sukhanov had been thorough and to tidy up a little. But she was very wrought up and she, as Sukhanov before her had done, overlooked some materials for making bombs and some cheese labels, which the police eventually discovered.

On leaving the flat, she went to Vera Figner's flat, where Kibalchich, Grachevski, Sukhanov and Figner were busy making the grenades. She offered to help them, but was in such a state that the others urged her to go to bed so that she would be fit for the part she was to play next day. Sensibly she did as she was told. Figner, who had been mixing the chemicals for Kibalchich, joined Perovskaya at two o'clock, since she could do no more to help. At seven o'clock on 1st March the two girls woke. Kibalchich and Sukhanov had completed only two of the bombs out of the four, but they took these two to Helfmann's flat, where the young men were to congregate, and where Kibalchich was to follow them with the other two bombs as soon as they were ready.

Chapter Fifteen

1st MARCH 1881

After the arrest of Zhelyabov and his threat that the attacks on
the Tsar would continue relentlessly, Loris-Melikov had tried to
persuade His Majesty to cancel his attendance at the parade in
the Manège next day. Alexander refused saying that now
Zhelyabov was safe in custody, if normal police precautions
were taken he did not think he would be in any danger.

On 1st March, therefore, the Tsar rose at his usual time, 8.30,
and took his customary walk in the gardens with his children,
after which he went to church, following his devotions with
breakfast with Princess Yurievskaya, his former mistress, and
now, since the death of the Tsarina, his morganatic wife, with
whom he was deeply in love. After breakfast he went to his
study and there, at last, put his signature to Loris-Melikov's
draft Law. He handed the signed document to the Chairman of
the Supreme Commission when the latter presently called to
report on the Trigone-Zhelyabov development.

Princess Yurievskaya was fully aware of all that had taken
place, but she was by no means so sanguine as her husband that
the arrest of Zhelyabov had removed all danger. She would have
liked him to have accepted Loris-Melikov's advice and cancelled
the visit to the Manège, but as he was set on going she implored
him to avoid the Nevski Prospekt and the Malaya Sadovaya.
In her view the Ekaterinski quay offered far more security, with
the public square on one side and the canal on the other.
Alexander promised to do as she suggested.

Alexander left the Palace at five minutes to one, thoroughly enjoyed himself at the parade and on leaving went to call on his cousin, the Grand Duchess Catherine. When he left the Grand Duchess, he told his coachman to drive back by the way they had come, by the Ekaterinski quay.

A good hour or more before the Tsar got out of bed the four bomb-throwers had risen, breakfasted or not as the whim took them, and set out for Helfmann's flat. According to the testimony of Rysakov's landlady, he had appeared to be in extraordinarily good spirits, and had done what he had never done before, gone to her room and talked to her. She had given him a glass of tea, she explained, because he had told her that he had to go to work that day.

By the time that Perovskaya arrived with the two bombs, the quartet were waiting for her. Having explained that the other two bombs would be along presently, she had then told them about Zhelyabov's arrest. This was the first they had heard of it, but before they could question her, she told them that she was taking his place as their leader, and they would carry out the plan already devised by Zhelyabov. She produced the map of St Petersburg on which Zhelyabov had marked the positions which the grenadiers had to take up. The scale, however, was too small for them to be exactly certain where they should be, so she drew diagrams on the back of an envelope. Grinevitski and Timofey Mikhailov were to be at the two corners where the Malaya Sadovaya joined the Bolshaya Italianskaya; Rysakov and Emilianov further down the Malaya Sadovaya, nearer to the Nevsky Prospekt. They were to be in place by noon. They were not to throw their bombs until they heard a loud explosion; then they must move towards where the noise came from, and if the Tsar were still alive they were to go into action.

This plan, of course, depended for its accomplishment on the Tsar coming by his usual route via the Nevsky, the Malaya Sadovaya and the Italianskaya. If he should change his route, then Perovskaya, who would have stationed herself at the corner of the Nevsky and the Malaya Sadovaya, would walk down the latter street and give them the signal by blowing her nose.

The only alternative to the route just described was via the Ekaterinski quay and the Italianskaya. If they received her signal the four young men were to make their way to the

Ekaterinski and post themselves at intervals of thirty yards between the Teatralni bridge and the corner of the Inzhenernaya. She, herself, in this case, would go to the other side of the canal to a spot from where she would be able to see up the Inzhenernaya, and when she saw the Tsar coming she would signal to them, again by blowing her nose.

The instruction to wait until they heard a loud explosion was the first indication that three of the four—Grinevitski was in Zhelyabov's confidence—had that a mine was to be used as well, though it is clear from the later depositions of Timofey Mikhailov and Emilianov, that they suspected something was in the wind.

Isaev had laid the mine, primed it and attached the wires late on the previous evening. Frolenko was to have the honour of firing it. Everyone except Bogdanovich and Yakimova had been forbidden to go near the shop on the day and even Bogdanovich and Yakimova were to leave before the firing.

Bogdanovich was to leave at eleven o'clock. Yakimova was to stay to serve any customers who might call, but as the time approached for the Tsar to come by, she was to go outside and as soon as the Imperial carriage turned from the Nevsky into the Malaya Sadovaya, she was to give Frolenko the signal. A table had been placed near the sitting-room window for Frolenko to stand on so that he could see the street and calculate the right moment for firing the mine.

As to the rest of the conspirators, Vera Figner had to stay at her flat until two o'clock at least, in case she should be required to shelter any of the cheese shop party who might be in need of assistance. Helfmann and Sablin were to remain in their flat to perform the same service for any of the others.

At ten o'clock Figner received a visit from Frolenko. To her amazement, with scarcely a word, he produced half a loaf, some sausage and a bottle of wine and set about making a hearty breakfast. When Figner expressed her surprise that he could eat anything with such a task before him, he replied that a great deal depended on him and he could not concentrate if he was hungry.

When he had finished eating, he set out for the cheese shop, which Bogdanovich had already left. The time dragged by and H-hour came and went without any sign of the Tsar. At two o'clock Yakimova went to the corner of the Nevsky and there learned that the quarry had taken another route. She returned and told Frolenko, who disconnected the wires, hid the battery, coil and plunger, and departed.

Kibalchich, a strange figure in the battered top-hat he habitually wore, had been wandering about the neighbourhood hoping to see how effective the mine had been. When he heard of the change of route, he went home. He had no faith in his bombs. He had not slept for forty-eight hours, so he went to bed, and consequently knew nothing until he read the newspapers next day.

Perovskaya, disappointed at the first change of route, had gone to the entrance of the Manège while the parade was being held. There she waited until the Tsar emerged, and as soon as she saw that he intended to return by the way he had come, she hurried to give the signal to the grenadiers.

Had the Tsar gone straight back to the Winter Palace instead of calling on his cousin, the four young men would have been unable to get themselves into their new positions in time. As it was, the quarter of an hour that Alexander spent with the Grand Duchess Catherine gave them the precious minutes.

The imperial procession was led by a body of mounted Cossacks, with others on each flank of the royal carriage. Following the carriage were two sleighs, the first bearing Colonel Dvorzhitski and his personal assistant, the second, Captain Koch of the police and a fellow officer.

Emerging from the Inzhenernaya, the procession turned right up the Ekaterinski quay, no doubt intending to return to the Palace by the Teatralni bridge. It moved at top speed along the quay.

Timofey Mikhailov ought to have been standing on the corner of the Inzhenernaya and the quay, but his heart failed him at the last moment, and he moved away. Rysakov was next, some fifty yards further on. He lobbed his bomb, but it fell short and exploded under the back axle of the carriage, dropping one of the Cossacks and hurting a small boy who had waited to see the Tsar go by.

The back axle was damaged but somehow held together. The horses, frightened by the explosion, bolted, but when the Tsar ordered him to stop, the coachman was able to pull up in about eighty yards. Colonel Dvorzhitski jumped from his sleigh, opened the door of the carriage and helped the Tsar down. The

Colonel suggested that they should not waste any time, but return as quickly as possible to the Palace. The Tsar, however, wished to see what had happened.

There was a good deal of confusion on the quay. The Cossacks had seized Rysakov, and Captain Koch had searched him and found his revolver. Police, soldiers and civilians were all pressing round trying to discover what was going on.

Somebody called out, "Where is the Tsar?"

"I am safe, thank God!" Alexander replied, "But what about the wounded?"

The boy was still lying on the ground, screaming. He died two days later.

The Tsar went to Rysakov and asked him if he had thrown the bomb. Rysakov said that he had.

"What is your name?" Alexander asked.

"Glazov, artisan," Rysakov answered.

His curiosity still not completely satisfied, the Tsar wished to inspect the spot where the explosion had actually occurred, and he walked along the narrow pavement, followed by Dvorzhitski. The people made way for him—all except one. That one was Grinevitski, who was leaning against the parapet of the canal. When Alexander was two yards away from him, Grinevitski threw the bomb at his feet.

When the smoke had cleared, the sight on the Ekaterinski quay was terrible to look on. The snow was red with blood, and twenty people, maimed and insensible, sprawled in the litter, all of them badly wounded. The Tsar was still alive, but both his legs were broken and he was breathing with difficulty.

No one seemed to know what to do. Some cadets lifted him and put him on the police sleigh. An officer suggested he should be taken into a nearby house and the doctor summoned, but the Tsar overheard him and commanded that he should be taken back to the Palace.

The Grand Duke Michael, his brother, who had been two streets away when Rysakov's bomb exploded, and who had rushed to the scene, helped by an officer and two Cossacks, propped him up on the police sleigh and drove him towards the Palace. A messenger was sent ahead, but at the Palace there was worse confusion. No stretcher could be found, so they carried him to his study, and put him on a couch there, and there he died at half-past three.

Grinevitski, who had been seriously wounded, was taken to hospital with the other casualties. About nine o'clock in the evening he came round and the police tried to question him, but he refused to answer. He died at half-past ten without even saying what his name was.

Chapter Sixteen

THE UNPREPARED-FOR AFTERMATH

One of Zhelyabov's greatest fears had always been that the conspirators would be so obsessed by the preparations for the attack that they would forget to make preparations to meet the consequences. It seemed that this was exactly what had happened.

After the attack Emilianov and Timofey Mikhailov returned with their unused bombs to Helfmann's flat, and then went their ways. At half-past two, Perovskaya, very quiet and composed, entered a café where she had arranged to meet Arkadi Tyrkov and another member of the reconnaissance party. She told the two men that the Tsar had either been killed or very badly wounded. Rysakov, she said, had been caught and she thought Grinevitski had been killed.

Late that evening a few officers of the Fighting Services' Section were holding a discreet celebration in Sukhanov's rooms. Presently the door opened and Perovskaya walked in, tears streaming down her wan, drawn cheeks. The party crowded round her to congratulate her, but she brushed aside their compliments, saying over and over that the Party must now concentrate all its efforts on rescuing Zhelyabov from prison.

On 2nd March, *Narodnaya Volya* issued a manifesto which had already been prepared, it is thought by Zhelyabov and Grinevitski. Addressed to the "Workers of Russia", it revealed that the Socialists had killed the Tsar, and gave their reasons for the assassination. "He was killed because he did not care for his people. He burdened them with taxes.... He cared only for the rich.... He himself lived in luxury.... He hanged or exiled any who resisted on behalf of the people or on behalf of justice ..." and so on and so on.

Despite its rhetoric and heroics, the manifesto appealed to many and the prestige of *Narodnaya Volya* rose to heights never before achieved, and countless offers of help began to pour in. If only the Executive Committee had been prepared to cope with both! But it was not. Nemesis struck quickly.

During the night of 2nd/3rd March, the police raided Helfmann's flat. According to custom, they took the concierge with them to tell the tenants to open the door. Both Helfmann and Sablin were in bed and asleep and it took a little time to rouse them, but presently a woman's voice asked who was at the door. The concierge replied that it was the police and again asked her to open the door.

There was silence for a moment, then just as the police were preparing to break in the door two bullets crashed through the panels. The police hurriedly took cover and returned the fire while one of them went for reinforcements. Presently the firing inside the flat stopped. There came a woman's scream and a woman's voice calling for a doctor. The police broke down the door and found a distracted Helfmann in one of the bedrooms bending over a dead Sablin. After coming to the door the first time, Helfmann had returned to her own room, but when the police began to answer Sablin's fire she was afraid a bullet might strike one of the bombs returned by Mikhailov and Emilianov, which were in Sablin's room. It was when she went to bring the bombs to safety that she found Sablin had shot himself with his last round.

When the police had searched the flat thoroughly and taken away two live bombs, a plan of St Petersburg and a rough sketch drawn on the back of an envelope (by Perovskaya when she was instructing the grenadiers that morning) they left behind two or three men to seize anyone who should come to the flat. It was thus that Timofey Mikhailov walked into the trap at eleven o'clock next morning.

Kibalchich was the first to hear about the raid, and he summoned an urgent meeting of the Executive Committee before noon. It was clear that someone was talking, and they suspected

Rysakov. That meant that Emilianov, Bokdanovich, Yakimova, Sukhanov, Frolenko, Tikhomirov, himself and Perovskaya were all in great danger, though none in such peril as Bogdanovich and Yakimova. They must clearly lose no time in getting away. As usual, Yakimova stayed in the shop to serve any customers who might call, while Bogdanovich caught the next train to Moscow.

When evening came and she was still safe, Yakimova tidied up the basement, left some money on the table with a note to the butcher asking him to feed the cat, and then left for Moscow via Smolensk. The police swooped early next morning, found the tunnel and the mine this time, and sent up a hue and cry for the "Kobozevs".

Of all those engaged in the plot, it was the gallant and courageous Perovskaya who seemed to be most in need of help. After Zhelyabov she had been the most ardent of the conspirators and it would not be unreasonable to suppose that the success of the attempt would have pleased her and encouraged her to even greater activity. As it was, she seemed scarcely to have taken in that they had killed the Tsar, that the tyrant was dead, that they had achieved their object after so many failures; instead she thought only of her lover Zhelyabov and of his plight, for on 3rd March the newspapers had carried the story that Zhelyabov had at last spoken and that he had claimed to be the organiser of 1st March. Thereafter she could think only of rescuing him.

Tyrkov realised what was happening to her and devoted himself to looking after her, a devotion which was the direct cause of his subsequent arrest. Later he wrote of her at this time:

> She kept talking about rescuing Zhelyabov. It was out of the question, of course, but she could not or would not accept it. She could not rest for a moment; she had to try every possibility.... She concocted all sorts of plans. It would have been hopeless to try to discourage her.... She seemed to have lost all sense of realities and had become quite irresponsible. So I made a point of agreeing with everything she said and of going with her wherever she wanted to go. People said "Sonia has lost her head." It was quite true. They tried to make her leave St Petersburg and go into hiding for the time being, but she would not hear of it....

The news that Zhelyabov had claimed to be the organiser of the attack surprised his friends. Up to that time, because he had been arrested on 27th February, there had always been the possibility that he could escape being implicated. Some did not believe that he could have been so foolishly reckless as to throw away his life. Perovskaya herself at moments could believe that he had made the claim attributed to him, and then at other moments was full of doubts. She had to know the truth and she managed to persuade a girl who had shared a flat with her until Zhelyabov had become her lover, but who was not a member of the Party, to go to a high official of the administration who would know the truth. The girl, Rina Epstein, had to report to her that it was true.

What had happened was this. At 2 a.m. on 2nd March, Zhelyabov had been awakened and confronted with Rysakov. He did not deny knowing the boy, and, in fact, went straight to him and shook his hand. When Rysakov had been taken away, Zhelyabov asked why he had been disturbed in the middle of the night, and then learned for the first time of the Tsar's death. He made no attempt to hide his pleasure.

The duty officer asked if he would care to make a statement. He said he would, and at once sat down and wrote that the attack could only have been made by the Fighting Groups of the Executive Committee, but that he did not know any of the individuals involved, except Rysakov, who was a revolutionary of high calibre; and that while he had taken no active part in the attack, his moral involvement was beyond question.

By the following morning he seemed to have changed his mind, for he called for paper and pen and wrote to the Public Prosecutor demanding that if Rysakov was to hang, he should hang too. "It was by pure chance that I was not physically involved in his death. I demand to be associated with the deed of 1st March, and if necessary I will make such disclosures as may be required to implicate me."

As a result of this second statement, he was taken before Count Plehve, Minister of the Interior, and General Komarov of the Third Division. To both he kept his promise to make such disclosures as would implicate him.

At first sight this act of self-destruction appears quixotic in the extreme, but Zhelyabov had a very good motive. He realised that at the trial of Rysakov the prosecution would do all in its power to belittle the revolutionary movement. The trial would attract not only the attention of the Russians but of the people of every country in Europe. The prestige of the Party was in the scales. The execution of an inept boy of eighteen would threaten that prestige, whereas the trial of a revolutionary of his own stature could only enhance it.

When Rysakov had first been arrested he had flatly refused to answer questions or to make any statement. On the following day, however, he was handed over to Dobrinski, who had so cunningly deceived the unhappy Goldenberg. Rysakov was frightened, morally weak and ignorant; he stood no chance against this most brilliant of all Russian interrogators. Before their first meeting was over, Rysakov had—more likely than not unwittingly—betrayed Helfmann's flat. For the next month Dobrinski talked to him every day, and every day Rysakov disclosed more and more.

It was a direct result of Rysakov's disclosures that Helfmann had been seized, that Sablin had killed himself, that Timofey Mikhailov had been arrested, that the tunnel in the cheese shop was discovered with the mine in situ. It was also a direct result of Rysakov's disclosures that Perovskaya was arrested on 10th March. She was spotted as she drove down the Nevsky Prospekt in a cab by a policeman who was accompanied by the woman who kept the dairy where Perovskaya bought her milk. The policeman gave chase and caught up with her. She had a fifty rouble note in her purse and she tried to bribe the policeman with it to let her go. He refused. Rysakov identified her as "the blonde who was in charge of the grenade party." It was a direct result of Rysakov's disclosures that Natalia Olovennikova was arrested on 14th March, though Tyrkov's arrest on the same day was the result of his devotion to Perovskaya. Kibalchich was arrested on 17th March, also as the result of Rysakov's betrayal. Frolenko was with him at the time, so he was taken into custody as well. Rysakov identified Kibalchich as the man who had made the bombs, but he did not identify Frolenko.

By 20th March the authorities decided that they had a cast-iron case for a charge of assassinating the Tsar against Zhelyabov, Perovskaya, Kibalchich, Helfmann, Timofey Mikhailov and Rysakov. The trial was set for the end of the month to take place before the Senate.

Chapter Seventeen

THE END OF THE SIX

The Trial of the Six began at 11 a.m. on 26th March. All except Zhelyabov were represented by counsel. All, except the wretched Rysakov, were in good spirits, Zhelyabov particularly so. Until he was told to stop by an officer of the court, he chatted quietly to Perovskaya, who was sitting next to him.

The trial lasted for three days, the court sitting from 11 a.m. to 2.30 p.m. and from 8 p.m. to midnight. Nineteen officials and soldiers were called. Eye-witnesses described all that had happened on the Ekaterinski quay.

From the beginning Zhelyabov, and he alone, set out to harry the court and the prosecution all he could. He challenged any statement, however trivial, which he knew or believed to be false. At one of the most dramatic moments in the prosecution's case, when a witness was describing with a wealth of flamboyant detail the removal of the wounded Tsar to the Palace, Zhelyabov à propos of nothing, suddenly interrupted.

"May I ask for guidance on a matter of procedure?" he said.

"Well?" said the President.

"Am I supposed to stand or sit when addressing the Court?"

"When addressing the Court you should stand," the President told him.

The tension in the court-room relaxed; the dramatic moment had passed, and could not be recaptured.

Kibalchich also interrupted a good deal when expert evidence

107

was being given concerning the mine and the bombs. He insisted that even the smallest point should be absolutely accurate. When it was suggested that the explosive had been imported, he exclaimed: "I really must protest. This substance was made in our laboratory. The formulae for it can be found in the *Russian Artillery Journal* for August 1878."

The other prisoners seemed content to answer merely the questions put to them.

The third day of the trial was devoted to the final speeches for the prosecution and the speeches of the counsel for the defence. Muravyev, the Acting Public Prosecutor, whose speech, when allowances are made for the then fashionable florid style of his oratory, was rightly regarded as a *tour de force*, spoke for a little over five hours. He dealt fully with the whole question of Socialism and Nihilism at home and abroad, the aims of the Social Revolutionary Party, the characters of the prisoners, their views and aims, and the terrible heinousness of their crime.

The counsel for the defence had been appointed by the Court, and four of them, probably realising the effect it could have on their careers if they defended their clients too well, made only half-hearted speeches. The exception was Kibalchich's counsel, Gerard. He explained how it was that Kibalchich had become a revolutionary, how he had been arrested for lending an "illegal" book to a peasant and had spent three years in prison before being brought to trial (Trial of the 193) when he was sentenced to two months imprisonment; and how he had been prevented from resuming his medical studies. Again and again he was called to order by the President, but went doggedly on.

As Zhelyabov had declined to be represented, he had the right to address the Court himself. This was, perhaps, the one part of the trial the Court most feared, and the President constantly interrupted in order to keep him within well defined limits, although the greatest lattitude had been granted to the Public Prosecutor.

The correspondent of *The Times* who was present, reported that Zhelyabov's speech was the most remarkable of all. "With an air of assurance, changing to one of defiance when interrupted by the Court or the disapproving murmers of the audience, Zhelyabov tried to lay bare the state of things and the social conditions which had made him and his fellow-conspirators what they are now."

When Zhelyabov had finished, each prisoner was allowed to say a brief final word, then the court retired to consider the verdict. It was midnight, and they did not return until 3 a.m. when they pronounced all six Guilty. The Public Prosecutor then demanded the death sentence, and once more the Court retired. Another three hours passed before they came back again at 6.30 a.m. and pronounced formal sentence—all six condemned to death by hanging. The prisoners had the right to appeal, which had to be lodged before 5 p.m. on 31st March.

None of the six appealed, but Rysakov and Mikhailov petitioned the Tsar. Rysakov had become completely demoralised and pleaded abjectly for his life. "Your Imperial Majesty and All Merciful Ruler: Fully aware of the horror of the crime which, under the influence of others, I have committed, I have decided most humbly to beg Your Imperial Majesty to spare my life so that I may unceasingly attempt to atone for my appalling deed," he began.

When both petitions were rejected, Rysakov tried to barter his life for information which would lead to the arrests of terrorists still at liberty, in particular Isaev and Vera Figner. He offered to track them down himself. But no one was interested in him any longer. The long account of the Party, its organisation, aims and methods which the Public Prosecutor had given had all been supplied by Rysakov.

On 31st March Kibalchich made two requests. He had designed an aircraft—he was decades in advance of his times; he had even foreseen jet propulsion—and he asked to be allowed to discuss it with a scientific expert. This request was refused as also was his wish to speak with Perovskaya and Zhelyabov.

Also on this last day of March Hessia Helfmann declared that she was pregnant. A medical commission was appointed to examine her, and when they confirmed the fact, her death sentence was commuted to life imprisonment. A daughter, whose father was Kolotkevich, was born to her in September 1881. Helfmann died in prison in February 1882.

The execution was fixed for 3rd April. On the previous evening, at eight o'clock, five Orthodox priests called on the prisoners. Rysakov confessed and took communion; Timofey Mikhailov confessed but did not take the Sacrament; Kibalchich, who did not confess or communicate, had a long discussion with the priest; neither Perovskaya nor Zhelyabov would see a priest.

Before going to bed between eleven and midnight, Kibalchich, Mikhailov and Zhelyabov wrote letters to their parents, which, unfortunately, have not survived. The sentries later deposed that all five slept peacefully. They were called at six o'clock and given tea, and when dressed were taken to the prison waiting-room. Here they all changed into the black clothes prescribed by law for those about to be executed. Perovskaya became very distressed as she changed, but when Mikhailov told her to cheer up, she took a hold on herself.

When they were ready they were taken to the prison yard, their hands and feet were fettered, and they were bound to the seats of their tumbrils, their backs to the horses, strapped to an iron bar behind them. Attached by a cord round their necks were placards with the word *Tsaricide* in large letters.

At five to eight, the prison gates opened and the procession emerged. First came a cart carrying guards, then the first tumbril with Rysakov and Zhelyabov, followed by the second, with Perovskaya sitting between Kibalchich and Mikhailov. Priests followed in the next cart, and then came the cart carrying the five coffins. Beside the tumbrils marched drummers, who had been instructed to beat their drums loudly enough to drown anything the prisoners might try to say. Twelve thousand troops, police and detectives lined the route and guarded the scaffold in the Semyonovski square.

Apart from Rysakov, the prisoners were completely composed. Rysakov could not take his eyes off Zhelyabov, but Zhelyabov would not look at him or speak to him. When about half the distance to the square had been covered, Zhelyabov suddenly began to shout to the great crowd at the top of his voice. But he was unable to make himself heard above the drummers.

About eighty thousand people, it is estimated, had gathered in the fine early April weather, pressing round the scaffold which had been built in the middle of the square. It was a platform reached by a flight of six steps. Round the outer edge was a railing three-foot-six high, thirty feet by twenty-four. In the centre of the platform was the gallows, a long cross-piece supported by two uprights. In the cross-piece were six iron rings. Behind the gallows were three tall posts with chains and manacles. Below the scaffold was a platform reserved for the officials.

When the tumbrils with the prisoners arrived in the square

at half-past eight, Frolov, the executioner, and his assistants, had already been on the scaffold for an hour. The carts with the priests and the coffins, having taken a shorter route, appeared shortly after the arrival of the Prefect of St Petersburg, who supervised the fixing of the ropes through the iron rings.

The prisoners, having been unstrapped, were led up to the scaffold. Mikhailov, Perovskaya and Zhelyabov were manacled to the posts behind the gallows, Kibalchich and Rysakov to the railing in line with them.

The representative of the Ministry of Justice then read out the sentences. This took several minutes, and during this time Zhelyabov was seen to lean towards Perovskaya and speak to her.

When the reading was over, the five priests went to the prisoners and held out crosses to them. All five kissed the crosses. The priests then blessed them and withdrew.

Frolov then released the prisoners from the posts and railings, and led them under the iron rings. Zhelyabov, Kibalchich and Mikhailov went to Perovskaya and kissed her. Rysakov also went to her, but she turned away and refused to kiss him. They they stood under the gallows in the following order: Kibalchich, Mikhailov, Perovskaya, Zhelyabov and Rysakov.

It was ten-past nine when Frolov placed over Kibalchich's head the prescribed shroud, which had a hole at the neck to allow the rope to pass through. He then passed from one to the other enshrouding them.

The prisoner stood on a kind of low stool. The rope was pulled tight, and the stool was taken away. Death came by strangulation only after some minutes of convulsions.

In his diary Count Milyutin, a spectator, wrote: "They did not even know how to hang them!"

Mikhailov was a heavy young man. He had been hanging for about a minute when the noose slipped and he crashed to the platform. Amid the mocking shouts of the crowd, Frolov made Mikhailov climb up again on to the stool and retied the noose. Once more the noose slipped, and Mikhailov, who was now too weak to move, was lifted up by Frolov's assistants. He had been hanging for about three minutes the third time, when another roar came from the crowd. The ring from which he was hanging was seen to be slipping out of the cross-piece. Frolov quickly seized a ladder and ran a second rope from the hook meant for Helfmann.

All this time Perovskaya was awaiting her turn. She was slightly built and was despatched without a hitch, but Zhelya-bov was as heavy as Mikhailov, and to avoid accidents with him, Frolov tied a double knot in the noose. Though this secured the noose, it delayed strangulation, and the convulsions lasted for seven minutes.

Finally came Rysakov. He struggled and tried to fix his feet in the stool, but the assistants pulled it away.

By half-past nine the bodies hung still from the hooks. The coffins were brought, the bodies cut down and packed into them under the supervision of the military doctor on duty. They were then loaded into carts, driven to the railway station and taken by train to the Preobrazhenski cemetery, where all prisoners were buried.

By ten o'clock the Semyonovski square was empty. There was nothing now to detain the crowds.

Chapter Eighteen

REACTION SETS IN

"The murder of Alexander II had in Russia the effect of a railway collision," Sir Bernard Pares has written in his *History of Russia*. "With the bureaucracy even Liberalism stood condemned, and repression seemed the one road of salvation; the murder of the Tsar Liberator filled the Slavophils with devotion to the throne; the Liberals were shocked at the outcome of a movement in which they had almost looked upon the revolutionaries as colleagues; the Radicals if anything gravitated closer to the revolutionaries; several addresses of Zemstva on this occasion show general bewilderment and confusion."

The reign of Alexander III (1881–94) and the reign of Nicholas II up to 1905 constitute a period of almost continuous reaction, and this was due not so much to the lingering shock of Alexander II's assassination or the continued activities of the revolutionaries as to the fact that the dead Tsar's two successors were narrow-minded and convinced reactionaries who not only rejected further reforms but did all in their power to limit the effectiveness of many of the changes which had already taken place. Historians of Russia, seizing upon this reaction, have labelled the period of the two reigns as the times of *counter-reform*.

The fact that Alexander III and his son were such reactionaries can be traced very largely to the influence which one man had in both their lives. This was Constantine Pobedonostsev, who, before being appointed tutor to Alexander III had been a noted jurist at Moscow university. Alexander had in his turn made him the tutor of his heir, and he was to continue to impose his ideas upon Russian internal policies until his death.

These ideas, which reveal him as the high priest of reaction, Pobedonostsev summarised in his book, *Moscow Conversations*. They were based on deep and unshakable mistrust of both human nature and intellect. This mistrust sprang from his very personal interpretation of western democracy which he held to be rotten to the core and therefore to be prevented at all costs from contaminating Russia. When this yard-stick was applied to Russia, he contended, it could be seen that the events of the last reign and particularly the attempted reforms of the early period had already allowed Russian vital organs to be infected. The Press, for example, had frequently been misused and could therefore not be trusted; nor did it represent public opinion and so ought to be gagged. The elections and parliaments of the west had proved indisputable breeding grounds of corruption; Russia should find no place for such institutions but rather put her faith in the personification of power as represented by the Tsar who should be the total embodiment of autocratic rule.

Pobedonostsev was personally able to practice what he preached by virtue of the powerful position he held as Chief Procurator of the Holy Synod, "the Tsar's eye" to control the Church, to which he had been appointed in 1880 and was to hold until he died. Since he believed that to counter the weakness and viciousness of men and the dangers of the fallibility of reason the state must have as its main purpose the maintenance of law, order, stability and unity among men, and that this could only be achieved by autocracy aided by the influence and example of the Orthodox Church, his work as controller of the latter allied to his relationship with the two Tsars reposed in him a tremendous potential for putting his stamp on the development of Russia. His direct contribution, as has been said, lay in his control of the Church. He proscribed every form of dissent and carried out a vicious persecution of all non-Orthodox and non-Christian communities, involving particularly the followers of Count Leo Tolstoy's doctrine of non-resistance, to the lengths of demanding and getting, in 1897, the excommunication of Tolstoy himself on the grounds that his teaching was dangerous both to Church and State. He also turned the village priests into a secret political police force by insisting that they should report to the civil authorities all their parishioners whom they deemed to be *politically* untrustworthy; and he curbed the free speech of the priesthood by ordering all priests who showed the slightest signs of support for liberal ideas to send their sermons in for censoring before they delivered them.

Though the reactionary tendencies of Alexander III must have become apparent before he came to the throne, nevertheless it was hoped by the more prominent of his predecessor's ministers that out of filial affection he would at least try to implement the scheme drawn up by General Loris-Melikov shortly before Alexander II's death. Melikov, it will be remembered, had been appointed chief of a Supreme Commission of administration in an attempt by Alexander II to try to counteract the growing influence of the revolutionaries. Even before drawing up his scheme for "associating elective representatives of the public with the government in legislative work," he had abolished the Third Division, given the Press a freedom they had not enjoyed before and put liberal ministers at the head of education and finance and himself in charge of the Interior.

Before dying, Alexander had not been able to make public his intention of accepting Melikov's proposals, which would undoubtedly have gone a long way in restoring some measure of the confidence between people and administration which the general was personally convinced was necessary in order to ween public support from the revolutionaries. That it would have been effective in this respect is apparent from the confession of *Narodnaya Volya* that the measures already instituted were separating them from the public and that they had had to act quickly in carrying out their programme of regicide before they were totally cut off from the public. After Alexander's death Melikov and his supporters remained convinced that this separation could still happen if the murdered Tsar's successor would implement the scheme, and they added that in their view it would be the surest way of overcoming future revolutionary plans.

But the scheme ran completely counter to all Pobedonostsev's ideas and as a result Alexander III rejected Melikov's advice. Pobedonostsev was asked by the new Tsar to draft an accession manifesto and naturally he seized the opportunity to strengthen the influence of his own views. The manifesto, published on

11th May 1881, made it quite clear that Alexander was determined to put down all revolutionary opposition and maintain
autocracy. With regard to the latter the wording was, "with
faith in the power and the right of autocracy", and it was to
this phrase even more than to the fact that he had not been
consulted in the drafting of the manifesto that Loris-Melikov
took exception, since it spelled the rejection of his own policies.
He resigned, and with him Dmitry Miliutin, Minister for War,
Alexander Abaza, Minister of Finance, and the Grand Duke
Constantine.[1]

Unfortunately this was merely playing into Pobedonostsev's
hands, for those appointed in these ministers' places were
supporters of reaction. Indeed, after Pobedonostsev, the most
ardent reactionaries were Dmitry Tolstoy, Minister of the
Interior, and Ivan Delianov, Minister of Education.

Alexander III was unlike his father in several respects. Born
in 1845, when he mounted the throne at the age of thirty-seven,
he was physically huge and so strong that he could straighten
out a horse-shoe with his bare hands. He also differed from
Alexander II in his liking of domesticity. Morally courageous—
he had strenuously opposed Loris-Melikov's policies during the
last months of the previous reign—honest, strong in character,
completely straight-forward in his views, he was narrow in his
outlook as a result of a rather slow-working mind and the education he had received from Pobedonostsev. He was, in fact, such
an adherent of the latter's reactionary doctrines that he regarded
the murder of his father as the direct result of the drift towards
liberalism. Taking all things into account, therefore, it was not
surprising that he governed Russia as he did.

One of his first acts was to introduce Temporary Regulations
designed to protect the security of the state and public order.
By them officials in defined areas were endowed with wide
authority for controlling the Press and for dealing with people
who might endanger the state's safety, and within a short time
widespread summary searches, arrests, trials by courts-martial,
imprisonment and exile returned as the order of the day.

The main target of the Temporary Regulations was *Narodnaya
Volya*. But even when that organisation had been utterly
smashed they were not withdrawn, and in fact they remained

---

[1] This was the first joint resignation in Russia on a question of
political principle, as Sir Bernard Pares points out.

4. Contemporary impression of the attempt to blow up the Imperial train near Moscow on 1st December 1879.

Radio Times-Hulton Library

5. From the *Graphic*, 6th March 1880. The scene after the explosion at the Winter Palace.

Radio Times-Hulton Library

6. Assassinat[ion]
of Alexander I[I],
1st March 188[1]

(*Above*) The b[omb]
explodes.

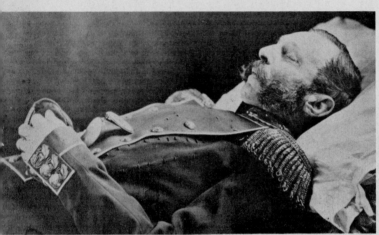

(*Left*) The Tsa[r lying]
in State.

(*Below*) The T[rial.]

Radio Times-H[ulton Picture]
Lib[rary]

in force and became one of the chief instruments of tsarist government right up to the Revolution of 1917.

The counter-reforms, to which reference has been made, affected first the liberty of the Press. The new regulations governing the Press not only restricted the subjects which might be discussed in the columns of old-established newspapers and journals, but prevented the existence of radical journals altogether. This counter-reform was followed by others of the same kind among which was one revoking the liberal university statute of 1863 and almost completely abolishing the traditional autonomy of the universities. Defining the students as "individual visitors" the new statute (1884) forbade the formation of all student organisations whatsoever.

Looking upon the peasants as wards of the state rather than mature citizens, Alexander and his advisers also introduced a bureaucratic control of the peasantry. At the same time the role of the gentry in the countryside was emphasised and to underline their position as the main bulwark of the social structure in 1885 a State Gentry Land Bank was founded.

Perhaps the most outstanding of Alexander's counter-reforms, however, was the creation in 1889 of a zemstvo chief or land captain. This official, while having absolutely nothing to do with the zemstvo (local self-governing authority) was allotted the task of supervising the peasants, and in effect managing them. He confirmed the election of zemstvo officials, could prevent them from operating once in office, and indeed possessed the power to arrest, fine and imprison them if they did anything which, in his opinion, warranted such punishment.

The land captains were selected, on the recommendation of the provincial governors as approved by the Ministry of the Interior, from gentry who fulfilled certain property qualifications. Each administered several townships (*volosti*) thus giving rise to a new administrative system.

In 1890 the zemstvo came under attack. The original qualifications laid down when the system was introduced in 1864 to distinguish the eligibility of the landowners for membership of the zemstvo had been based on property only, so that no difference was made between the gentry and others who held land. Now these qualifications were changed to give the gentry the advantage, and as a result the zemstvo membership of the gentry greatly increased. At the same time the peasants lost the right to elect members to the zemstvo; they could elect only candidates for membership, who were confirmed or rejected by the provincial governors on the advice of the land captains. Two years later urban local government was also subjected to a counter-reform which raised the property qualifications for voters to such a degree that the electorate was drastically reduced.

Early on in this account I suggested that reforms in Russia were essential if the country was not to suffer an economic condition which would not only put her completely out of the running in Europe but bring about internal economic collapse. I also suggested that it was his recognition of this fact, and of the role of the peasant in the essential economic development which had motivated Alexander II to assume the role of Emancipator. This aspect of Russian affairs has rather been lost sight of during the narrative of revolutionary activity, so it is necessary now to refer briefly to it again.

Despite Alexander II's return to out and out autocracy and the withholding of further reforms in his reaction to the failure of his emancipating plans and the activities of the revolutionaries, the "great reforms", as they are known, which he had introduced in the early period of his reign had produced an effect which could not be counteracted and an impetus to development which could not be halted. Every social class felt the impact of the "great reforms". Certainly the gentry remained the dominant social group, providing not only the great landlords of whom the Court largely consisted, but the upper echelons of the bureaucracy. Nevertheless, the gentry did begin to go into a decline.

Censuses taken in 1877, 1887 and 1905 show a definite deterioration in the amount of land owned by the gentry—197 million acres in 1877, 186 million in 1887, 143 million in 1905. This does not reveal the whole story, for much of the gentry's wealth had been mortgaged to the state before the emancipation, and though the terms of the settlement were fairly generous, the compensation had to be devoted in the first place to redeeming the debts to the state. In many cases nearly the whole of the compensation was swallowed up in this way, and this, together with the loss of serf labour, made the lot of the landlord extremely difficult. Besides, many of them lacked the education which might have made them successful capitalist farmers. Altogether the conditions were such as to make the decline in the wealth of the gentry inevitable. One result was to make large numbers of them decide to opt out, sell up what remained of their property and move into the towns.

At the same time that the aftermath of the "great reforms" was thus adversely affecting the gentry, it was also causing a movement in the opposite direction which led to the creation of a middle class whose rate of expansion outstripped the rate of decline of the gentry. The interesting thing about this rise of a middle class is that it took place in spite of the preoccupation of the government with the maintenance of autocracy and the deliberate policy of bolstering up the gentry. That this should happen lends weight, I submit, to my suggestion that the economic requirements of Russia willy-nilly compelled the economy to turn from the land to industrialisation; and that this was an irresistible movement which no amount of reaction could block.

The industrial expansion in the second half of Alexander III's reign—that is, at the time when the Tsar's reactionary policies were taking effect—was astounding, and has been estimated by the Russian-American economist Alexander Gerschenkron, at eight per cent per annum.[1] This was largely due to the almost fantastic development of the Russian railways—the mileage of permanent way increased by forty per cent between 1881 and 1894 and doubled itself again by 1905—which provided a transportation system until then unknown in Russia. This, in turn, encouraged would-be industrialists to overcome the various difficulties confronting them until the time arrived when the government could no longer close its eyes to what was happening. By this time, nothing could be done to check the advance of industrialisation, and fortunately there came to the Ministry of Finance a man of sufficient vision to realise that what could not be stopped could be helped along to the eventual great advantage of the country.

It is, perhaps, stating a truism by saying that Russia was still a predominantly agricultural country. She had always been so, of course, but the Emancipation had emphasised this character-istic. Under the Emancipation arrangements the peasants were *given* half the cultivated land, though a great deal of it had to be communally held. To evade the restrictions of communal ownership, increasing numbers of peasants rented land from the

[1] "Problems and Patterns of Russian Economic Development" in *The Transformation of Russian Society* (ed. C. E. Black), London.

gentry,[1] while almost as many more began to pioneer Siberia. On the other hand, there were still far too many peasants for agriculture to provide all with a reasonable living, and since the individual peasant could now leave his commune provided he undertook to continue to bear his share of his village's taxes, many decided to forsake the land and move into the cities.

It was this movement which was the prime factor in causing the inevitability of the development of industrialisation in the teeth of reactionary pressures. For with the influx of labour into the towns the industrialists would have been inhuman not to have made use of it; and this, in turn, led to a programme of factory expansion. At the same time the discovery of rich deposits of coal and iron in the Donets basin, and a little later the discovery of oil in the Caucasus, added their weight to the impetus which had been given to the industrial movement, since foreign investors saw that rich pickings might be had in return for a reasonable outlay and the employment of pioneering enterprise.

Sir Bernard Pares gives a succinct account of the sort of thing that was happening. "Moscow," he says in his *History of Russia*, "became an important centre of textile industry; the American Civil War, by stopping the cotton import, contributed to its prosperity; the flax industry, almost the most important in the northern provinces of Russia, also grew rapidly. In 1850 there had hardly been any private trading companies in Russia; by 1873 there were 227, but the number increased enormously by 1889, especially in mining, and from 1896 to 1899 innumerable new companies were founded."

The man who played the major role in this exciting development was the Minister of Finance from 1892 to 1903, Count Sergius Witte. He had begun his career on the railways and had been promoted from station-master to director of the South-western Railways to Minister of Communications before being appointed Finance Minister. As Minister of Communications he had been the moving spirit in the expansion of the railways, the majority of which were state-owned.

As Minister of Finance he was endowed with the powers—so long as his policies received autocratic approval—to play an equal part in the overall development of industry. He received

---

[1] By the 1917 Revolution three quarters of all the cultivated land was in the hands of the peasants, either owned or rented.

this support from both the tsars he served and in his early, critical, years at the Ministry, from Alexander particularly; for, despite his deep-seated reactionary tendencies, Alexander was alive always to the necessity for a sound economy; while, by the time Nicholas came to the throne, the effects of Witte's policies were too well established for them to be undone, even if the new Tsar had wanted them to be.

Witte's greatest contribution, from which all the rest sprang, was his establishment of a gold standard. This had the effect of winning western confidence for it enabled Russia to hold her own in the foreign exchanges. By gaining this confidence he attracted essential foreign capital and by extending official assistance to all who wished to set up shop in Russia, foreigners and natives alike, he added an impetus of his own to the natural impetus towards industrialisation already operating.

This then is the background to the next part of our narrative; the rapid expansion of industry served by a movement of the peasants to the cities and industrial centres; and the creation of two new classes of citizens, a bourgeois middle class and a proletariat. While intent upon transforming themselves into capitalists, the former exploited the latter. The majority of the proletariat having been drawn from the peasants, with whom they still had ties through the laws requiring them to contribute to the taxes of their former villages, they brought at the outset the peasant mentality to their new circumstances. On the other hand, as time went by they were to begin to develop characteristics of their own; for while, as we have seen demonstrated only too well in their response to the movement "to go to the people", the peasants had little or no interest in changing their lot by revolution, the proletariat was soon to be prepared to fight against exploitation.

The period from the assassination of Alexander II to the October Revolution of 1905 then, represents a period of tremendous changes taking place against a back-cloth of reactionary government. It presented a paradox which could only be resolved in the way that it was eventually resolved—the clash of the new socialist ideology with a mode of government entirely unfitted to meet the changing structure of Russian society as it formed under the influences of the industrial revolution.

Chapter Nineteen

AFTER THE EPILOGUE

"The 1st March (1881)," Vera Figner has written in her memoirs,[1] "was the epilogue to twenty years of struggle between the government and the people. Twenty years of persecutions, brutalities, oppression and hardships inflicted on the minority, but overwhelming everybody, the culmination of everything being summed up in Rysakov's phrase: 'We shall see if all is well!'"[2]

In the weeks following 1st March the situation of *Narodnaya Volya* rapidly deteriorated as the result of the good use to which the Minister of the Interior, Count Plehve, put the information supplied by Goldenberg and Rysakov. During the remainder of the month alone nearly one hundred and fifty men and women were arrested, many of them resulting from the betrayals made by Okladski, the carpenter who had taken part in the Alexandrovsk attempt, and especially by Merkulov, another workman whom Zhelyabov had converted. The latter walked the streets accompanied by a detective to whom he pointed out those to be arrested. Among his early victims was Emilianov, the only

[1] Vera Figner, *Mémoires d'une révolutionnaire* (Gallimard, Paris), 1930.

[2] One account of the assassination has it that when Rysakov's bomb failed to kill Alexander, in answer to the question "Where's the Tsar?" the latter got down from his carriage exclaiming, "Thank God, all is well!" to which Rysakov had retorted, "We shall see if all is well!"

member of the bomb-squad still surviving. On 1st April, Isaev, the Party's sole remaining technician, was arrested and before the month was out Sukhanov and Anna Yakimova of the cheese-shop on the Malaya Sadovaya, were caught. Early in the follow-ing month the secret printing-press was discovered, but fortunately Vera Figner, in whose flat it had been concealed, remained at liberty.

The Executive Committee was now reduced to five men and three women while the auxiliary force upon whom these not very effective people could call had dwindled to the point of almost total disappearance. Zhelyabov seemed to have foreseen that this might happen, for shortly before his arrest he had told two members of the Moscow organisation, "Remember, if your Moscow does not come to our rescue, it will go badly with us."

Moscow did try to come to St Petersburg's rescue, but failed, and in the summer *Narodnaya Volya* moved its headquarters there. The move was virtually an admission of defeat, for opposi-tion to the existing order had to be concentrated in the city where Tsar and government were if it was to be most effective. On the other hand, the Moscow police were less vigilant than those of the northern capital, and this gave the tiny band of revolutionaries a breathing-space in which they made a strong attempt to pull themselves together. However, when Vera Figner arrived in Moscow in the late autumn she found a distressing state of affairs. "Both brain and brawn," she wrote, "were lack-ing, and there were neither leaders capable of initiative nor skilful executants." The Executive Committee was no longer a fighting body and was capable only of making propaganda and carrying on organisational work. The whole movement might well have ceased to exist altogether but for the almost fanatical devotion of one woman to the teaching and policies of Zhelyabov —this same Vera Figner.

Vera Figner has already appeared briefly in our narrative. She had helped with the making of the grenades, and her flat in St Petersburg was designated as an hide-out for the conspirators should they need one. Though her active participation in the plot had been small, she was a revolutionary of some standing already, and she was subsequently to carve for herself a promin-ent niche in revolutionary history.

Vera Figner had been born in Kazan province on 7th July 1852, where her father Nikolai Alexandrovich, was employed in the state forestry department. She was the eldest of six children, four girls and two boys.

Nikolai Figner, a man of violent temper, was a stern disciplinarian, who overawed his "gentle and good" wife, Yekaterina Khristoforovna, and his family whom he ruled with an iron rod. He drew up a set of rules to regulate the lives of his children, and if one of them was broken, even ever so slightly, harsh punishments were meted out. Bed-time and rising-time were fixed; silence was imposed at table; and boys and girls alike were conditioned to withstand extreme heat and extreme cold in a paternal attempt to free them of all physical weaknesses.

The compliant mother was a broken reed so far as her children were concerned, but, Vera was to write later, "there was one bright spot in this ghastly barracks atmosphere, one comfort and joy—our old nurse. No one else in our home understood in the slightest degree either children's natures or children's needs; we were surrounded by cruelty and harshness. Only in the nurse's room, which my father never entered, only when we were with her did we feel that we could be ourselves. With her we felt like human beings, like children and like masters. Her room was our sanctuary where we could recover our self-respect after we had been hurt and humiliated."

Normally the children were kept completely isolated from others of their own age, only very infrequently leaving the estate for visits to elderly relatives who lived nearby. This isolation naturally fostered in the children a particular devotion for one another.

At the age of eleven Vera was sent to the Kazan Institute, a girls' school for the daughters of the gentry. It was a move from the frying-pan into the fire, for except for two occasions in the school year when the pupils were taken for country walks, they were not allowed outside the school grounds.

Though her fellow pupils had the opportunity of meeting their contemporaries in one another's homes, this was denied to Vera. Her only contacts with young girls of her own age were at school during term-time.

The institute provided little in the way of education. Mostly it was rules and regulations and lessons learned by heart. A weekly dancing lesson provided the only physical exercise beside the sedate daily walks in the school grounds. Reading was discouraged, and in later life Vera Figner could recall receiving only once a book from the school library in all the five years she spent there.

Despite all this, when she left school she hoped to be able to continue her education at a university, if she could persuade her father to allow her to do so. But on her return home she quickly discovered that he had lost none of his bullying sternness and would be unlikely to listen to her plan, let alone consider it.

However, now that she had come home, for the first time in her life she came into contact with intelligent, progressive people, her mother's brother and his wife who had taken to paying frequent visits to the Figner home, and to whose house she was permitted to go and where she met the Kupryanovs' friends.

The Kupryanovs and their circle were Liberal-Democrats. Kupryanov himself was an admirer of the economic doctrines of Nikolai Chernyshevsky. It did not take him long to discover that despite her lack of education, his niece possessed a lively and inquiring mind, and he took pains to talk to her about the social shortcomings of Russia, to introduce her to some of the new ideas filtering through from the west and to lend her Darwin among other progressive books.

Vera Figner always remembered with gratitude this uncle who "first awakened in me the desire to find some useful activity." Nevertheless, he seems to have had no direct influence on her subsequent embracing of socialism. Some time was to pass before, as she declared at her trial, "a comparison of my own situation with that of so many other human beings first made me realise that my aim in life must be to help these fellow-creatures."

But once she had reached this realisation she decided to waste no time in equipping herself for the task she was determined to undertake; and for her this meant qualifying in medicine. Horrified by her suggestions, her parents at last began to wonder whether they might not have encouraged this unwonted and inconvenient feminine seriousness by having deprived her of the companionship of young people of her own age, and at once set about trying to rectify their mistake. They took her to Kazan and threw her into a round of social gaieties which frightened her and made her unhappy.

However, this visit to Kazan was not a complete failure; indeed, it was to have extremely satisfactory consequences from her own point of view. She had been the guest in Kazan of some friends of her parents called Filipov, whose oldest son, Alexey Viktorovich, a judge, fell in love with her. Shortly after she returned home, he arranged to be transferred to the district in which the Figners lived, and began to call almost daily on her. Presently he declared his love, and they were married on 18th October 1870.

Filipov was a staunch supporter of higher education for women and was in full agreement with his wife's wishes to study medicine. By now Vera had become fully aware of the lot of the Russian masses, which only increased her determination to implement her plans. But she was irked by the restrictions imposed on students in Russia and decided to go to Zurich to study. Somehow she managed to persuade her husband to give up the law and go to Switzerland with her to study medicine.

The Filipovs set out in the spring of 1872 accompanied by Vera's sister Lydia who was also to embrace whole-heartedly the revolutionary cause and to suffer for it, as was her sister Evgenya. Arriving in Zurich, Vera threw herself into her studies with a single-mindedness which left no time for social or any other contacts. However, her lively inquiring mind soon began to involve her in subjects outside medicine, and in a short time she had joined a group formed to study the theory of socialism and the history of social oppression.

There were twelve members of the group, and all of them were young Russian women, students like herself. Everyone of them was later to become an active revolutionary, and all were to suffer extreme penalties for The Cause in *The Trial of the Fifty*.

A grossly exaggerated account of the activities of the group having reached the government in St Petersburg the Tsar took fright and in the summer of 1873 he issued a *ukase* demanding the immediate return of the twelve to Russia, threatening that if they did not obey they would be prohibited from sitting for the Russian examinations which alone would give them a right to work in Russia. Some of the twelve obeyed, but Lydia Figner moved on to the university of Paris, while Vera, the Lyubatevich sisters and Kaminskaya went to Berne.

A complete change had come over Vera Figner since her arrival in Zurich. Not only had she matured intellectually, but whereas before she had had difficulty in expressing herself now she was able to speak fluently, vividly and with force. Filipov, a conservative at bottom, was unable to accept her extreme political doctrines and when she moved to Berne he would not go with her, but giving up his study of medicine, returned to Russia and resumed his career in law. Later they were divorced.

Vera herself had also altered her attitude towards her medical studies. As she saw her future work now, she believed she must try to cure not only the symptoms of the social disease attacking Russia, but to remove the causes; and she argued that the medical treatment of the masses would not permanently cure their ills while their living conditions stayed as they were. On the other hand, it does not seem to have occurred to her to give up her studies, probably because she realised that she must have a profession by which she could support herself.

In Berne she met even more exiled Russian socialists and became interested in *Rabotnik* (*The Worker*), a newspaper published monthly by the Bakuninists and printed in Geneva. The organisation to which she belonged, later to become known as the Moscow Circle, now had twenty-five members, among whom were her sister Lydia, Sofia Bardina and the three Subbotina sisters and their mother, busily engaged in socialist propaganda in Moscow. Though they had agreed to give what help they could to workers in strikes and other forms of protest demonstrations their basic belief was that the masses had to be educated to socialism by peaceful means, and their basic aim was to build up a democratic association of workers. To further this aim they took jobs—in Moscow factories, in the Ivanovo-Voznesensk weaving industry and the sugar plants at Kiev—so that they could work alongside the workers they were trying to educate.

As I have already described, the Circle was discovered by the police in 1875 and a number of its leaders, including Lydia Figner, were arrested. The result was the *Trial of the Fifty*. Many of those who had escaped the onslaught of the Third Division at once wrote to Vera Figner and others still abroad, and urged them to come home. Vera was within six months of qualifying and if she left Berne before she did so she would never be able to qualify. Undeterred by these considerations she at once responded to the appeal and returned to Russia in 1876.

The activities in which she now engaged brought her for the first time into contact with the realities of the situation, and her first reaction was one of keen disappointment at the difficulties of spreading the gospel, not only on account of the lack of response among the workers but because of the patent disorganisation of the Circle. She went through a period of depression in which her friend and adviser was Anton Taksis, a Lavrovist, who helped to convince her that most of their problems sprang from inexperience. Taksis believed that though enthusiasm in this kind of work was necessary it was not so important as an ability to carry out hard, often dull, routine work. At his suggestion she decided to go into the country and work as a nurse.

Before she left Moscow for Samara she joined *Land and Liberty*, which, it will be recalled, advocated the holding of mass demonstrations in order to awaken public awareness to what was required. She was present at the first of these demonstrations on 6th December 1876, which was addressed by Plekhanov and at which a young worker, Jakov Potapov, unfurled the Red Flag, thereby inciting the police to arrest him and break up the meeting. Vera and her sister Evgenya narrowly escaped arrest by hailing a cab as police seized a friend who had asked them home for lunch.

Early in 1877, Vera, accompanied by Evgenya Figner, went to the country districts around Samara, where both undertook nursing work. Later they moved to Saratov where they arrived in March 1878.

Their experiences among the illiterate peasants here served to underline the hopelessness of the task of trying to teach the tenets of socialism to people unable to read or write. However, for two years the young women persevered, but they were gradually coming to believe that more drastic measures would be necessary to achieve their ultimate aim. These thoughts were further strengthened by a visit from Alexander Solovyov—who was later to make an unsuccessful attempt on the Tsar's life—and when she returned to St Petersburg in 1879 she was not only convinced of the necessity for violence but joined the faction of *Land and Liberty* which decided to break away from the main body of the organisation after the conference at Voronezh and form *Narodnaya Volya*, committed from the first to regicide.

As we have seen it was she who took the explosive to Odessa for the attempt to derail the imperial train on its way back from the Crimea, and though her role in the successful attempt of 1st March 1881 had been relatively small, as it turned out this was all to the good, for of those still at liberty, she was not only perhaps the most committed but the most level-headed. In the two years following the assassination it could be claimed that she was *Narodnaya Volya*.

Chapter Twenty

THE EXAMPLE OF VERA FIGNER

It will be recalled that the appearance of Mikhail Trigony in St Petersburg while Zhelyabov was preparing the attempt in the Malaya Sadovaya had led directly to the arrest of both men. In some way the police had managed to identify Trigony as the revolutionary leader who was known under the cover-name of "My Lord", and had kept him under surveillance since his arrival in the capital.

Trigony, whose parents were landowners in the Crimea, had been a fellow-student of Zhelyabov at Novorossik university, and when the latter had been expelled, since his own studies were at an end, he had embarked on a career as a lawyer, and had only joined *Narodnaya Volya* in 1880. He had come to St Petersburg at Zhelyabov's request to advise him on certain aspects of the uprising which the organisation believed would follow upon the assassination.

Trigony's base was Odessa, and here he had formed a group which, since his arrest, had been leaderless. The Executive Committee had intended that Isaev should take over the group from Trigony, but when he, too, was seized, they decided that they had better send someone from headquarters who would help to resolve the difficulties in which they now found themselves. They chose Vera Figner.

Vera Figner had already met the Odessa group, and counted them among her good friends. They included a lawyer called

Svedentsev, a former officer, who though an idealist supporter of the group, at the age of thirty-five was not very active; Olga Purits, an energetic and capable young woman who belonged to a wealthy family; a student called Drey, the son of a doctor popular among the poor Jews; and Professor Martynov, an old friend of Trigony.

The group had also, at one time, had as one of its most prominent and influential members, Vladimir Zhebunev who had "gone to the people" and whom Vera Figner had met in Zurich. Zhebunev had been a fluent and very effective speaker and being rather more ambitious than most revolutionaries one of his dearest wishes was to achieve membership of the Executive Committee. Since Vera Figner knew him she had supported his candidature and he was summoned to Moscow. There, however, he had been arrested in somewhat mysterious circumstances and brought to trial with the 193. Fortunately his revolutionary background was unknown to the authorities and he was exiled to Yakutsk in Siberia. But he had exerted a considerable influence in Odessa where, believing that the proletariat was the sole hope of those planning revolution he had devoted himself chiefly to establishing relations with the workers.

The workers of Odessa were, in fact, among the most militant and best organised in Russia partly due to Zhebunev's activities and partly to the systematic propaganda disseminated by the owner of a printing-press, Zaslavsky. Following upon Markulov's treachery after the assassination they unfortunately lost their most active members.

Shortly after Vera's arrival in Odessa, the group was joined by an exile called Georgievsky, who had escaped from Siberia, and by a young woman whom Vera had summoned from the provinces, and at once they had set about planning the rescue of their imprisoned comrades. "We also set up a secret press," she has written and confesses with one of her occasional flashes of dry humour, "but it printed only one thing—a proclamation on the occasion of the death of an old fighter—before it was discovered and Georgievsky and his young friend were arrested."

Svedentsev put Figner in touch with army circles and she met once again Lieutenant-Colonel Akenbrenner, who was later, in 1884, to be confined in the Schüsselburg fortress where he was to remain a prisoner for twenty years. Akenbrenner had known Zhelyabov when the latter was in Odessa in 1879. He was opposed to acts of violence and terrorism, arguing that all they could achieve by such acts would merely lead to changes in the government and at the same time do nothing to solve the social problems. Svedentsev had recommended Akenbrenner to Figner as a socialist revolutionary, but she did not take to him, considering him lazy, and likely to prove a thorn in their side if they recruited him. She found, too, that many of the other officers shared Akenbrenner's views. They were mostly older, mature men, quite different from the enthusiastic young people always ready to take any risk, who gathered around Sukhanov. Nevertheless, she introduced them to naval circles among whom they found many opportunities for propaganda.

After the arrest of Isaev the Executive Committee's choice for permanent leadership of the group had been Sukhanov. But before he could go south he was arrested. Then it happened that Butsevich who worked in the Ministry of Roads and Communications, was transferred to Nikolaev, and he was given the task. Vera Figner helped him to settle in, and as a result of the preparations she had been able to make during her stay in Odessa, Butsevich was able to establish a liaison between the southern and northern military groups.

Towards the end of October 1881, Vera Figner was recalled to Moscow where the Executive Committee had now transferred *Narodnaya Volya* headquarters and found there conditions which I have described in the previous chapter. New members were appointed to the Committee—Martynov, Lebedev and Romanenko—and these, together with P. A. Tellalov and Savelyi Zlatopolski, Grachevski, Leon Tikhomirov and Juri Bogdanovich plus the three women, Anna Korba, Maria Okhanina and Figner, all original members, constituted the directing body of the movement. But the arrests went on and by the spring of 1882 Tellalov, Martynov, Lebedev and Romanenko had been removed from the scene as well as other outstanding *narodniki* like Stefanovich and Olga Lubatovich. Figner herself had a narrow escape, for on the evening Lubatovich was arrested she had gone to her friend's hotel. She had noticed that contrary to his custom the porter was not in his place by the door and there was no one about in the corridors and when she came to Lubatovich's room she had received no reply to her knocks. She then tried the door and found it unlocked and on going in found the room empty. From the look of the room she received the impression that her friend had been arrested and hurried away, only to hear later that Romanenko had been seized with Lubatovich.

All these inroads into their ranks, and the constant danger under which they lived seemed to have sapped both the physical and mental vitality of the survivors. Only Vera Figner had any drive and it was she who, by her constant urgings at last got them to agree to organise the assassination of the particularly odious General Strelnikov, military procurator in the south.

Strelnikov was personally responsible for the hundreds of arrests that had been taking place all over the south, but especially in Odessa and Kiev, during the past year. He was not at all nice about the persons he arrested, seizing many who had no connection whatsoever with the revolutionary movement, and proudly announced that he did so on the principle, "Better to arrest nine innocent people than let one guilty one escape." He would bluntly inform those he arrested that they would not be released until they had signed statements concocted by him. When they refused his rage was indescribable, and he would rave like a madman, "Soon you will beg me on your knees to accept these dispositions, and I shall refuse, and you will stay where you are for ever."

Vera Figner had received many requests from the revolutionaries in the south that *Narodnaya Volya* should do something about him. Each request was accompanied by particulars of the latest brutality committed by the sadist. During one interrogation, for example, he had seized his victim by the throat and almost strangled him. When Urussov, who was a bona fide revolutionary, had tried to escape from his escort, Strelnikov had said to the soldiers, "Ah well, so you've killed him?"

"Why, no," he was told.

"Then you've beaten him up?"

"No."

"Then you've made a very great mistake."

He terrorised the parents of those arrested, saying to the mothers, "Your son will be hanged." Only with the greatest difficulty could he be persuaded to allow the prisoners to receive visits. "Jews," he would say to the parents of Jewish prisoners, "are as shameless as cats and as lascivious as hares." Indeed, his cynicism and brutality towards the weak had given him the reputation of being a volunteer executioner.

While reporting all this to the Executive Committee, Figner also pointed out to them the great damage that Strelnikov was doing to Narodnaya Volya's image by discrediting it to the public by his gratuitous denunciations and by terrorising people entirely innocent of all revolutionary attachments. For the public had not the means of distinguishing revolutionaries, from the moment that they were accused of political crimes, from other criminals. In fact she reminded the Committee that in many of his pleadings he had actually represented the socialists as common criminals hiding their misdeeds under the flag of revolution. She insisted that they owed it to their dead or imprisoned comrades to make the removal of Strelnikov the order of the day, and clever advocate that she was, she assured them that it would be the easiest thing in the world to collect the necessary information for the carrying out of the plan in Odessa, where it would be easier to act than in Kiev.

"My proposal was adopted," she remarks laconically.

So off she went to Odessa where she immediately set about gathering all the information she could about Strelnikov's habits and movements whenever he was in the city. By the time that one of the two men selected by the Committee to carry out the assassination arrived—he was none other than Stepan Khalturin, the carpenter who had narrowly missed blowing up the Tsar in the Winter Palace—she was able to tell him Strelnikov's address, the times at which he granted interviews, the times he went out, the hours at which he went to the barracks to conduct his interrogations, the routes he took, the houses he visited. Khalturin had already encountered Strelnikov several times when the latter suddenly left Odessa for Kiev. At the end of a month he reappeared, by which time Khalturin was being consumed with impatience.

It was in early February 1882 that Strelnikov came back to Odessa and embarked on a new series of arrests. He had already seized fifteen victims when the second agent, Klimenko, arrived, and the two men went into conference with Figner to decide on the final details of the plan, all agreeing that speed was of the essence in order to prevent further arrests.

After he had dined, every day towards five o'clock in the afternoon Strelnikov was accustomed to take a walk on the

Marine Promenade, and it was decided that he should be killed while enjoying this post-prandial constitutional. Klimenko was to approach him and shoot him through the head, if possible at point blank range, and then escape in a cab driven by Khalturin who would be waiting nearby.

The escape-cab was an essential feature of the plan, and the conspirators were now faced with a situation all too familiar to them—they had no money to buy the cab. They contacted Moscow asking the Committee for three hundred roubles; the Committee sent the money, but it got lost en route. Every day brought news of more and more arrests, and the necessity to carry out Strelnikov's assassination became increasingly urgent. To raise money Figner decided to approach the members of the Odessa group and in small amounts she collected six hundred roubles. But this visiting of so many of the local organisation unfortunately attracted the attention of the police to her. She was warned that they were bringing the traitor Merkulov to Odessa to identify her. A new wave of arrests came very close to her; many of her friends, among them Svedentsev, were seized. Khalturin and Klimenko urged her to leave Odessa, pointing out that her presence was superfluous now that the plan had been drawn up and the money for the horse and cab raised. Wisely she agreed and set out for Moscow on 15th March.

Three days later, shortly after five o'clock, Klimenko walked up to Strelnikov and shot him through the head. Unfortunately the Marine Promenade was unusually crowded and when the explosion rang out the crowd closed round Klimenko and made it difficult for him to reach the cab, which was itself so hemmed in that Khalturin found that he could not force a passage through the people without hurting some. In consequence both men were arrested on the spot. Four days later they were hanged.

On her arrival in Moscow Vera Figner stayed for a time with Nadezhda Andreyeva, who, with her brother, was a member of the Moscow group. Andreyeva's room was in an apartment owned by a schoolmistress who was out all day. The schoolmistress's maid, a very old woman, bent and toothless, who chewed incessantly as she moved restlessly through the rooms with the help of a stick, muttered as she went, "Misfortune is coming. I can feel it." Figner found it all rather sinister, but the old woman's intuition proved to be right.

Not long before she had come to Moscow, the group there

had been decimated. Then on 10th March its headquarters had been discovered, and Juri Bogdanivich had been seized, while Okhanina had barely escaped the same fate. No one knew who had been compromised, who was being watched, who would be arrested next. A general, indefinable anxiety enveloped everyone, and put an end to all meetings. As many as could decided to leave the city. Franjoli and his wife went to Saratov, Tikhomirov to Rostov-on-Don, from where he presently escaped abroad, while Okhanina made her way to Paris, never again to return to Russia.

The only visitor Figner had was Zlatopolski, who brought her a copy of the Executive Committee's proclamation relating to Strelnikov's assassination. He insisted that she should leave Moscow at once and decided that she should make for Kharkov, where the Executive Committee was represented only by a local group. Once again she had a narrow escape, for on 13th April Zlatopolski was himself arrested, the Moscow printing-press was shut down, and the Moscow group was dead.

Chapter Twenty-one

VERA FIGNER ALONE

In Kharkov Vera Figner found a small but very energetic group, whose main work consisted in making propaganda among the workers. Since there were not many workers in Kharkov, the group had extended their activities to other towns—Rostov, Elizavetgrad and Poltava. Nevertheless, it had few contacts and at the moment of Figner's arrival their fighting fund amounted to just one rouble and twenty kopeks. Though in such conditions journeys were impossible, the work of the group went forward.

This was the state of affairs when news came from St Petersburg of the arrests of Anna Korba, Grachevski and the naval lieutenant Butsevich. The *Narodnaya Volya* "workshops" in the charge of Pribylev were also discovered and all its staff arrested. This last blow put an end to the Executive Committee, of which, after the departure abroad of Tikhomirov and Okhanina, Figner was the only member on Russian soil.

Very few men or women faced with such a débâcle could have produced the courage and determination that Vera Figner now produced. It is a measure of the strength of her personality, her firm belief in her political doctrines, and her single-mindedness of purpose, that no catastrophe could deter her from devoting all her energies to carrying on single-handedly, the work of *Narodnaya Volya* inspired by Zhelyabov. With tremendous determination she at once set about trying to reconstitute the movement, her aim being to bring together the best of those still at liberty and form them into a group which would replace as soon as possible the Executive Committee destroyed by the police. Some idea of the task confronting her can be gained from the briefest of recitals of the disasters that had overtaken the *narodniki*: the Moscow and St Petersburg groups had been wiped out, nothing was left at Odessa after Strelnikov's assassination and Merkulov's treachery, while the Kharkov and Kiev groups lacked practically all experience.

Besides the Moscow printing-press, there were two others in the provinces, at Vitebsk and Minsk. These also had to be closed and the material safely hidden for the time being. On the other hand she could not afford to lose contact with the skilled men and women who operated the presses since she believed she would have need of them in the future. They represented, she says, a special charge for all those who symbolized the old organisation and for her particularly, because she alone wielded the greatest authority "in the formal sense of the word." But what could she do with one rouble and twenty kopeks?

She paid a visit to Kiev to see the group there, and was most impressed by the men and women she met. After the Moscow group, the Kiev group, she believed, was the best. Nevertheless she decided to take into the directing committee which she was trying to form, only one man, a certain Spandoni.

There appears to have been an ulterior motive behind her choice of this man. Spandoni had joined forces with Evgenya Subbotina when the latter had been exiled after the *Trial of the Fifty*. Like her two famous sisters, Evgenya Subbotina had already given the greater part of her personal fortune to *Narodnaya Volya*, but she still had left some eight thousand roubles. Now, to demonstrate her trust in Spandoni, she proposed giving this sum to Figner provided the latter would send her twenty-five roubles each month to Siberia.

The money was in the possession of one of her relatives, Vera Shatilova, who lived in Orel. Vera Figner had been a very close friend of Shatilova in the Moscow group in 1876, and had the greatest respect for her. Though rather ugly, there were few to whom Shatilova did not appeal through her liveliness, her sense of humour and her seriousness. The fact that there was in the archives of the Third Division a file marked *Vera Shatilova, enemy of the State, aged eighteen*, amused her greatly.

Having escaped involvement in the *Trial of the 193*, she brought many of those who were imprisoned or exiled much comfort with the vast correspondence that she kept up with them, though she risked her life each time she wrote a letter. She was arrested eventually, but acquitted, and after the three Subbotina sisters were deported, she lost contact with the revolutionary movement.

It was arranged that Vera Figner should go to Orel to pick up the money, and that she should also go to Voronezh and there try to persuade a wealthy land-owner who had once been a member of another organisation called *Liberty or Death*, but who had now retired from revolutionary activity to give her a contribution. In the past he had contributed at least twenty-three thousand roubles to *Narodnaya Volya* for the use of the Executive Committee, and she hoped that he would still be sympathetic. She set out on these journeys in the middle of summer.

"The weather was hot," she has written. "I was feeling very melancholy. The St Petersburg débâcle, the complete disruption in Moscow, the setbacks I had had in trying to re-establish contacts with the North weighed heavily on me. From Kiev I sent a comrade to St Petersburg and she had scarcely arrived when she was arrested. I had subsequently sent the best militant from the Kharkov group, Komarnitski, and he had disappeared. Some extremely unpleasant rumours were going round about the activities of the police-agent Sudeikin who was purported to be representing himself to everyone arrested as a socialist, a believer in pacifist propaganda and the firm opponent of terrorism. He suggested to all, without exception, that they should join the secret police, not, he said, to betray anyone, but to keep the police informed about the morale of the Party and the young people. He offered to pay a high price for their future co-operation. Komarnitski, although young, at least gave the impression of being an honest, intelligent and serious man. Sudeikin did not hesitate to offer him twenty-five roubles a month."

The movement had few men, in any case, and they disappeared mysteriously. A kind of imperceptible treason undermined all morale; who could be trusted?

Arrived at Orel, Figner went at once to Vera Shatilova's house. Shatilova's affectionate welcome brought her a resurgence of hope, but it was to be short-lived. For when they came to talk about the money, Shatilova told her that she had not yet received any word from Evgenya Subbotina, and until she did she could not hand it over. Very dispirited, Figner went on to Voronezh.

There she made her way to the homes of two bank employees who were members of *Narodnaya Volya*. Both were at their respective offices but the wife of one of them asked her in to wait for her husband's return. She had hoped that one of them would put her up, but both said that it was out of the question for both of them were being watched. Nor could she go to an hotel, for that would have meant registering with the police, which would have been extremely risky. At last one of them suggested a solution. There was a woman living nearby who sometimes took in as paying guests people who came from the country.

Later Vera Figner was often to recall this woman. She lived in an apartment near the church for which she made communion wafers, thus providing herself with a frugal living. "I felt some misgivings, which many intellectuals feel, at becoming the guest, a dangerous guest, of a poor woman. But I was so warmly welcomed that my uneasiness disappeared. The good woman showed me a sympathy so spontaneous that I felt at ease at once. She treated me, who was a complete stranger to her, as an old, dear and familiar friend. Compared with the welcome of the two bank clerks, the contrast was striking. I learned that, in addition to everything else, she was sheltering a young student dismissed from the university and who was in consequence under surveillance. But what really endeared me to both was their attitude towards a comrade called Surovtsev, whom they regarded as their friend. I learned, with great surprise, that he was living in the open air, down by the river. During the day he lit a fire to boil his tea and cook his potatoes; at night, when the weather was bad, though suffering from malaria, he slept under an upturned boat."

When the time came for Figner to leave, the woman told her that Khalturin had often stayed with her. "And though I don't know what you are doing and why the government persecutes you, I know that you are good people and I am prepared to do my best to help you."

A little later, the man who lived by the river, Surovtsev, joined Figner in Kharkov, bringing with him six hundred roubles.

"Where did you get the money?" she asked him.

"A comrade has borrowed it from the good woman who makes the communion wafers," he told her. "We have promised to let her have it back as soon as possible."

The roubles did in fact represent the life-savings of the woman and the dowry of some young girl. Figner was very upset at the thought that if Surovtsev had been arrested on his way to Kharkov all the woman's hard-earned savings would have been lost. Fortunately, she was able to return the money quite soon, for Vera Shatilova received authorisation from Evgenya Subbotina and handed over the eight thousand roubles. But this was all she could raise at the moment for the Voronezh land-owner had made all kinds of difficulties and put forward all sorts of excuses for not being able to help her.

In September Sergey Degayev and his wife arrived in Kharkov from the Caucasus. Shortly after their arrival news came of the arrest in the Caucasus of a group composed of officers in the Mingreley regiment, which Anna Korba had formed the previous autumn. Figner had met Degayev and his family in St Petersburg in 1880. He was a short, broad-shouldered man with expressive features, quiet-spoken and with gentle ways. The Executive Committee had been impressed by him, and Zhelyabov, Kolodkevich, Anna Korba, Alexander Mikhailov and Tikhomirov—who was attracted by Degayev's sister Natalya—told him about what they were hoping to achieve.

Nor was it only Degayev himself who appealed to the Committee; his whole family enjoyed an equal admiration. This family comprised his mother, his sisters Lisa and Natalya and his brother Volodya. Figner says that Degayev had a very high opinion of his sisters, while they, in their turn, much admired their brother. He certainly seemed a glutton for work. Having passed his examinations at the Institute for Bridges and Roads brilliantly, he obtained a job with the railways where he worked from ten to four. Besides his work he gave lessons in mathematics, maintained contact with his comrades at the artillery school, from which he had been expelled for political reasons, and still found time to carry out missions for the Committee. He was the sole support of his mother and brother and sisters.

One gets the impression from her description of them that Figner was not whole-heartedly attracted by the Degayevs. At one point she says, "A certain penchant for exaggeration, for effect, even for extravagance, was discernible in this family. Lisa was continually saying that she would make only a rich marriage. It was just a phrase, for she later made a poor one. Natalya Petrovna related with relish how one evening they had created a sensation at the theatre by appearing in a box one dressed entirely in white, the other entirely in black."

On the day that The Six were executed, Lisa had tried to get into the square, though the spectacle was bound to try the nerves of a young woman who had personally known Zhelyabov, Perovskaya and Kibalchich. And indeed she was taken ill. A man in the crowd, however, took her home and subsequently became a frequent visitor at the Degayev house, until Kletochinikov discovered that the man was a professional informer.

Volodya Degayev at eighteen had not really grown up. He had been expelled from the naval school because his loyalty was suspect, and he waited "only for the revolution to begin." With the approval of Zlatopolski and his brother he became one of Sudeikin's agents. He proved an excellent false agent, for he was able to deceive the police chief without betraying the revolutionaries and at the same time succeeded in keeping them *au courant* with police activities.

When Degayev and his wife arrived in Kharkov, he told Figner what had happened to them during the past eighteen months. He had been arrested in connection with the mine in the Malaya Sadovaya, but had somehow managed to get himself out of this very serious situation. One thing, however, he did not tell Figner, and that was how, in the spring of 1882, when Sudeikin had decided Volodya's usefulness to him was finished, he had himself made contact with the policeman, and had met him twice, afterwards reporting their conversations to Grachevski. He had then left for the Caucasus without having obtained the slightest information that was useful to Gratchevski.

Figner comments, with a kind of sinister foreboding, that Degayev set out for the Caucasus at the moment that Grachevski himself came under the surveillance which ended so disastrously on 3rd June.

On this day, it will be recalled, Grachevski, Anna Korba, Butsevich, Pribylev and others were arrested in St Petersburg. This catastrophe made it essential to elect Degayev to the Executive Committee. This had always been his ambition, and he had lost the respect of some of the revolutionaries because of his frank avowal of it, which was not considered quite the thing. Besides the fact that he had a certain right to be appointed on account of his many years' work on behalf of *Narodnaya Volya* and because he had the confidence of those who had been arrested, other suitable candidates were not in a position to act for various reasons. Franjoli, for example, was ill and could not undertake the work, and Prascovya Ivanovskaya had been arrested when Figner had sent her to the South with material for the printing-press.

Making the best of what she clearly looked upon as an un-satisfactory situation, Vera Figner took both Spandoni and Degayev into her confidence and told them her aim of setting up a central directing body. Degayev listened to her in silence and immediately agreed to accept membership of such a body.

She had been looking for strong characters, men who had ideas about how the Party should be directed and had the ability to put them over. Neither Spandoni nor Degayev was this kind of man; they had no idea about what ought or ought not to be done, and she could not make up her mind whether this in-ability sprang from inexperience or lack of capacity. The fact was that they never showed any initiative, never made a single proposal and were always willing without argument to accept everything she put forward.

"I did not want to exercise the authority my position gave me, because I was only too aware of my lack of strength," she says. "What I wanted was to belong to a group in which all the members were the counterparts of one another."

As she saw it, *Narodnaya Volya* had carried out the task it had set itself—roused a passive and quiescent Russia, and created a movement which ought not to be allowed to perish. Conscious-ness of the necessity for political liberty and of the struggle for that liberty ought to exist in the spirits of many generations. In its ambition to achieve this liberty *Narodnaya Volya* had represented the *avant-garde* of Russian intellectuals sprung from the privileged classes and from the workers. Now it looked as if even the new organisation was going to die for want of the power to act.

Figner explained all this, and more, to Degayev and Spandoni as she outlined her plan for the reorganisation of the Committee. She proposed that five of the staunchest and most capable of the military organisation should take over the functions of the

Committee which had disappeared. They would be detached from the military organisation entirely except on those occasions when it was necessary to issue orders to it. She explained that she was thinking along these lines because in her view only the military organisation could provide the necessary men, while, if everything went well, it was not unreasonable to hope that the military organisation would eventually fulfil the role for which it had been created, of supporting a popular uprising.

The men she proposed to second were the serving officers: Rogachev, Akenbrenner, Zavalichin, Kravsky and Pokhitonov. Spandoni and Degayev agreed with her as usual and they decided that Degayev should visit the military groups in St Petersburg, Odessa and Nikolaev, after which he and his wife would establish themselves in Odessa so that he could take charge of a printing-press which Figner would set up there in the meantime.

When she approached Pokhitonov, he told her that he could not help her. He was suffering from a malady which, the doctors diagnosed, would send him mad if ever he were imprisoned, and he felt he could not take the risk. Through him, she made contact with Rogachev at Poltava, with whom she had several long talks, which resulted in his agreeing to fall in with her plans, and the decision that he would resign his commission so that he might devote all his time and energy to revolutionary work.

At the same time, Kravsky refused to be moved by Degayev's persuasion. On the other hand, Akenbrenner agreed, and applied for an eleven months' leave, which was granted, and which he used to try to resuscitate the military organisation at St Petersburg which had become completely inactive.

On 15th October, while Degayev was still on his travels, Figner received a visit from Mikhailovsky, the great Russian writer and one of the founders of Russian revolutionary socialism. He arrived in Kharkov without warning and not without difficulty, to tell her that he had been commissioned by the lawyer Nikoladze, acting for a high-ranking personage, who later became identified as Count Vorontzov-Dashkov, a member of the government, to mediate between the government and *Narodnaya Volya* with the object of negotiating an armistice between the government and the Executive Committee.

According to Mikhailovsky the government was weary of the struggle, were aware of the necessity of expanding the framework of the social structure and were ready to undertake reforms, but they could not do so under the threat of revolutionary terrorism. If *Narodnaya Volya* would undertake not to commit any act of terrorism between now and the coronation the government for its part would undertake the promulgation of a *ukase* which would grant an absolute amnesty for all political criminals, would assure the liberty of the press and complete freedom for socialist propaganda. The government was prepared to demonstrate its good faith by releasing one of the *narodniki*, Isaev, for example.

Mikhailovsky regarded his mission very seriously, but Figner saw in his proposals only a repetition of those made in 1879 by the public prosecutor Dobrinsky in his attempt to seduce Goldenberg. Although Goldenberg had not betrayed anyone in the physical sense of the term, he had given away several addresses and had described some of those he knew. For several reasons Figner believed that a trap was being set for them either by the government in order that the coronation might pass off without any trouble or by the police in an effort to discover the situation of the organisation and the whereabouts of its important executive members.

She said as much to Mikhailovsky, who retorted with the question, "Is the revolutionary party able at this moment to carry on with its terrorist activity?"

"I had to tell him the truth," she says, "that it was not possible for us to do so."

"Then you've nothing to lose," Mikhailovsky replied, "and everything to gain."

Eventually it was decided that while categorically refusing to negotiate with Nikoladze in Russia, a comrade should go and explain what had been suggested to Okhanina and Tikhomirov and to seek their advice. In the meantime Mikhailovsky was to tell Nikoladze that since all the members of the Executive Committee were abroad, he had been unable to consult them. If Tikhomirov and Okanina approved of an armistice, Figner intended to ask the government to release Nechaev, who had been in prison for nearly ten years, as a sign of its good faith, because their own suggestion, Isaev, had not been very influential in the Committee.

While waiting for Tikhomirov and Okhanina's replies, Figner sent Surovtsev to Moscow to transport the type from there to

Odessa, which had been chosen as the base for the new printing-press. Surovtsev was to have the Degayevs as his tenants, and Figner engaged Maria Vassilevna, sister of Ivan Kaluzhnaya who had been sentenced to hard labour in Siberia to look after them and also help in the press. Maria, in Figner's view, was just the right person for this post, for she was good, gay, and though not an intellectual was sympathetically disposed towards the movement. So round about 10th November the Degayevs and Maria left Kharkov for Odessa to await the arrival of Surovtsev.

The new press had been in operation for two or three weeks only when on 20th December news reached Figner in Kharkov that it had been discovered and the Degayevs, Surovtsev, Maria and Spandoni had been arrested. It was a rude shock, for it meant that the last hope of publishing the Party organ, from which both Government and people would have learned the truth about the movement, was lost.

This new disaster plunged Vera Figner into the depths of depression. It seemed to her that all her past efforts had been in vain, and that try as she might to make *Narodnaya Volya* an effective organisation again, she was doomed to fail. On the other hand, she felt that she must persist because there were many eager young people who looked upon her as their one great hope. As one young woman had written to her, "You are the only star on the horizon." Even if she had wanted to give up her dangerous work, it is doubtful if she could have brought herself to do so, for she was now so immersed in clandestine activity and more than ever convinced that *Narodnaya Volya's* ideas and ideals were the right and only ones if Russia were ever to become free, that not to carry on must have been physically and psychologically impossible. So once more she tried to pick up the pieces.

Describing her private feelings at this time, she has written: "Even more than in the previous months, I led a double life. I had to keep up an outward show of calm and courage, but in the night silence I asked myself with painful anguish if there would be an end to it—my end. But in the morning I put on my mask again and once more set about my work. When on saying goodbye Mikhailovsky had asked me what I hoped to be able to do, I had answered him with a metaphor, 'I shall take up the broken threads and join them together again.' Mikhailovsky had taken my head in his hands and covered my face with kisses.

I only understood later, when I read some lines which he had dedicated to me that he was thanking me for my stubbornness."

But bad though the latest disaster had been, worse was still awaiting her. On 23rd or 24th January 1883 some of her friends insisted that she should call to see them, though they would not say for what reason they wanted her to do so. To her extreme surprise, when she did call she found there the Odessa printer, Degayev, who should have been in prison.

Chapter Twenty-two

TRAITOR OR PATRIOT?

Moved and very happy, Vera Figner asked Degayev what had happened, and how he could be here.

"I managed to escape," Degayev stammered.

He seemed to be in the grip of a perpetual anxiety. He explained that he had no idea how the police had managed to track down the printing-press, though he thought that the boxes of type which had been brought from Moscow might have raised some suspicions among the railway officials at Odessa because of their weight.

From the moment of his arrest, he went on, he had thought only of escaping, and with this in mind had told his captors that he came from Kiev and that he must insist on being ques-tioned there. After hesitating for some time, the police had at length decided to transfer him to Kiev, and while they were taking him to the station in a carriage, he had thrown a packet of tobacco in the eyes of his guards, leapt out and was immedi-ately swallowed up by the darkness.

"Some officers hid me in Odessa," he said, "and then took me to Nikolaev where I got your address."

"But where did you pass the night?" Figner asked him. "In the street?"

The question seemed to confuse Degayev and all he could say was, "In a bad place."

This reply made Figner somewhat uneasy. By "a bad place"

she understood him to mean a brothel, though he made no mention of girls. However, Degayev's appearance roused her sympathy. He was not at all happy to be free because his wife was still in prison. She tried to console him by saying that she was sure his wife would have wanted him to do what he had done, and would herself have escaped had she had the opportunity, and to cheer him up a little she said she would send a special messenger to tell his mother and sister that he was safe, and that they should go to Odessa and try to bail out his wife.

She admits that she did not think to question Degayev's story. "Complete confidence in one's fellow members had always been the rule of revolutionary movements," she explains, "and Degayev, after all, was not a newcomer among them. Several times during the preceding years he had brought himself with honour out of some very dangerous situations. . . . Later I was to recall certain strange phrases that he had used that could have been taken for veiled allusions or even warnings, but we were certainly far from being on our guard on his account."

One day he said, "One of the Odessa prisoners has betrayed us."

"But who would possibly do that?" she had asked.

"One of the *narodniki*," he had persisted.

"But," Figner had pointed out, "there are only your wife, Surovtsev and Marie Kaluzhnaya. They are trustworthy and besides they know nothing to betray."

But Degayev repeated that one of them had betrayed *Narodnaya Volya*, and Figner felt herself quite put out by his insistence. What, she wondered, did he mean? Later she was to realise they had been warnings, but for the time being she put them down to the reactions of a man who was compelled to remain inactive.

The authorities quickly freed Marie Kaluzhnaya, the maid, and soon, Figner heard, the rumour was going about that it was she who had betrayed the press. Marie heard the rumours, too, and to free herself from this terrible suspicion she shot at a policeman, was rearrested and sentenced to hard labour in Siberia. In 1889, while in the penal settlement at Kara, she committed suicide with Marie Kovalevskaya and Nadezhda Smirnitskaya in an act of protest against the flogging of a fellow-prisoner, Nadezhda Sigida.

On another occasion Degayev asked Figner, "Are you absolutely safe at Kharkov?"

"Absolutely safe," she had assured him.

"You are quite sure?"

"Unless I run into Merkulov in the street," she had replied, "and that's hardly likely to happen."

A little later still, Degayev questioned her about the times she normally went out, and without thinking she had told him, "I usually go out about 8 a.m., when the student nurses are doing their errands because I have the passport of one of them."

Yet another time he had asked her, as he was leaving her, "Is there another exit besides the gate into the paddock?"

"Yes," she had told him, "there is a way out through the grocer's shop, but I never use it."

A day or two after this last conversation—on 10th February —she went out at her usual time of eight o'clock. She had scarcely taken a dozen steps when she found herself face to face with the traitor Merkulov. She could tell by his reactions that he had recognised her at first glance, and she was surprised when she realised that he was alone, without his customary attendant detective.

She continued on her way deep in thought. There was nowhere where she could hide, no "safe house" she knew of that had more than one exit. She wondered what she had in her pocket, and found a pocket-book containing the names of two or three members of the organisation, the receipt for a registered letter and that was all. She tore both up as she walked along and dropped the pieces in a discreet trail.

By this time she was in Ekaterinskaya street where, at that time, near a small oval-shaped garden stood a small wooden house where a turner had a workshop. In this house she had some friends, and it appears that the police were aware of this, for just as she was about to enter the house, she was surrounded by men "who came from I don't know where." In less than a minute she found herself seated in a carriage between two policemen on her way to police headquarters.

Chapter Twenty-three

THE END OF VERA FIGNER

Arrived at police headquarters, she was put into a small room and searched. She realised at once that the women who had been sent to carry out the search were inexperienced and opening her purse she took out two or three pieces of the receipt which she had not disposed of and put them into her mouth.

The women saw her and shouted. The shouts brought a policeman running into the room and he seized her by the throat. She tried to laugh in order to indicate to him that it was too late, but it was only after he let her go that she was able to swallow the remains of the receipt.

A police officer conducted a brief examination in which he recorded evidence of her arrest. Asked what her name was, she replied, "You ought to know whom you've arrested."

At that moment Merkulov came into the room, went up to her and said, "You weren't expecting this, were you?" She let out an expletive at him and made a threatening gesture, and the traitor slunk back towards the door.

Presently she was taken to prison and put into prison uniform. In answer to her request for something to drink, she was given some milk, for the authorities were certain that she had poisoned herself. They had taken a few grains of solid ink found in her purse for potassium cyanide.

On the following day she was transferred to St Petersburg,

where she arrived late on a Saturday evening. Placed in a small cell at the Police Department, she was left to her thoughts over Sunday.

Her arrest had created a good deal of excitement among the authorities and in government circles. Alexander on hearing of it exclaimed, "Thanks be to God, this horrible woman has been arrested at last!" She believed it was the Tsar who had ordered that she should be photographed, because when the public prosecutor, Dobrzhinsky, examined the photographs in her presence he turned and said to his colleague Muravyev, "Pick out the best for you know who."

Immediately she was taken from her cell she was at once surrounded by a crowd of officials wishing to see what she looked like. She was taken to see Count Plehve, the director of the Police Department, the Under-Secretary of the Interior Orzhevsky, and even the Minister of the Interior, Count Dmitry Tolstoy.

Plehve was a large affected fat man. Nodding towards a line of chairs which stood by the wall he shouted at her, "Take a seat," and then began to mock her, saying that all the young people who had been arrested spoke of her with enthusiasm.

"And do you find this enthusiasm satisfying?" he asked, then shrugging his shoulders he went on sarcastically, "Perhaps now you won't mind the social conditions to which you have the right?" Then as if he wanted to look into the mind of a revolutionary tired out by her underground activities he concluded, "Perhaps you are so weary that you are glad it's all over for you?"

Orzhevsky was an elegant man of the world. He wanted to have a political discussion with her, but she told him that she would prefer to expose her ideas at her trial. Dmitry Tolstoy was a good-natured elderly man. "How modest you are," he said to her amiably. "I had expected someone quite different," and then began to speak about the revolutionaries, telling her that he knew they had tried to kill him. From this he went on to attempts on the lives of politicians and of the Tsar. Referring to the latter he asked, "But what good would it do you? You kill one tsar and another succeeds him." He spoke like a grandfather lecturing a grand-daughter, and she could find nothing to say to him. "It's a pity," he said, "that I haven't the time, for I am sure I could convert you." This did rouse her, and she retorted, "Yes, I feel it's a pity, too, since I am sure I could make you a supporter of *Narodnaya Volya*."

It seems that Tolstoy appreciated her joke, for at her first encounter with the public prosecutor Dobrzhinsky asked her with a smile, "Do you really believe you could convert Count Tolstoy?"

"And why not?" she asked.

After her interrogation at the Police Department she was taken to the Peter-Paul fortress, where she remained for twenty months awaiting trial. When she had been there about six weeks, she was visited in her cell one day by an old general of the gendarmerie, the Third Division, who told her that his name was Sereda, and that the Tsar had instructed him to discuss with her the matter of revolutionary propaganda among the armed forces.

He took her hand, and though she tried to prevent him, kissed it. "You're a good-looking woman," he said. "Your misfortune is that you've never had a child."

After this rather original introduction, they sat down, and she asked him what his intentions were; did he propose holding a show-piece trial in order to further his career or would he be content with just a few accused? He replied that he did not intend to organise a great trial; only the most active would be tried. Fourteen others had been arrested at the same time as Figner, among them six officers, though he had no doubt that several dozen could have been seized.

Later the general told her that he was neither a reactionary nor a sympathiser with the regime. He had had to resign his commission in the army because of his debts. "But for them I wouldn't be here," he said. "I love liberty, but I do not approve of political assassination. I understand the battle of the barricades, but not street-corner murders."

Sereda was the last official to interrogate her, and she was able to devote her time to writing her memoirs. When these were finished they made quite a sensation among the police officers. "They were passed from hand to hand, and we read them like a novel," one of the officers revealed.

When she had completed the writing of her memoirs what she describes as "a period of calm opened up in my life." Naturally, one so active as she had always been inevitably found it monotonous. Her mother and sister were permitted to visit her for twenty minutes every fortnight. They sat behind grills placed a metre apart. Though she pleaded to be allowed to kiss her mother's hand, the rules of the fortress would not permit it, and this distressed her. Then in the summer the visits ceased; her mother had gone into the country. "Then there was silence, eternal silence."

By the time her mother returned in the autumn, Figner found the prospect of the fortnightly visits being renewed disquieting. She had now become accustomed to her solitude and she could see no point in upsetting the interior calm which she had achieved by twenty minutes of painful conversation about nothing in particular. Nevertheless, each time her mother came to the fortress she had not the heart to refuse to see her.

Quite a long time had passed when suddenly her seclusion was broken by a very unsettling event. Called one day to the registrar's office she found one of the assistant prosecutors waiting for her.

"Vera Nikolaevna," he said, "I have come to see you for a very special reason and because I know you will tell me the truth."

Taken aback by this introduction, Figner asked what the reason was, and learned that as a result of the escape of Vasilyi Ivanov from the Kiev prison, two of the prison guards had been accused of helping him and had been sentenced to hard labour in Siberia. But, said the assistant prosecutor, Tikhonovich, an officer who was to be tried with her, had deposed that he alone had helped Ivanov to escape during his tour of duty, and this had been confirmed by Nikitina who had planned the escape. But Ivanov had denied that the officer had helped him, and that he had been allowed to escape by the two guards. The fate of the latter depended absolutely on Figner's testimony, the prosecutor explained.

He put before her two large files and let her read the depositions of Tikhonovich and Nikitina, which coincided exactly with what Ivanov had originally told her shortly after his escape. She could not understand why he was now trying to have two guards sent to Siberia, but this did not resolve her dilemma: ought she to denounce the lies of a Party comrade or become his accomplice and leave the two guards to their fate? After a few moments' reflection she decided to tell the truth.

The incident troubled her very much, and she had scarcely

relegated it to the past when one day in the spring of 1884 she was once again taken to the registrar's office. This time Dobrzhinsky himself and General Sereda were waiting for her. When she went in they were bent over some large files, and appeared to be tired, preoccupied and particularly serious.

Presently Dobrzhinsky asked her if she recognised some hand-writing in one of the files. She did not know it, and said so. Taking back the file the public prosecutor then showed her the signature of Sergey Degayev, which corresponded with the handwriting. Below the signature was the date 20th November. She was sure this must be wrong, because the Odessa printing-press had been raided on 18th or 20th *December*. However, Dobrzhinsky made her read certain passages from what was certainly a statement by Degayev and certainly a highly impor-tant document also, since it virtually handed over to the govern-ment all those whom the author knew were members of *Narodnaya Volya*. All the officers of the North and South military organisations, without exception, had been named.

Little by little she began to take in what it all signified—that Degayev was a traitor almost without equal. For several minutes she paced up and down the room in great agitation while Dobrzhinsky and Sereda continued to pore over the document. When she was somewhat quieter, Dobrzhinsky made her sit down again and then began to show her all the depositions made by the arrested officers. They, too, without exception, were ad-missions of guilt and assurances of repentance. Even Kravsky, in whom she had always had absolute faith, whom she had summoned to work with the Party, in whom she had placed so high hopes, even Kravsky had reneged!

She wanted to die, yet she had to live in order to achieve the ultimate goal of all revolutionaries—to be brought to trial, for only death or trial was regarded as the crown of all revolutionary activity. To stop herself from brooding too much over her dis-coveries, she threw herself into a frantic regime of study. She attacked English with such purpose that at the end of two weeks study she was able to read Macaulay's *History of England* in the English text. "Books," she was to say later, "helped me to live . . . they lessened the pain of our defeat, they helped me to get over even Degayev's treachery."

At last on 16th or 18th September 1884 she was taken with thirteen other defendants before the regional military court and the indictment was read to them. Counsel had been designated by the court to defend her, but she said she would defend herself.

Left with the lawyer alone for a brief moment, he whispered to her, "Sudeikin is dead. Degayev has killed him and fled."

For a moment everything went black, she has recounted, and even when she had somehow controlled her emotions she still did not know what to think. Had Degayev been a traitor or not?

The trial of the fourteen opened on 24th September 1884. There was little any of them could say in their defence, and had there been anything at all most would have disdained drawing attention to it. When the prosecution had presented their case, the defendants were told that they might speak.

When Vera Figner's turn came she made a long speech which has since become famous. After reviewing her life up to the time of her arrest, she went on to explain her motives.

"All my experience," she said, "had convinced me that the regime could only be changed by violence. Without liberty of the Press the dissemination of ideas through the written word is impossible. If some social institution had shown me some other way of achieving Russia's liberty perhaps I would have adopted it. I would certainly have tried it. But I saw that there could be no solution except by violence.

"My way chosen, I had to follow it to the end. . . . From the moment that I was convinced that violence was necessary I had to take part in the acts of the organisation to which I belonged. I would not have had the right to incite my comrades had I not had the experience myself. To tell the truth the organisation would have preferred me to make propaganda among the intellectuals but I demanded another role; I knew that the judges and the only opinion that could be expressed would always inflict the extreme penalty on those who used violence. Also I would have considered myself to be guilty of the greatest cowardice had I called upon others to perform deeds in which I had never taken part and for which I had had no responsibility.

"That then is the explanation of my thirst for blood which appears to you frightful. . . . The essential point of the programme which I drew up was the abolition of absolutism. I do not attach any great importance to supporting a republic or a constitutional monarchy, but I do believe it to be essential that conditions should be created in which the individual should have the possibility of developing to the full all his talents and of devoting them without reservations to the service of society. It seems to me that these conditions do not exist under the present regime."

Eight of the accused, including Figner and six officers, were condemned to death by hanging. When she was back in her cell a retired naval officer came to her and told her that the officers sentenced to death had decided to sign a plea for mercy. One of them, however, a Baron Stromberg, was undecided, and he wanted to have Figner's opinion on what he should do.

"Tell Stromberg," she said to the officer, "that I never advise anybody to do what I would not do myself in any circumstances."

"How cruel you are!" commented the man as he turned and left her.

Because the execution of Sofia Perovskaya had created such a bad impression throughout Russia, it had been decided that no other woman should henceforward be executed. So Figner was reprieved and sent to hard labour in Siberia. This in turn was commuted to imprisonment and she was confined in the Schlüsselburg fortress where she remained for twenty years. After the 1917 Revolution she lived in retirement in Moscow, greatly respected by the Soviet authorities. She died there in 1942 aged ninety.

Chapter Twenty-four

THE TRUTH ABOUT DEGAYEV

It is not absolutely clear when Sudeikin, the Kharkov police-agent, actually decided to make contact once again with Sergey Degayev. As we have seen the date under his signature on the document shown to Vera Figner had been 18th November, a full month before the Odessa printing-press was raided and he and his wife and associates arrested. But whether this was a true error or whether it indicated that he and Sudeikin had joined forces either in or before November cannot be said with any degree of certainty. On the other hand there was the series of arrests in the Caucasus shortly after he had arrived in Kharkov from there in September 1882, which does raise suspicions; and if he was already co-operating with Sudeikin then and had betrayed the officers of the Mingreley regiment, it is more than possible that it was he who had informed Sudeikin about the Odessa press.

In order the better to understand the strange relationship which developed between Sudeikin and Degayev a little should be known about Sudeikin's character. Holding the rank of lieutenant-colonel in the Third Division, he was the head of the secret police in St Petersburg. This gave him tremendous powers, and after the death of Strelnikov the revolutionaries regarded him as the arch-enemy. Not content with this, he wanted even higher things for himself. In fact he was possessed by what we should nowadays call a power-complex. His burning ambition was to make himself absolutely indispensable to the Tsar and the great ministers of state, and he was so determined to realise this ambition that he had actually conceived a plan for achieving it.

This plan rested upon his being able to convince Alexander and the members of his government that he alone stood between them and assassination by the revolutionaries. In its furtherance he intended to organise a terrorist group, and having arranged for himself to be attacked, he would resign from his post giving it out that he had sustained injuries which prevented him from carrying out his duties adequately. Presently two or three high-ranking dignitaries, including the Minister of the Interior, would be murdered, Alexander would send for him and urge him to return to his service, and he would agree on condition that he was appointed a minister, preferably of the Interior. Soon he would make himself so powerful that he would rank second only to the Tsar, whom he would mould with his advice.

He carried his plan so far that he actually selected men from the ranks of the gendarmerie and trained them in terrorist tactics. But then it struck him that if he could somehow secretly seize control of *Narodnaya Volya* his power would be such that he would be able to control all events in Russia.

This was where Degayev came in.

Sudeikin could hardly have made a better choice, for Degayev also believed himself destined for great things. It seems that when Sudeikin summoned him, apart from being impressed by Sudeikin's blackmail—he told his victim that he had enough evidence of his revolutionary work to be able to have him exiled to Siberia for life—Degayev was equally impressed both by Sudeikin's grandiose schemes and by his argument that only with his help would *Narodnaya Volya* be able to seize power. For this version of the whole sordid affair we are indebted to Tikhomirov, the expatriated member of the Executive Committee, to whom Degayev related all the details, and to the corroborative account of Degayev's sister in whom he confided shortly after joining forces with Sudeikin. Lisa Degayev has written:

> Sudeikin told my brother that only with his help could the *Narodnaya Volya* seize power. He spoke less like a police officer than like a fellow populist, admitting that the existing order was in need of a thorough overhaul, but arguing that the Party's

tactics were all wrong and that for this reason it was getting no-where. My brother realised that his collaboration with Sudeikin would inevitably involve the loss of some of the comrades, but he told himself that no revolutionary enterprise had ever succeeded without sacrifices.

Lisa Degayev maintains that the two strange men did not make their pact until her brother was arrested at the Odessa printing-press, though I am inclined to suspect that all was agreed between them before Degayev left St Petersburg for the Caucasus. Degayev had been involved in the preparations for the Malaya Sadovaya assassination and had been arrested after Alexander II's murder. The fact that he had been released and no charge brought against him seems to me quite strong evidence in support of my theory. When the printing-press was raided it would have appeared rather strange if its director had been permitted to escape from the police. Having acquired sufficient information about the press to justify a raid on it, it could be reasonably argued that the police must have known who was in charge of it, and even if the raid had been timed for an hour when Degayev was absent, he could not have got far before he was eventually traced.

Since it is now known as a matter of fact that Degayev's escape was faked, it may reasonably be supposed that his arrest and reappearance were planned before the operation was carried out. The police may have thought that a man alleged to have escaped from them would make a greater impression on his revolutionary comrades than if he merely escaped arrest. Alter-natively, they could have argued that if he were not arrested, he might be suspected of having betrayed the press, since so few people knew about it.

But whatever happened, after the seizure of the press Sudeikin began to increase the tempo. It seems that at the beginning Sudeikin had assured Degayev that he was more interested in gaining the control of *Narodnaya Volya* than in making arrests. Very soon, however, he changed his mind and argued that if the Party as then constituted were virtually smashed he and Degayev would more easily seize control of the remnants and their plan more quickly succeed. Degayev was quite power-less in preventing Sudeikin from doing whatever he wanted to do, for he had already betrayed Figner and the military organisa-tions; but perhaps he could find nothing to disagree with in

Sudeikin's arguments. At all events these arguments were justified by the events which followed the seizure of Figner and the officers. Though *Narodnaya Volya* was, to all intents and purposes, utterly crushed, there were still a few groups remaining. Though not of very great importance they were sufficient to form a useful nucleus for the plans of the two men. Within a short time they were all answering to Sudeikin's strings; even the false passports with which they were supplied were provided by his office; and he has even been described as the editor of two issues of the *Bulletin*, the Party organ, published in 1883.

In Figner's account of Degayev's behaviour when he reappeared to her after having been "arrested" there are certain signs that he was already becoming "mixed-up", even of having developed certain conscientious scruples. These seem to have increased after the arrest of so many of his comrades, and it has been suggested that his motive in persuading Sudeikin to let him go abroad sprang from his difficulty in meeting members of the Party with equanimity. Be this as it may he did go abroad in the spring of 1884.

He went first to Geneva where Tikhomirov was living. Sudeikin had instructed him to lure the latter to Germany where Third Division agents would kidnap him and bring him back to Russia. Here we can see Degayev's conscience more apparently at work, for during one of the many talks he and Tikhomirov had, Degayev suddenly blurted out what had happened.

Somewhat naturally he expected Tikhomirov to show anger at such treachery or if not that, then some sign of approval for what he had done. But Tikhomirov remained absolutely impassive, so that Degayev had no idea of what his thoughts were. In a last emotional outburst, seeming apparently unable to stand Tikhomirov's utter lack of reaction, he demanded that the Executive Committee—that is, Tikhomirov and Maria Okhanina—should "either mete out to him the punishment he deserved, or allow him to make amends for his crime, at least to some extent, by doing the Party some signal service."

Tikhomirov has related that he found himself in what for the moment seemed an insoluble dilemma. Degayev had told him that he had given Sudeikin information relating to certain Party members of which the police chief had not yet made use. If he had Degayev liquidated these people would be exposed to Sudeikin's vengeance.

After some thought he told Degayev that he would keep his treachery secret provided he would make it possible for the people he had betrayed to escape abroad, and once this had been accomplished, kill Sudeikin with his own hands.

Apart from telling Maria Okhanina, Tikhomirov kept his side of the bargain. Degayev, on the other hand, was dilatory in keeping his, and in August Tikhomirov demanded that he should visit him again in Geneva. Once more Sudeikin made no difficulty about his going abroad. But whatever passed between him and Tikhomirov on this second visit, when he returned to Russia Degayev still made no move, and continued to play his double role, even to the extent of dominating the Party conference held in October which, quite ignorant of anything that had taken place, either between Degayev and Sudeikin or between Tikhomirov and Degayev, decreed that Sudeikin must die.

But now one other person learned Degayev's secret, a kind of unattached revolutionary called Hermann Lopatin. He was sitting with Degayev one evening in Palkin's Restaurant in St Petersburg when he asked Degayev to tell him the details of his escape from the Odessa police. Degayev began to do so, but as he continued he seemed to become confused to the point of incoherence. Then suddenly he stopped, took a deep breath and told the startled Lopatin the truth and of how he had confessed to Tikhomirov who had demanded that he should kill Sudeikin. Since a revolutionary of Tikhomirov's stature had handed down his verdict, Lopatin undertook not to disclose Degayev's information to anyone else, but he did keep the traitor under almost constant watch from this time on.

Sudeikin was still planning the fake attack on himself, and Degayev had decided that he would turn the fake attack into a real one. But when Sudeikin seemed in no hurry to put the plan into effect, on 16th December Degayev invited him to his flat. Degayev had two accomplices with him, neither of whom knew of his double role. When Sudeikin's attention was temporarily distracted, Degayev drew a revolver and fired at him. Though the range was short, he succeeded only in wounding the police chief, who was then finished off by the two others with the help of sawn-off crowbars.

Tikhomirov had expected that the assassination of Sudeikin would automatically mean the end of Degayev. However, somehow he managed to evade arrest and escaped abroad, going to Paris where he surrendered himself to Tikhomirov. Tikhomirov set up a revolutionary tribunal of three charged with making a full investigation of Degayev's treachery and passing sentence on the traitor. Because he had successfully killed Sudeikin, his own life was spared, but he was forbidden to take part in any revolutionary activity for the rest of his life, and banned from membership of any revolutionary organisation.

Eventually he made his way with his wife to the United States. They lived for a time in St Louis, where Degayev returned to his studies and in 1897 became a doctor of philosophy of John Hopkins university. He now embarked on a teaching career under the name of Dr Alexander Pell, and for the next ten years was on the staff of the university of South Dakota, latterly as Dean of the College of Engineering. This was followed by an appointment at the Armour Institute of Technology, where he worked until failing health led to his retirement.

None of his American colleagues learned the true background of Dr Pell until after his death. To protect himself from the embarrassment which disclosure would have entailed, in 1910 he had his brother Volodya insert in a Russian newspaper an announcement that Sergey Degayev had died in New Zealand. In fact he lived to see the Bolsheviks take over in Russia. He died at Bryn Mawr in 1921.

Chapter Twenty-five

"A DOZEN MEN AND WOMEN"

Within a short time of Sudeikin's death, the Executive Committee drew up a statement denouncing Degayev. For one reason or another it was not published until nearly a year later, though the news had become known to the revolutionaries by the time he had escaped abroad. The most widespread reaction was one of great indignation, first, because the Executive Committee had not punished him as he so clearly deserved, and second, because the Party had not been kept informed.

All this added to the dissatisfaction that had been growing for some time among various factions of *Narodnaya Volya*, particularly among the younger members. As one direct result of it, early in 1884 a number of the dissidents broke away and formed their own organisation which they called the *Younger People's Will* and which came to regard itself as *Narodnaya Volya's* successor.

The *Younger People's Will* differed from *Narodnaya Volya* in aims and objectives. They believed in terrorism but advocated that it should be used not against far-off politicians but against local economic exploiters. Their main aim was to compel the Tsar to call together a Constituent Assembly as soon as possible. They rejected dictatorship by the Party. They appealed to the urban proletariat instead of to the peasants. In contrast to *Narodnaya Volya's* insistence on a strong central controlling body, they wanted local autonomy. They proposed the reorganisation of *Narodnaya Volya* along more democratic lines.

164

The *Younger People's Will* presented quite a challenge to Tikhomirov and his Old Guard, but the latter realised that a reconstitution of *Narodnaya Volya* was essential. In the hope of contributing something towards this, Tikhomirov went to Paris where that other famous veteran Pyotr Lavrov was living, and planned with him to found a new revolutionary review. Calling it *Vestnik Narodnoi Voli* (*Messenger of the People's Will*) they issued the first number in September 1883. It failed to appeal to its intended readership, however, and made little impact.

In February 1884 representatives of active groups, though not of the *Younger People's Will*, met in Paris, and accepting the authority of Tikhomirov and Maria Okhanina, they decided to set up a commission of three who were to go to Russia and try to revive the Party without making any change in its traditional programme. One of the three was that Hermann Lopatin to whom Degayev had confessed his treachery, who was quite a lively figure. He had never been able to train himself to accept Party discipline and had therefore refused to attach himself to any group. But this had not prevented him from being active in the revolutionary cause. He had been instrumental in getting Lavrov safely abroad, and had tried, though unsuccessfully, to get Chernyshevsky out of Siberia. He had often been in prison himself, and on several occasions had escaped.

Lopatin and the other two members of the Commission of Three arrived (separately) in St Petersburg in March 1884, and found the *Younger People's Will* in an aggressive frame of mind, refusing to accept the authority of the Executive Committee. Lopatin tried patiently to overcome their objections and though he had little success a truce was effected in June. This led within a short time, however, to the withdrawal of the opposition of the *Younger People's Will*, which was brought about chiefly by the deep inroads made into its strength by the police.

The Commission of Three was now able to set about their appointed task of reconstituting the Party. In this work Lopatin was extremely energetic but the response to his efforts was disappointing. There were a reasonable number of converts, but too much energy was wasted in stupid meaningless quarrels. Despite everything, however, two printing-presses were set up and in the autumn of 1884 an issue of the Party organ, *The Bulletin of the People's Will*, was published.

But Lopatin's days were numbered. He was a staunch believer in terrorism and believed that the time was ripe for another practical expression of *Narodnaya Volya's* chief doctrine. So he planned the assassination of the Minister of the Interior, Count Dmitry Tolstoy, who had only a short time previously been the target of two unsuccessful attempts by the *Younger People's Will*, one by poisoned dagger, the other by shooting. Lopatin's choice of weapon was the bomb. Dynamite stolen from a government plant was fashioned into bombs at Lugansk, now called Voroshilovgrad, and brought to St Petersburg by Lopatin himself. But before he could use them he was arrested on 6th October while carrying two of them.

Lopatin's arrest ought to have brought about *Narodnaya Volya's* eclipse, for bombs were not the only things found on him when he was seized. There was a small book containing the names and addresses of many of the members, and numerous scraps of paper on which there were passwords and keys to codes used by the Party. As a result of these finds the police swung into action in thirty-two cities and the situation was made even worse when several of the prisoners decided to turn informer. By the time police and informers had completed their respective tasks all that remained of *Narodnaya Volya* were a few scattered individuals and even fewer cells who had no idea that any others existed.

The fact that the movement did not entirely disappear at this point was due to two things: the existence of the revolutionary spirit in the minds of many who so far had had no direct contact with any organisation, but who only needed an opportunity for expression; and the appearance on the scene of Boris Orzhikh.

Orzhikh was just twenty in 1884. Two years previously he had entered Odessa university and almost at once had become involved in mild revolutionary activity which, as time passed, became such a serious involvement for him that when Lopatin was arrested he was already an "illegal", the revolutionary jargon for a member of the organisation who had to live under an assumed name because the police were on his trail.

Now, although at first sight the Party appeared to have been practically wiped out, its actual plight was not quite so serious. This was because the secret police in the south, in contrast with that in the capital, in Moscow and one or two other larger provincial centres in northern and central Russia was grossly incompetent. As a result there were in Kiev, Odessa and Kharkov, and one or two other places, cells which were entirely untouched. Orzhikh heard of the existence of some of these cells and with the help of a few students and factory workers he made contact with them. With the nucleus they provided he planned the rehabilitation of the movement.

Orzhikh was soon very pleased with the progress he was making towards achieving his aims of revivifying Narodnaya Volya; and at the same time he was delighted to find that there were still in existence a batch of bombs which had been made for Lopatin, because he, like Lopatin, felt that the movement needed some action in order to give it encouragement. Also like Lopatin, he chose Count Dmitry Tolstoy as his target and planned to blow him up when the train carrying the Minister of the Interior to the Crimea for a rest in the spring of 1885, stopped at a southern station. So, concealing a number of bombs in his baggage he made for Kharkov. On the way, once or twice he barely escaped disaster. Arriving at Kharkov, however, he learned that Tolstoy had gone insane, and decided that the killing of a madman would not be a gesture that would serve as an inspiration to his fellow revolutionaries.

For the time being he put aside plans for seeking another target for terrorism and busied himself with other secret activities, particularly with the founding of a press, in which he was helped by two fellow students, Natan Bogoraz and Lev Sternberg. Since he did not believe that the Party he was trying to reconstitute owed any allegiance whatsoever to the old Executive Committee safely ensconced in exile, he did not inform it of what he was doing. As a result, the veterans were excluded from the new Party's ranks, a fact which, when he did eventually hear of Orzhikh's efforts, acted as the final straw in Tikhomirov's disillusionment, as we shall presently see.

Many difficulties placed themselves in the way of the publication of Orzhikh's first Bulletin of the People's Will, but at last it was issued towards the end of December 1885. Its appearance made a considerable impression for it proved at last that Narodnaya Volya had not been wiped out. It gave the movement a new impetus and soon, largely owing to Orzhikh's personal efforts, groups were organised in the northern and central provinces, and in Moscow, though not in St Petersburg.

Unhappily history was now ready to repeat itself. Early in 1886 a member was arrested in the south and turned informer. One of the presses was seized and the other had to be abandoned. Many arrests were made, and in February Orzhikh was himself caught. Then a Moscow member fell into police hands and also turned informer, which led to the erasion of the Moscow group. This was followed by the arrest of Bogoraz in December shortly after he had managed to issue what was to be the last *Bulletin*.

The Geneva counterpart of the *Bulletin* had also breathed its last a little earlier. Even at the time of Degayev's visit to him Tikhomirov had begun to lose faith in the revolution, but Degayev's story had reawakened his interest in the movement. In the last couple of years, however, he had been finally disillusioned, but had grown so lazy he could not work up the energy even to declare his change of heart. His closing down of the Geneva *Bulletin* stemmed from this same laziness, but apparently he still had some principles left which prompted him to announce his withdrawal from the movement in a pamphlet *Why I Have Ceased to Be a Revolutionary*. The effect of this startling announcement was two-fold: it caused the defections of many fellow-travellers while it acted as a spur to the more dedicated. Tikhomirov completed his separation from the movement in September 1888 by writing a most abject letter of repentance to the Tsar whom he implored to allow him to return to Russia. His request was granted and within a short time he had transformed himself into a leading reactionary journalist. Nicholas II was to present him with a gold ink-pot as a token of appreciation for his services to the Crown.

The assault on Orzhikh's organisation really did put an end to *Narodnaya Volya*, but even while the police were putting the final touches to its destruction yet another organisation was being formed in St Petersburg. Though they had absolutely no connection with *Narodnaya Volya* they called themselves all the same the *Terrorist Section of the People's Will*, and thus kept alive at least the name.

The prime-mover in the Terrorist Section's founding was a certain Pyotr Shevyryov, who gathered round him a small band of students utterly inexperienced in the ways of clandestine behaviour and organisation. In character Shevyryov was not unlike Nechaev—fanatical, quite unscrupulous and with a similar liking for enveloping himself in mystery.

One of his most prominent supporters was a fellow-student called Alexander Ulyanov, who, though reserved and serious, was nevertheless the most articulate of the group. It was Ulyanov therefore who drew up the statement of the Section's doctrines. These differed from orthodox beliefs of Narodnaya Volya principally in the emphasis they put on the role of the proletariat in the march to revolution, instead of on the peasants. As the name they took proclaimed, the main immediate aim of the Section was political assassination. Shevyryov and one or two others were so intent on the murder of Alexander III that it had become an obsession with them, and this being so the Tsar's death was placed first in their programme. Already by the first weeks of 1887 their plans were far advanced. They were to use bombs which had the added refinement of pellets of strychnine packed in them, the idea being that if Alexander was not killed outright by the explosions he would be struck by one or more pellets which would bring about his death by poisoning.

By February three of these bombs, the material for which had been bought by the group—Ulyanov pawned a gold medal he had been awarded for a paper on fresh-water Annelida—were ready. News now reached them that Alexander was on the point of leaving St Petersburg and as they wanted the assassination to take place in the capital they hurried forward their preparations. Three were detailed to watch the Tsar's movements and three, each carrying a bomb, were appointed assassins. On 26th February the three watchers, who were to give the signal of Alexander's approach, and the three assassins stationed themselves at selected points in the Nevsky Prospekt.

It was now that their lack of conspiratorial experience really became dangerous, for when the Tsar did not leave the palace at the time they had expected, instead of dispersing the six paced up and down the Nevsky for most of the day, waiting in vain. Not unsurprisingly they were spotted by Third Division agents who, however, decided not to act at once, but to keep them under constant surveillance.

Two days later they carried out the same procedure. But once more the Tsar stayed indoors; and when on 1st March they appeared again on the Nevsky the police decided they must act. All six were arrested and charged with attempted regicide, to which all pleaded guilty. They still hoped that a second group led by a worker and supplied with dynamite might be successful, but two of the arrested men talked and as a result almost every member of the Terrorist Section was seized.

Fifteen—twelve men and three women—were eventually arraigned before a senatorial tribunal. None of them attempted to minimise their crime except, perhaps, Shevyryov. Ulyanov claimed responsibility for the organisation of the group. In his statement to the court he said, as Dmitry Karakozov, who had tried to murder Alexander's father twenty years and more earlier, had declared, "There will always be found among the Russian people a dozen men and women who believe so ardently in their ideas and feel so keenly their country's plight that to lay down their lives for The Cause will seem no sacrifice for them."

All the accused were sentenced to death. The three women and seven of the men had their sentences commuted to hard labour in Siberia, and the other five men might also have saved their lives had they agreed to ask Alexander for mercy. The sentences were not harsh taking all things into consideration. Three minors, for example, were given only ten years, while the supplier of the poison, Bronislaw Pilsudski, received fifteen years, and his brother Josef, who was only slightly involved, five years. The latter survived to become President of the Republic of Poland.

The executions of the five were carried out on 8th May. Among them was Alexander Ulyanov, whose family lived in Simbirsk where the recently dead father had been an inspector of elementary schools. When Alexander's seventeen-year-old brother heard the news of the executions he declared, "I swear I will revenge myself on them." Thirty years later, then known throughout the world as Vladimir Ilyitch Lenin, he kept his promise.

Anyone regarding the Russian scene in the eighties and nineties could have been forgiven if he had decided that on the face of things the mass of the Russian people were not really interested in political and social liberty. The Terrorist Section of the People's Will had said openly that it was lack of support from the public which was the fundamental reason for their adoption of the doctrine of political assassination on the grounds not only that assassination was their sole weapon available, but that terrorism might at last stir the people from their lethargy.

Nevertheless, as Ulyanov had said, despite everything there were always to be found "a dozen men and women."

But the sacrifice of life or liberty was really meaningless if The Cause for which it was made did not advance towards the attainment of its goal. Nevertheless, on the face of it, "a dozen men and women" scattered here and there could not hope to achieve any great success, for they were too isolated, always in too great a state of flux to present the formidable challenge which alone could have hoped to overthrow the forces of reaction.

Several small groups advocating political assassination appeared in the wake of the Terrorist Section's catastrophic demise. But for them political assassination, though they might not admit it, had become a policy of despair, which was not at all the right basis for the struggle for the achievement of their aims. Practically every one of them fell into the hands of the police without even having successfully made a gesture.

One of the great drawbacks which the revolutionary movement suffered from at this period was a general ideological confusion. On one hand there was the militant Populism as represented by *Narodnaya Volya* and on another there were the ideas being propagated by men like Georgy Plekhanov. Plekhanov argued that the hope of Socialism everywhere lay in the industrial worker. He believed that the present Russian capitalism was an "historically inevitable" phase and that progress towards Socialism in Russia was equally inevitable. The coming upheaval, he declared, would be and could not avoid being, merely a political change-over. To expect the overthrow of the monarchy to coincide with the socialist revolution was "to retard the achievement of both goals." (In pamphlets in which he set out these ideas he was, in fact, groping towards the formulation of what has since become Russian Marxism.) Militant Populism and this view of Russian Socialism represented the two poles of revolutionary thought; in between there were others who tried to find a solution in a combination of parts of both ideologies thereby creating confusion among themselves and uncertainty among potential supporters.

For a time, too, events in the country hindered progress in the straightening out of revolutionary thought and, indeed, effectively countered any urge there might have been towards revolutionary activity. Between the winter of 1891 and 1893 famine overtook thirty million Russians living in the eastern and south-eastern provinces and was made worse than it might otherwise have been by widespread outbreaks of cholera. None of the measures taken by the government and other bodies was adequate for the alleviation of the suffering caused by starvation and disease, and this gave rise to the hope among a few of the more militant revolutionaries that the official incompetence might spur the peasants into revolt. There were indeed a few outbreaks of violence, but history has shown that it is not possible to sustain a revolution on an empty belly. On the other hand by focusing public attention on broad national problems both famine and epidemic did go some way to dispersing the lethargy of the eighties. The famine had disclosed the really precarious state of Russian agriculture which was still Russia's economic mainstay, despite the fantastic rate of industrial development, and this led to large numbers at last facing up to the fact that progress under the present regime would be an impossibility. These people believed that the Tsar and government must see the situation in this light also, and would take the necessary steps of their own volition; in other words demonstrate the rightness of Plekhanov's theory that the changes would grow out of events of their own accord. These hopes, however, were decisively destroyed when, in January 1895, not long after he ascended the throne, Nicholas II dismissed all thoughts of a constitution as "senseless dreams".

Alexander III had died peacefully in his bed on 1st November 1894. Of the event Sir Bernard Pares has written, "This makes a division in the period we are considering (1881–1905). The difference was not in any change of government policy; it was that something which had been present during the life of Alexander III now dropped out. An autocracy, to be real, presupposes will-power in the sovereign."

Obstinate and narrow-minded though he had been, Alexander III had been endowed with a strength of will which had made it possible for him to implement his policies. If only he had not been so utterly reactionary he might have achieved for Russia the emancipation at which his father had aimed, or at least a part of it.

In contrast the new Tsar was an almost indescribably weak character. True, he possessed a tremendous personal charm, but, despite the fact that it may be persuasive if backed by determination, personal charm is no substitute in an autocrat for the ability to define purpose and the strength of will to see that this purpose becomes realised fact.

As stated earlier, Alexander, who had drawn up quite a practical scheme for Nicholas II's education, had appointed his own former tutor to take the formation of his son's mind in hand. But even the redoubtable Pobedonostsev had complained that he had been unable to judge Nicholas's capabilities because though his pupil was attentive he never revealed his own thoughts. Perhaps he had no significant thoughts of his own; but at all events he came thoroughly under Pobedonostsev's reactionary influence which was soon seen to be at work, in the reply he made to the address of the Zemstvo of Tver.

The background to this statement was as follows. It was the custom in Russia for public bodies of all kinds to present congratulatory addresses to the new sovereign on his accession. Among such addresses received by Nicholas in January 1895 was one from the Zemstvo (municipal council) of Tver, which rather outspokenly expressed the hope that the Tsar "at the beginning of his service to the welfare of his people" would listen to "the voice of the people and the expression of its dreams ... that the law will henceforth be respected and obeyed not only by the nation but also by the representatives of the authority that rules it ... and that the law would stand above the changing views of the individual instruments of the supreme power."

Nicholas did not appreciate the significance of these statements until Pobedonostsev explained them to him and it is more than likely that the Procurator of the Holy Synod drafted the reply which was designed to remove all doubts in those who thought along the lines of the Zemstvo of Tver. Proclaiming that he would maintain "an unswerving adherence to the principle of autocracy," he described all thoughts of "the participation of the zemstva in the general direction of internal affairs of state" (which had been part of Loris-Melikov's recommendations to his grandfather) as "senseless dreams".

It is certain that Pobedonostsev was so confident in the ability of the Crown and government to resist all the attempts of the revolutionaries to overthrow reaction, that it would never have occurred to him to ponder the effect that such a categorical pronouncement would have on them. For their part they saw it as a challenge, and they took it up with a new access of determination.

In 1889 delegates of various Socialist political organisations had met and decided to unite their groups into one comprehensive organisation to which they gave the name of the Social Democratic Workmen's Party, more commonly known as the Social Democrats. Though from the very beginning there were differences between various factions, based mainly on whether there should be a central authority and organised political action or whether the aim should be a workers' movement whose policy would be the redress of economic grievances, the Social Democrats constituted the main expression of organised socialism in Russia at this time. Plekhanov's group comprised of some truly great revolutionary personalities such as Axelrod, Vera Zasulich, Martov and Lenin, who was one of its most outstanding components; and the Party took its chief aim from Plekhanov's own conception of how the changes should be brought about—that is, by working through the state instead of seeking to overthrow it; in other words, non-terrorism, non-militancy.

Now, following Nicholas's reply to the Zemstvo of Tver, the Social Democrats found a rival in the field alongside them. The prime-movers in the new organisation, which called itself the Socialist Revolutionary Party, were former militant members of *Narodnaya Volya*, for though as an action movement it had been crushed, some men and women had escaped arrest; and for this reason the Socialist Revolutionaries are regarded by some to be a continuation of *Narodnaya Volya*, which is not strictly true.

The Socialist Revolutionaries in contrast to the Social Democrats concentrated their efforts on the peasants instead of on the workers, and based their socialism on the very simple belief that all the land should belong to the peasants. More than any other movement before them they fired the enthusiasm of the peasants and in a very short time they outnumbered the Social Democrats. Their programme was aimed at the overthrow of the existing order by revolution.

The birth and rise of the Social Revolutionaries—as they called themselves now—was in direct response to Nicholas's declaration of continued reaction. Though industry was growing fast during that period Russia still remained a predominently agricultural country. Hence the violent opposition of the Social Revolutionaries remained for the time being more effective than that of the Marxist socialists. As we shall see they were to be at the root of most of Nicholas's discomfiture.

"Nicholas II," says Sir Bernard Pares, "was almost entirely deficient in will. Alexander had been his own Prime Minister; Nicholas had no Prime Minister at all. He was by no means deficient in personal courage, but his courage was that of a fatalist. . . . Alexander had conscientiously chosen his own ministers. Nicholas often took them from the recommendation of the last person who had been in his cabinet. When he intended to dismiss them, he did not dare to hurt their feelings by telling them so; and they often received their *congé* un-expectedly by messenger or by post or even through the news-papers, just when their last audience had convinced them that they were securely in power. This weakness and duplicity threw the door open to every kind of ministerial and extra-ministerial manœuvre."

They also led to his being served by a series of ruthless men whose main aim was personal aggrandisement, such men as Plehve and Sipyagin, and even Stolypin, described as the last great minister of imperial Russia; while Witte, financial and administrative wizard though he was and great as were the services he rendered to Russian industrialisation, thought chiefly of his own status. They acquired for themselves almost un-limited power, and because of Nicholas's weakness they governed Russia according to their own devices so long as they remained in office.

It was against this somewhat strange background that the dream of liberty began to take a greater hold on the imaginations of increasing numbers of Russians, and seizing upon this the Social Revolutionaries decided to take action which they hoped would shorten the period of the transformation of the dream into reality. One of the instruments they chose to achieve this end was the re-introduction of the terrorist methods of *Narod-naya Volya*, and within a short time they had formed a section known as the Battle Organisation which was soon practising terrorism on a vast scale. In the active struggle between the power of reaction and the revolutionaries the activities of the Battle Organisation were to dominate the scene.

And the story of the Battle Organisation over a period of several years was to be dominated in its turn by the activities of one man who was strangely not a bona fide revolutionary and who, since his role has been revealed, has been held up as the model for that most perfidious of all individuals—the double-agent.

His name was Eugene Azeff.

Chapter Twenty-six

BIRTH OF A JUDAS

In 1869 there was living in the town of Lyskovo, in the province of Grodno, a Jewish tailor called Fishel Azeff, to whom was born during this year a second child, a son, whom he named Eugene Filippovich. Fishel Azeff's business was not a thriving one, and the appearance of five more children after Eugene did nothing to alleviate the economic standing of the family.

At this time the Jews in Russia were subjected to many restrictions. They were very numerous especially in western Russia, as the result of the policy of the late medieval Polish kings who had invited them to populate the then empty spaces of this area, and it was their numbers that were at the root of many of the restrictions that were placed on them. In our period they were to suffer from the aggressive policies of Orthodoxy and Russification, and older curbs, which over the centuries had grown lax, were tightened up and new curbs enacted. Under this stricter policy they were rigorously confined in the Pale of Jewish Settlement—the area in western Russia where the majority of them had settled—and even within the Pale they could live only in the towns and smaller settlements inhabited by craftsmen and merchants, but not in the countryside. Educated or prominent Jewish families could overcome most of these restrictions, but families like the Azeffs suffered great hardships. They were limited as to educational facilities, especially in secondary and university education, where their numbers were controlled by quotas. Total escape could be achieved only by conversion to Orthodoxy.

It was the increase in his family that decided Fishel Azeff to leave Lyskovo in 1874 and move to Rostov-on-Don. Rostov was just beginning to develop rapidly as an industrial centre following upon the discovery of mineral wealth in the Don basin, and Azeff senior believed that he might have greater opportunities in the expanding atmosphere of such a place. Perhaps a little foolishly he decided to forsake his trade and set himself up as a draper in a small way. That this was a mistake is obvious from the fact that twenty years after the move the police records of Rostov still described the Azeffs as a "poor Jewish family".

Despite his poverty, however, Fishel Azeff managed to provide his children with a reasonable education; all three of the sons went to secondary schools. But that was the limit of the help he could give his children in equipping them for life, and when Eugene Azeff left the Rostov gymnasium in 1890 he was unprepared for any trade or profession which might have provided him with a progressive career.

At the gymnasium he had already begun to exhibit some of those qualities which were later to make him notorious. There were a good number of revolutionary-minded boys among his fellow-pupils, whose rebellious ideas appealed to the young Jew very conscious of the social restrictions under which his race placed him. On several occasions he became the ringleader and incited his followers to acts of disobedience. But having done so he then revealed the strange quirk in his character which was to dominate a good deal of his adult life. For, having made sure that his companions really intended to disobey school regulations as he suggested, he then secretly denounced them to their teachers.

His progress through his various schools was somewhat slow, and when he left Rostov gymnasium, he was already twenty-one. Unable to decide what he wanted to do, he wandered from one unremunerative job to another. He gave lessons, he became a reporter on the small local newspaper, and worked in an office as a clerk.

In 1892 he fell under suspicion as being involved in the dissemination of a revolutionary manifesto. Rightly believing that his arrest was imminent, he decided that his safety lay in flight. But he had no money—of his own.

For a short time now he had been working as a commercial

traveller, and just at the moment when his need for money was great, he had received a consignment of butter. By selling it at well below the normal market price he quickly disposed of it for eight hundred roubles, and with this money, the equivalent of about £85, he fled to Germany, where he made his way to Karlsruhe.

In Karlsruhe he enrolled as a student at the Polytechnic for a course in electrostatics and soon discovered that there was already a small Russian colony in the town, among whom were a number of his acquaintances from Rostov. He was accepted into the group and shared a room with another student called Kozin on the fourth floor of 30 Wertherstrasse.

It was not long, however, before he found himself faced with a problem. The money which he had brought with him began to run out. He was living only just above the starvation line and was in a constant state of hunger and cold. How was he going to provide himself with funds, he wondered, for jobs were not easy to come by?

It was while he pondered how he might solve his problem that he suddenly realised what he could do. All his Russian friends were attached to one or other of the revolutionary movements. He himself had been accepted into the Social Democrats, and even those who did not belong to this group made no secret of the activities and aspirations of their own particular organisation. The secret police at home ought to welcome the services of anyone who could tell them what was happening among the revolutionary expatriates, he believed.

So on 4th April 1893 he sat down and wrote a letter to the chief of the Police Department, exploring the possibility of being placed on its pay-roll. "I have the honour to inform your Highness," he wrote, "that two months ago a group of revolutionaries was formed here whose aims are. . . ." His own aim was to make it clear to the Police Department that he was able to supply information not only about the revolutionary activities of Russian students abroad but also about the propaganda which was being circulated in Rostov. A few facts concerning these points and a list of names ought to be sufficient to prove that he was not inventing, he thought. With caution he signed the letter with a pseudonym.

At the same time he wrote a similar letter to the Rostov gendarmerie.

Like all the other government departments of imperial Russia —and for that matter of Soviet Russia—the Police Department was a slow-moving bureaucracy. Azeff had asked that a reply should be sent him by registered letter, and now he had to wait patiently for any moves that St Petersburg and Rostov might make.

The Police Department did not reply until 16th May, and was then very cautious. It appeared that the chief of the section concerned, with the approval of the Vice-Director of the Department was anxious to do a deal and yet was not willing to betray any eagerness. "We know of the Karlsruhe group and we are not very interested in it. For this reason you are not worth very much to us. Nevertheless we are prepared to pay you providing, however, that you will disclose your identity, since our principles are strict and we will have nothing to do with certain people."

Azeff interpreted the letter correctly and sent an immediate reply in which he said that his price was not very high—a mere fifty roubles a month. He still did not sign his real name, pointing out that the revolutionaries might intercept his letter and expose him.

By the time this letter reached St Petersburg, however, the Police Department had already found out who their correspondent was. Since he had mentioned the Rostov group of students they had concluded that he was a Rostov man himself. So they had sent his letter to the Rostov gendarmerie with a request for tests to be made of the handwriting and a possible identification of the writer.

The Rostov gendarmerie could have done this in any case, given time, because they had specimens of Azeff's handwriting in their archives. They were able to reply at once, however, because they had applied the same procedure to the letter they had received from him. "The writer is a certain Eugene Azeff," they told the Department. "He is intelligent and a clever intriguer. He is in close touch with young Jewish students living abroad and he could be of real use as an agent. It can also be assumed that his greed and his present state of need will make him zealous in his duty."

This reply was highly satisfactory in the view of the Department and when they received his second letter an immediate reply was despatched. With the approval of the Under Secretary of the Interior, given under seal on 10th June, Azeff was taken onto the strength of the secret police—which from now on will be referred to as the Okhrana—and at the end of the month he received his first payment. He was to remain an employee of the Okhrana until December 1908.

He had some of the qualities of the natural spy, particularly with regard to security. Though his financial condition had now very materially changed for the better, he realised that if he appeared to be too well off—compared with his former dire penury—the suspicions of his Karlsruhe friends would be aroused. On the other hand he did not see why he should continue to suffer too great hardships, so he wrote a number of appeals to Jewish charitable organisations begging for assistance. On the pretext of asking them to correct his German he showed these begging letters to his friends, and after a time he put it about that one of the organisations to which he had written had agreed to help him. He now changed his practical way of life, but still kept his expenditure at a very modest level.

Another change came over him, too. In his first months in Karlsruhe he had tended to be moderate in his political views, opposing extreme revolutionary methods and leaning rather towards the Marxists. Now, however, he veered rapidly to the Left and by 1894 had established a reputation for being an out and out advocate of terrorism. He had a dislike of speaking in public, and excused himself from doing so by claiming that he was a man of action and no theorist; and to support this claim he readily undertook various technical tasks.

His reputation in student circles soon brought him recognition from wider circles, and he expanded his contacts by making visits to nearby towns in Switzerland and Germany. In August 1893 he attended the public meetings of the International Socialist Congress and the private gatherings of the Russian delegates and others.

In 1894, while on a visit to Berne, he made the acquaintance of two leading revolutionaries who were to have a great influence on the shaping of his career as a double-agent. These were the Zhitlovskys, husband and wife, who had founded the Union of Russian Socialist Revolutionaries Abroad. It was this contact with the Zhitlovskys that gave Azeff his later entrée into the Socialist Revolutionary Party in Russia.

Although he was very careful in everything he did, unpleasant rumours presently began to circulate about him. Many

of them were put about by people who had taken a dislike to
him on personal grounds. There was some justification for this
dislike for there was something in his character which prevented
him from making close friendships. He could never forbear to
jeer at the failings of others and he could not overlook any
injury, however slight, however innocently committed and
brooded always on taking revenge. Nor did his looks attract.
His photographs portray a heavily built coarse looking man,
with a puffy face and sallow complexion, protruding large ears,
squashed nose and thick lips. He was not the kind of person to
attract anyone with any aesthetic sensibilities, and he had no
other compensating characteristics.

Some of the other rumours came very near home, however.
There had been two or three waves of arrests in Rostov and the
revolutionaries there had discovered that they had been made
as a result of information supplied from abroad to the gendarmerie. Probably because he was generally regarded as an odd
fish suspicion fell on Azeff. But no attempt was made to investigate the stories and they remained just rumours. Some time
later, when the Karlsruhe students of Azeff's class had been
replaced by a fresh batch, one of them called Korobochin
heard of the old rumours and on the basis of them accused Azeff
a spy. Unable to substantiate his accusation when pressed,
Korobochin was expelled from the group and there was a wave
of sympathy for Azeff.

During this early period he was privately busy consolidating
his position in student circles as a revolutionary. He built himself up in the role of man of action by never losing an opportunity for advocating terrorism. When in the first number of
Narodvolets, Burtzev printed a call for the Tsar's assassination,
the only letter of approval he received was from Azeff. Azeff
also took a leading part in educating the younger students in
revolutionary doctrines; he collected a small library of illegal
works which he lent for a small sum to anyone who applied to
him, devoting the proceeds to the purchase of more volumes. In
these ways he stood high in the respect of his young acquaintances and was invariably asked to take the chair at student
meetings. Since he spoke very little, when he did make a pronouncement it seemed to carry an added authority.

If his student comrades admired him for his devotion to
revolutionary ideals and regarded him as a leading revolutionary

personality in the circles in which he moved, the Okhrana were no less pleased with him for his devotion to his duty towards them. There was not one of his reports so far which did not contain valuable information, and he was universally looked upon in the Police Department as a bargain at fifty roubles a month plus a bonus at New Year. In fact his value was so much appreciated that in 1899 his salary was doubled and he was given a bonus at Easter as well as at the end of the year.

Having completed the course at Karlsruhe, he had moved to Darmstadt where he had studied for a diploma in electrical engineering. This was awarded to him in 1899, and he applied for a post as an engineer with a firm in Nuremberg and was appointed. He did not remain here for long, however, for the Okhrana had other plans for him.

Chapter Twenty-seven

A MAN CALLED ZUBATOV

The chief of the Moscow Okhrana was Sergey Zubatov who had begun his career in a manner very similar to that in which his newest ewe-lamb had begun his. While at a Moscow gymnasium he had become involved in revolutionary circles, but soon decided that his real sympathies lay elsewhere. He seems to have been genuinely convinced of the wrongness of revolutionary ideas and particularly of revolutionary methods of activity and felt the conviction so strongly that he decided he must do something to combat them in a practical way. So he got in touch with the Okhrana and was soon, as he later put it, helping "to undermine the revolutionary conspiracies with counter-plots." In other words, he became a police agent. Though he was responsible for quite a number of arrests, his role as informer was soon discovered, and he then openly entered into the service of the Okhrana. Here his rise was rapid, and there are not a few well-informed people who see in him the greatest chief that the Moscow Okhrana ever had.

He was not a striking-looking man. Of medium height, he had chestnut coloured hair, a small beard and bright blue eyes which he habitually shielded with tinted spectacles. Judging by his appearance and manners one might have believed at first sight that here was a typical Russian intellectual.

There was, however, nothing of the dreamer about him. He had a quick and penetrating mind which enabled him to appre-

ciate at once the nub of any problem however complex. He was
a first class administrator, could write and speak lucidly and
persuasively, and was an ardent innovator. Within a few years
of becoming chief of the Moscow Okhrana he had introduced a
series of technical reforms which created in Russia for the first
time a corps of really expert detectives.

As chief of the Moscow Okhrana his influence and his writ
went far outside events occurring in the city. He was ultimately
responsible for political investigation in more than half of the
empire. As such the revolutionaries justifiably saw in him one
of their arch-enemies, yet he survived until the 1917 Revolution.

In his battle with the revolutionaries, he saw his role as going
beyond the mere apprehension of men and women who
threatened to endanger the state. From the very inception of
the mass socialist movement he regarded the struggle between
the revolutionaries and the authorities as a purely political
question. He believed, supporter of autocracy that he was, that
the greatest danger to the established order lay in the adherence
of the workers to the revolutionary cause. He was also convinced
that the best way of removing any threat which the successful
recruitment of the masses by the Socialists might constitute was
to concentrate on making the organised existence of the revolutionaries as difficult as possible.

In his view, this could not be achieved solely by repressive
measures. Far better results would be obtained if he could promote dissidence within the revolutionary ranks, while at the
same time making it unnecessary for the masses to support the
revolutionaries by improving their material conditions. It was
for this reason that he actively supported all labour legislation,
very often taking the side of the workers in their disputes with
their employers, and it was mainly through his efforts that
eventually the workers were allowed to form unions—naturally
under police control—for the protection of their economic
interests. And while he was doing this on the one hand, on the
other he was even more actively creating as much dissension as
he could among the revolutionary intelligentsia, using as one of
his major weapons the agent provocateur whose task it was
to incite to acts of violence. He once declared this openly:
"We shall provoke you to acts of terrorism and then crush
you."

To implement this policy of disorganisation his chief concern was with the creation of a kind of secret agency within the revolutionary organisations. In this he was to prove very successful, for he possessed a flair for picking out men with innate qualifications for this kind of work. This type of secret activity demands specialist qualities not required in secret agents employed on other categories of missions. Chief among these qualities, in my view, is the ability to simulate sincerity until it is absolutely indistinguishable from the real thing. This calls for a man of peculiar ethical standards, for he must fundamentally believe in deception as a way of life rather than as a weapon to be used occasionally on justifiably moral grounds, while at the same time he must be capable of unquestioning loyalty to those for whom he works. Such men are born, not made. Not even Eugene Azeff was a good example of such a man for though he did believe in deception as a way of life he was incapable of being loyal to anyone but himself. Azeff was perhaps Zubatov's greatest mistake.

Once having found his man Zubatov also had the ability to control him and to impart to him the specialist knowledge necessary for him not merely to penetrate the ranks of the enemy but to achieve the highest positions of influence in those ranks. While demanding absolute loyalty from his agents, he gave them the full support of his own loyalty. "Gentlemen," he would say to his Okhrana officers who had contact with his agents, "you must look upon your collaborators as you would upon a woman you love, and with whom you are conducting a secret intrigue. Watch over her as the apple of your eye. One rash step and you have dishonoured her in the eyes of the world."

Zubatov also actively involved himself in this assault on the revolutionaries. Standing orders required that every single revolutionary arrested should be brought to him personally. He would take them one by one into his private office and talk to them in a friendly way, explaining to them how detestable all revolutionary ambitions were, and how just the measures were that the government was taking against them. Very often he was so persuasive that if the arrested man or woman was not deeply immersed in revolutionary affairs or too indoctrinated he could convince them that they had been led astray. For these people he felt a kind of attraction and adopted them as special protégés, and kept an eye on their future interests. In the same way, when one of his special agents retired for one reason or another he would see that he was comfortably settled in a well-paid job and had pleasant accommodation.

This then was Azeff's new chief when in the autumn of 1899 he returned to Russia at the behest of the Okhrana.

Chapter Twenty-eight

THE BEGINNINGS OF A REAL DOUBLE LIFE

By 1899 the Social Revolutionaries were beginning to be numerous and active, and the Okhrana chiefs had realised that in combating them the service had need of outstanding agents. By his work up to this time Azeff qualified for the description of "outstanding" so it was decided to call him to Moscow and infiltrate him into the Social Revolutionary organisation there.

Azeff was not only flattered but pleased, for he saw that there would be far greater opportunities for personal gain working among the revolutionaries in Russia who numbered several hundred, than were to be had from his contact with the handful of revolutionaries abroad. Though he was to become the apple of Zubatov's eye, and though I have described him as the Okhrana chief's greatest mistake—as I shall presently show—Zubatov's assessment of him was not entirely a wrong one, though he did misjudge Azeff's capacity for disloyalty. Years later, when Azeff had been exposed, Zubatov wrote to a friend, "Azeff's was a purely mercenary nature. He looked at everything from the point of view of profit, working for the Revolution for the sake of personal gain, and for the government out of no conviction but also for the sake of personal profit." Unfortunately, he realised this rather too late.

To explain his return to Russia to the expatriate revolutionaries, Azeff told them that he felt the urge to do something of really practical value for the movement, and that though he appreciated the contribution which the exiles were making to

The Cause, he believed that greater opportunities existed for him in Russia. For their part the revolutionaries in Germany and Switzerland saw in this desire for action a gesture typical of the man, and since they realised that the Party at home could do with men of his calibre, they gladly endorsed his decision to return. The Zhitlovskys sent the most glowing testimonials to the Party chiefs in Russia ahead of him, and in consequence, his way along the road of perfidy was cleared of many potential obstacles. For the Zhitlovskys stood high in the regard and esteem of the leaders of the Social Revolutionaries, and particularly was this true of Argunov, one of the Party chiefs based on Moscow.

As a cover job in Moscow, Zubatov secretly used his influence to gain for Azeff a post with the General Electric Company at its Moscow headquarters. Exactly how much time he spent in the service of the G.E.C. it is difficult to assess, but it must have been sufficient not to arouse the criticism of his employers. Yet when one considers how much time he spent in his other double-role, one is left with the impression that either Zubatov had taken the chiefs of the G.E.C. into his confidence—which in my view could have been quite dangerous, or that Azeff was a glutton for work. There are, in fact, several aspects of Azeff's story which, despite the full disclosures that were subsequently made, have not yet been satisfactorily explained.

Within a short time of his arrival in Moscow this cover side of Azeff's life had been satisfactorily arranged, and he had already begun to feel his way into revolutionary circles. In this he showed a very delicate appreciation of the necessity for patience. He began by becoming a member of the Intellectual Aid Society which was composed mostly of the flower of the Moscow intelligentsia. He contributed to the society's paper, attended meetings and dinners which it organised and in this way gradually extended his revolutionary acquaintanceship.

Beginning thus was a very clever move, for though the men and women he met were liberal in thought to the extent of being revolutionary, the intelligentsia were not yet a powerful force in the revolutionary movement. Thus, while he was becoming known to these mild opponents of authority, he was behaving exactly as a bona fide revolutionary might behave who did not wish to attract official attention to himself.

His main objective, as I have said earlier, was to make contact with the Social Revolutionaries, but over this he took his time, being both cautious and circumspect in his initial approaches. For a long time after he had met the leaders and had been accepted into the movement, he continued to exhibit almost a lack of interest in its doings. What I mean is that while declaring himself to be a sympathiser, he in no way forced his presence on the leaders, nor indeed on any member of the movement; he never asked questions, never showed any curiosity which might have aroused suspicions. If he were drawn into a general discussion, he did not hesitate to state as his opinion that it was practically impossible to form large organisations and to found a clandestine press which could have any lasting security of function, simply because the police were too strong. He let it be known to the people who at this time were only theoretical terrorists that he believed terrorism to be the only weapon which could have any chance of success in achieving the revolutionary objectives. In all this, of course, he was being consistent with the portrait of himself which he had delineated while in Germany and Switzerland, a portrait known to the Moscow revolutionaries through the descriptions of him given by the expatriates.

On the other hand, though he always took the opportunity of saying that all other forms of revolutionary activity were trifling, he never refused a plea for help when it was made to him. For example, when the Social Revolutionary press had need of "a solid but not too unwieldy roller" and asked him if he could help in obtaining one, he readily agreed, saying that he knew an engineer who worked in a factory who could make one for him.

So by degrees he built up a reputation for being cautious and prudent yet not to the point of being cowardly. He also established himself as a man who had a practical approach to all problems, and in this role his advice was soon being constantly sought. In this way he soon became conversant with almost every ramification of the Party's activities, and everything he learned he passed on—at this stage—to Zubatov whose expressions of delight in his "beloved" agent grew ever more lyrical.

And Zubatov by the end of 1901 had every justification for his delight, for as Argunov was later to record, "We told Azeff all our passwords, all our connections, both literary and organisational, the names and addresses of our associates, and we recommended him warmly to all our friends. He enjoyed all our confidence . . . we looked upon him as a comrade and even perhaps as a friend. In the days of misfortune his active participation drew him closer to us."

Zubatov was not slow to show his appreciation of Azeff's efforts in the one way which the agent found most acceptable. In January 1900, after his return to Moscow, his salary had been increased to a hundred and fifty roubles a month. By the end of 1901 this had been doubled in recognition of his services in those two years, which, from Zubatov's point of view at least, had been most satisfactory, but from the point of view of the ignorant Social Revolutionaries had been quite disastrous.

Briefly the facts of these two years were these. On his arrival in Moscow the Social Revolutionaries had begun to publish their own paper, *Revolutzionaya Rossiya*. The press on which it was printed had been set up in Finland on the estate of a sympathetic woman landowner near Talu. Under the editorship of two of the leading populist writers, Nyakotin and Peshekhonov, it published its first issue in January 1901, and this, with the second issue which appeared soon after, was circulated fairly widely throughout Russia.

By this time Azeff had been able to supply Zubatov with information which would have been quite sufficient for him to arrest the leaders of the Party. But the Okhrana chief normally acted on the principle that it was useless to arrest individual leaders since almost invariably new leaders would be forthcoming. When he pounced he liked to make the largest possible haul. He acted on this principle now, and decided that little purpose would be served in raiding the Finnish press until he knew the identities of far more of the people connected with it than he knew at present. On the other hand the success of the two first issues had already imparted to the paper a quite considerable influence, so he decided to put it temporarily out of commission.

He planned this operation with great care. Numbers of police agents were sent to Talu with instructions not to act against the press, but to behave in such a way that those running it would believe a raid to be imminent, take fright and decide to find new quarters.

The plan worked perfectly. A search was immediately made for a more suitable place, and one was found at Tomsk, in Siberia, where Argunov's brother-in-law, Pavlov, was director of the detention centre. The centre itself, which was to be the new home for the press, was outside the town in an isolated spot in the forest; a better site could hardly have been found; and when it is also known that the staff of the centre all had revolutionary leanings, its full desirability can be judged.

The press was dismantled, the parts distributed to several people, who each travelled to Tomsk by a different route, making long detours to shake off the scent of any possible Okhrana followers. By September 1901 it had been reassembled at the detention centre and was ready to produce the third issue of *Revolutzionaya Rossiya*, which Zubatov decided he must prevent. But before he gave orders to this effect he called Azeff in and discussed with him carefully the possibilities of the agent being compromised if he did. As a result of this discussion he came to the conclusion that Azeff's position vis-à-vis the revolutionaries would not be endangered. So he briefed an officer of the gendarmerie called Spiridovich to go to Tomsk, raid the press, make the arrests and carry out an investigation. Before Spiridovich could reach Tomsk, however, intelligence reached Zubatov that the paper was already rolling off the press, so orders were given to the Tomsk police to make the raid at once before the copies could be distributed. The subsequent inquiry, however, was left to Spiridovich who went about it so skilfully that not only did the slightest suspicion not fall on Azeff but because of the operation his position with the revolutionaries was finally consolidated.

The raid in Tomsk was interpreted by the Moscow leaders as an indication that their own turn must soon come, and their only desire was to salvage as much as they could from the wreck that the Party would undoubtedly become with their removal. Their only chance was to put in charge of the Party's affairs a man who was not yet compromised, and therefore not in danger of arrest. Azeff, they believed, was the man they were looking for. "Azeff," Argunov has written, "shared to the full our sorrow at the seizure of the Tomsk press. It might have been a personal disaster. His whole attitude completely changed. From being a passive collaborator he now became an active member of our Party. There was no formal entry into the Party; it all took place naturally."

As soon as Zubatov learned that it was intended that Azeff should succeed Argunov, he ordered the strict surveillance under which he had been keeping the Moscow leaders to be relaxed.

Now that his brilliant agent had placed the entire Social Revolutionary Party in his power, Zubatov widened his horizons. He set his sights now on obtaining the same power over the All-Russian Organisation, which was based abroad. He therefore instructed Azeff to tell Argunov that for business reasons he must go on a trip to Europe and to offer to be of any service which Argunov might think he could render. Argunov immediately appointed Azeff to be his representative at the projected discussions which the All-Russian Organisation was planning in the near future with the object of uniting into one united movement all the various Populist groups within Russia. With Azeff was to go Maria Seliuk, whom Argunov thought might be useful to his delegate since she was familiar with all the ramifications of the Party's organisation with which, he believed quite wrongly, Azeff was not acquainted.

Zubatov now raised Azeff's salary to five hundred roubles a month, a sum hitherto unheard of in secret police circles for one in the double-agent's position, and at the end of November 1901 Azeff left Russia. Zubatov, who shared Argunov's view of Seliuk's value to Azeff, had made no attempt to stop her from leaving the country a short time previously. Two weeks after Azeff left Zubatov pounced and arrested Argunov and several other Moscow leaders. Argunov was subsequently sentenced to two years imprisonment and banishment to Siberia, from where he escaped in 1905.

In actual fact the negotiations between the Social Revolutionaries and the All-Russian Organisation had almost been completed before the Tomsk raid, and Azeff's role was really little more than acting as signatory to the agreement drawn up between the two parties on behalf of the Moscow Socialist Revolutionaries. Besides this, Argunov had commissioned him to make arrangements for the printing of *Revolutzionaya Rossiya* outside Russia. This Azeff faithfully now tried to do with the help of Seliuk and G. A. Gershuni, the representative of the organisations of south and south-west Russia, of whom we shall be hearing more presently. For two months the negotiations went on, until they were successfully concluded. At the same time Azeff was drawn into the planning of future activities and tactics to be followed by the new centralised organisation.

Revolutzionaya Rossiya, which was to be published in

Switzerland, was to become henceforward the organ of the
Social Revolutionaries. Gotz and Tchernov were appointed
editors, and with the addition of Gershuni, the executive members of the Party committee. Since the first two had their hands
full with the publication and distribution of the paper, Gershuni
became the chief practical organiser. Until his arrest about a
year later, in May 1903, he was continuously on the move,
visiting practically every part of Russia. Catherine Breshkov-
skaya, who became colloquially known as the Holy Ghost of the
Revolution, acted as Gershuni's deputy, like him travelling the
length and breadth of the country, converting and inciting.
Wherever she went Gershuni followed and organised and consolidated the effects of her enthusiasm and adding more and more
groups which became affiliated with the Social Revolutionaries.

As a young man Gershuni had fallen into Zubatov's hands
and had been subjected to his process of brain-washing. The
experiment in this case, however, had not been successful, for
though Gershuni had declared himself to be enlightened and
actually wrote out a confession of his errors, he betrayed nothing and no one. At once on his release he had returned to his
"bad revolutionary ways" but with an increased hatred of
authority. Few of his revolutionary contemporaries could equal
his passionate advocacy of revolution, while his constant
demands for the renewal of terrorism made him at least the
theoretical equal of Azeff in this respect. It was his quality as a
propagandist and as an inciter to action which made him one of
the most popular figures among the younger generations of
potential and actual revolutionaries.

Because of his reputation for calm practical judgment and his
ability to deal with the minutiae of any undertaking, the three
leaders kept in close touch with Azeff, who had made a very
deep impression on Gershuni by virtue of these qualities. Within a short time of their meeting, these two men, the one the
virtual leader of the largest revolutionary organisation to exist
in Russia up to this time, the other one of the most successful of
Okhrana secret agents, were on such intimate terms that they
decoded together the secret letters that arrived from Russia.
Azeff was for his part attracted to Gershuni because he had been
the very first revolutionary he had met to advocate an immediate return to terrorism. Subtly he played upon Gershuni's eagerness for this kind of revolutionary expression. Tchernov and

Gotz were not so attracted by the idea, and long discussions took place at which it was decided that the subject should not be mentioned outside the four of them. At last a decision was reached; while all admitted that there was no objection in principle to resorting to terrorism, in deference to Gotz's and Tchernov's reservations about its practical application they would make no public reference to it until the first important terrorist act had been successfully carried out. Once this had been achieved the Party would assume responsibility for it and declare that terror had become an official weapon in the Party's armoury.

This decision, somewhat naturally, spurred Gershuni to organise such an act as soon as possible. As he explained, he already had volunteers for its performance and had chosen the target—Sipyagin, the Minister of the Interior. If the plan were successful then he claimed the right to form a special section for terror which he proposed calling the Battle Organisation.

It is at this precise moment, too, that we see Azeff transform himself into the complete double agent. Not long after his departure from Russia, his relationship with Zubatov had undergone a slight change. The Moscow Okhrana chief was no longer his sole superior; Azeff now belonged as much to the Police Department as to Zubatov, and was required to send his reports to the Department in the first instance. Sometimes he sent a duplicate report to Zubatov, but for the most part Zubatov learned of the activities of his prize agent through the Department.

During these early months of his association with the triumvirate, he was sending full reports on Gershuni—and the others —to the Department. In them one may detect the deep satisfaction of a secret agent who had penetrated the sanctum sanctorum of the enemy without having been discovered. He told his superiors in one report, for example, "In Berlin and Paris I have penetrated into the very heart of the enemy's camp."

But as soon as the decision to give terrorism a trial, notably towards the close of January 1902, his reports on Gershuni underwent a subtle change. While he gave particulars of Gershuni's latest itinerary, he added with emphasis, "He must not be arrested yet under any circumstances; bear this in mind." Clearly the Department was as dazzled by their agent's fantastic success as Zubatov had been, for they were fully prepared to take his advice on what was after all purely a decision for the Department, and in consequence Gershuni went about his work unimpeded. They used the very argument which Azeff might have used himself had they asked him why Gershuni should not be arrested without delay. In a Department minute to Zubatov it was stated, "Gershuni cannot escape us since he is in such close contact with our agent. His immediate arrest would deprive us of information about the future plans of the Party and furthermore would compromise our agent." On the other hand, everywhere Gershuni went he would be followed, and every contact he made would be noted for future action.

Unfortunately they had not taken into account Gershuni's experience of underground work. He soon discovered that he was being trailed and with great ease threw his shadowers off his scent. Nor could they pick him up again.

Gershuni's main object in making this trip, as Azeff very well knew, was to arrange the details of Sipyagin's assassination. Sipyagin had replaced Goremykin as Minister of the Interior largely as the result of the machinations of Count Witte, Minister for Finance, in his intrigues against the proposal of Goremykin to extend the elective principle to the zemstva of the western provinces, which Witte regarded as altogether too liberal. Sipyagin was a thorough-going reactionary, and though he had not specifically been responsible for any particularly repressive measure, he was a legitimate target for revolutionaries.

In making the preparations for the assassination Gershuni was helped by P. P. Kraft and M. M. Melnikov, both members of the Saratov committee of the Social Revolutionary Party. These three, together with the volunteer assassin, a young Kiev student called Balmashev, met in Finland, and it was from there that Balmashev set out for St Petersburg on 15th April 1902 wearing the uniform of an aide-de-camp. There was one last minute hitch. On the way to the station Balmashev realised that he had forgotten his sword, and was therefore improperly dressed. Fortunately they were able to buy another.

The plan was that Balmashev should go to the Ministry of the Interior a few minutes before Sipyagin's normal reception time and announced that he had come from the Grand Duke Sergey with a personal message for the Minister. When Balmashev arrived there were already a number of petitioners in the anteroom, as the conspirators had hoped there would be, because although to kill the Minister in a confined space meant the virtual suicide of the assassin, Gershuni wanted there to be public witnesses to the "execution".

Exactly on the hour Sipyagin came into the ante-room accompanied by a small entourage of officials. He had already been informed by one of the secretaries that an aide-de-camp from the Grand Duke Sergey was waiting for him with a private message, and on seeing the young "aide-de-camp" he went up to him. Balmashev held out to him a sealed package which contained the sentence of death passed on him by the revolutionaries, and at the same time fired two shots at point-blank range. His victim fell dead at his feet.

After a moment or two of stupefied inaction, the Minister's aides seized Balmashev, who had made no attempt to escape. He was tried by court-martial and hanged in the Schlüsselburg fortress on 16th May.

Gershuni had followed Balmashev to St Petersburg and after the assassination remained in the capital for a few days. The killing of Sipyagin had been planned as the first of three assassinations which were to take place in quick succession. An officer called Grigoriev was to kill the arch-reactionary Pobedonostsev as he attended Sipyagin's funeral, and in the confusion which would thus be created, Grigoriev's fiancée, Yurkovskaya, was to shoot the notorious Governor-General of St Petersburg, Kleygels. This plan was foiled, however, because the Procurator of the Holy Synod did not attend the funeral.

The death of Sipyagin made a deep impression throughout all Russia, and particularly in the ranks of the revolutionaries who saw in it the opening of a new phase of direct action in their long struggle. Gershuni's own elation mirrored the general upsurge of hope which ran through the Social Revolutionary movement. A Party comrade who met him on a railway station shortly afterwards recorded, "Gershuni was cheerful and gay, and full of his first important success. 'It is just the beginning,' he said. 'The Gordian knot has been cut; terror has justified itself. All discussion has now become superfluous. The youth must now come forward at once. Time won't wait. We must act now.'"

He was not to be disappointed. For everyone who fell in the ranks of the Battle Organisation, a dozen volunteers came forward though all knew that because of the way the Organisation chose to work, they were condemning themselves to death.

Chapter Twenty-nine

GERSHUNI'S BATTLE ORGANISATION

The successful assassination of the Minister of the Interior and the comrades' reaction to it, particularly the latter, converted Chernov and Gotz to the use of terrorism, and they gave Gershuni the go-ahead for the establishment of his Battle Organisation; and the energetic and enthusiastic Gershuni lost no time. He had several daring plans already in mind which included the assassinations of the new Minister of the Interior, the former head of the Police Department, Viacheslav Plehve, the Governor of Kharkov, General Obolensky, who had recently put down a peasant rising in his province by mass floggings, and also Azeff's old friend Zubatov.

The Battle Organisation, as it grew up under Gershuni's guidance, became an autonomous body within the Social Revolutionary Party. In fact, in this early phase of its existence it might be said that the Organisation was Gershuni. He concocted plans and with his great powers of persuasion had no difficulty in obtaining general approval for them from the other Party leaders. They, for their part, had such confidence in him that they were prepared to leave all the detailed organisation to him, and were content to acknowledge whatever he succeeded in doing in the name of the whole Party.

Gershuni still travelled widely on general Party business, and though he carried out these assignments with a thoroughness which gave no cause for criticism, he used his trips to recruit

young men and women who in his view would make suitable
agents for his terrorism. Whenever he found such people, with
the Party's automatic consent he took them off whatever work
they were doing, then thoroughly indoctrinated them and
trained them for active work.

His actual method of working was interesting. He never made
detailed elaborate plans for any of the acts he organised. He
argued that it was quite useless to do so, as all former experience
showed, because the unforeseen was always likely to happen,
and this could throw even the most carefully prepared scheme
completely out of joint. He preferred to proceed, therefore,
according to the inspiration of the moment, and so long as he
was at its head the Battle Organisation had great success with
this method of operation, for he was a master of improvisation.
Zubatov was to describe him as "an artist in terror"; it was a
description which exactly fitted him. That he was able to operate
so long as he did was due entirely to the fact that Eugene Azeff,
his confidant along with Gotz in all matters pertaining to the
Organisation, had at last begun to play his double game in
earnest.

Azeff's holding back of information dates from the time that
the murder of Sipyagin was being prepared, and how he proceeded in a way that roused the suspicions of neither side,
presents a study in deception scarcely equalled in this sphere of
secret activity.

Vis-à-vis the revolutionaries his task of deception was comparatively easy. It required only that he should not be seen
visiting the Police Department or in the company of detectives,
and of providing himself with an alibi which would dissociate
him from any police activity originating from his information.
As we have already seen, the police took great trouble in protecting him from possible compromise.

Vis-à-vis the Police Department his task was much more complex. The Department knew that "he had penetrated to the very
heart of things" and were expecting him to continue to supply
them with the high-grade information which he had passed to
them almost from the time that he had entered their service.
Once he had embarked on what can only be described as a career
of "collaboration" with the revolutionaries, in order to safeguard his relations with the Police Department, he had to be
extremely selective in the material he left out of his reports. He

had to go on supplying information about revolutionary activities on which the police could base effective repressive action,
and at the same time also had to be ready with an explanation
should he ever be questioned about why he had either not known
or had not reported plans of which his very relationship with
the leaders of the Social Revolutionary Party made it virtually
certain he must have been aware.

The Police, as we have seen, were alive to the fact that he was
working for them for purely mercenary reasons; and since this
was certainly true, the matter of his motive for supporting the
revolutionaries becomes interesting as he made comparatively
little money out of them at least in the early years. What his
motivation was can really only be surmised, for he never disclosed it. Even if he had given reasons, one would be justified in
not accepting them, since he was such an inveterate liar.

Perhaps one may approach somewhere near the truth by
taking into account the fact that he held back from the police,
for the greater part of the time, only the plans and activities of
the Battle Organisation and the information that this Organisation was concerned only with killing. Could it have been that
there was in him a curious streak of sadism which could be satisfied by plotting to kill; a kind of long-range lust to kill; for
though he was later said to have prepared the actual bombs used
in assassinations, he never took part in any attempt nor ever
witnessed one? Or is one doing him an injustice by making this
suggestion and he was basically a sincere supporter of revolution,
whose betrayal of friends to their deaths was motivated by
another lust as irresistible as the lust to kill—the lust for money.
Considering how very little one has to go on, perhaps it is a
waste of time attempting to get into the mind of this strange
man.

Azeff first began to conceal information from the police when
Sipyagin's assassination was being discussed by Gershuni and
the others. There was even no general reference in his reports at
this time that the Party leadership was proposing to resort to
terror tactics. True, there is no evidence that he knew any of the
details of Gershuni's plans, but it is difficult to accept Chernov's
later suggestion that Azeff did not know that Gershuni had
chosen Sipyagin as his first victim in view of Azeff's insistence
to his police chief that Gershuni "must not be arrested yet
under any circumstances" while on the trip on which the

assassination was planned and carried out. Besides, the very close intimacy that had grown up between the two men makes it practically certain that Gershuni told his friend who was to be the victim of the first act of terror.

It is after the Minister's murder that we see Azeff adopting a technique of safeguarding himself from police suspicion. His first reply to the Department's questions about why he had not reported that the murder was being planned, stated categorically that he had known nothing at all about it. He was then instructed to discover whether, as the police already suspected, Gershuni had had any hand in it. For the next five weeks—the period during which Gershuni remained in Russia—he reiterated again and again that Gershuni was not involved in the affair and could not be involved because he was too immersed in general Party business. His information was, he said, that the assassination had been carried out by an independent terrorist group which had no connection whatsoever with the exiled revolutionaries.

However, as soon as Gershuni was safely out of Russia, towards the end of May he began to prepare the ground for revealing at least part of the truth. He said that he had offered Gotz five hundred roubles as a contribution to the terrorist group, and that Gotz had replied that he should wait for Gershuni to return and give the money to him. He went on that he had done precisely this, and had been startled to learn, for the first time, of the true role played by Gershuni in the Battle Organisation. At the same time he again urged that the police should make no move yet against Gershuni, since his own relations with the revolutionaries depended very largely upon his friendship with Gershuni.

Azeff and Gershuni met in Switzerland on several occasions in the first two weeks of June, and Azeff was drawn into the discussions of the Battle Organisation's plans to assassinate Plehve, Obolensky and Zubatov. Since he had reported to the Department that Gershuni was the leader of the Organisation he now had to inform it of some of its proposed activities. So he told of the suggestion to kill Plehve and Zubatov, but said nothing about that to kill Obolensky. At the same time he wrote to the Department (he was living in Berlin supposedly working for the General Electric Co. there), "We must have a personal conversation about my future work. My situation has become rather dangerous, as I am now playing a very active part among the revolutionaries. It would be unprofitable to withdraw now, but any action calls for the greatest care."

His statement that he was playing a very active part in revolutionary affairs was not untrue, for by degrees Gershuni was drawing him more and more deeply into the orbit of the Battle Organisation. This, too, was another reason for the fact that though he could not deny that Gershuni had a connection with the Organisation, he insisted that he was only a very secondary figure, and that the leaders were a group of independent revolutionaries who had no connection with the Party and whose names he could not discover.

The Department agreed with him that it would be wise to have a personal chat with him and in July 1902 Azeff set out for St Petersburg. By this time there had been several changes made in the personnel and organisation of the Department. Plehve had been succeeded by A. A. Lopukhin who had placed Zubatov in charge of all the political side of the work of the Department, and the two men between them had decided to concentrate on building up a secret police service whose main aim would be to penetrate revolutionary organisations. Plehve had given his approval of this reorganisation, and as Azeff was in a position, if all went well, to penetrate eventually the Battle Organisation's inner conclaves, he gave instructions that Azeff should be given carte blanche for effecting this.

When Azeff returned thus fortified by authority, he persuaded Gershuni to call a meeting of those most closely involved in the work of the Organisation. As a result Kraft and Melnikov, who had helped Gershuni with the preparations for Sipyagin's assassination, met Gershuni and Azeff in Kiev in October 1902. The four men chiefly discussed a plan for Plehve's assassination according to which Grigoriev, who was to have killed Pobedonostsev at Sipyagin's funeral, and his friend Nadarov were to attack Plehve's carriage as he drove through St Petersburg.

Having met Kraft and Melnikov for the first time at Kiev, Azeff now embarked upon a plan for protecting his friend Gershuni still further. He informed the Department that the two men were the real leaders of the Battle Organisation. As a result they were put under constant surveillance, and though Gershuni was also watched he was not so strictly kept under the official eye because of his allegedly minor role. This made it possible for him to escape when Kraft and Melnikov were arrested a few months later.

Upon Azeff's recommendation the Police Department agreed that he should return to St Petersburg and make the capital his base of operations for his specific assignment. In his revolutionary capacity as representative of the Party's general executive he was one of the most important revolutionaries in St Petersburg. It put him in effective control of the St Petersburg Social Revolutionary Committee; he supervised the smuggling of illegal literature into Russia via Finland; and he sought out and enrolled students prepared to do propaganda work among the proletariat. At the same time, at the behest of the Battle Organisation he collected as much information about Plehve's mode of life as he could as part of the preparations for the Minister's assassination.

Now, when he had reported to the Department that Kraft and Melnikov were the leaders of the Battle Organisation, he had also disclosed the details of the plan to kill Plehve. Naturally a watch was put on Grigoriev and Nadarov, and on 21st February 1903, when the Tsar was to take a review in which the two officers would be participating, they were arrested together with Grigoriev's fiancée. The official reason for the arrests was that it was feared that they might attempt to take the Tsar's life during the parade.

The arrests, which took Azeff completely by surprise, made matters very awkward for him as it turned out. During their examination of the prisoners the police hinted that they knew a great deal about the Battle Organisation, and the suggested extent of this knowledge so overwhelmed Grigoriev and Yurkovskaya that they turned informer and named all those with whom they had been working, including Azeff. Then again without consulting Azeff they arrested all those named except Gershuni who managed to escape, and Azeff, who was left untouched to carry on in St Petersburg.

The situation in which Azeff now found himself was a very serious one, from every point of view. From that of the revolutionaries, it must appear very strange that he should be left free while all his revolutionary friends were arrested. From the police point of view, Lopukhin and Zubatov were now convinced that Azeff was not telling them all he knew, and they wanted to know why.

Gershuni's escape threw Plehve into a rage, for it was now

clear, from the statement of Grigoriev, that he was the real leader of the Battle Organisation, and he summoned Zubatov to him and said that he would keep Gershuni's card-index record on his desk before him as a constant reminder until the man was caught. Even the Tsar took a hand, and announced that he would pay a handsome reward, rumoured at 15,000 roubles, to anyone who helped to arrest the terrorist leader. This set not only every policeman in Russia but many others besides on the watch for Gershuni, but he was so skilful in covering up his tracks that he always escaped, while many who faintly resembled him suffered the indignity of arrest.

Somewhat naturally relations between Zubatov and his "beloved" agent became very strained. The former Okhrana chief wrote to Lopukhin that he now had the gravest doubts about the validity of the methods Azeff was using, and Lopukhin summoned Azeff to him to try to get to the bottom of the matter. To all the charges made against him Azeff retorted with counter-charges. The gross incompetence of the police was entirely to blame for everything. If they had read his reports with proper attention they could not have blundered as they had. It would be a miracle to him if he were not permanently compromised in revolutionary eyes, and this was a disaster, not so much for him personally, as for the Department because only he could have helped them to bring about the downfall of the Battle Organisation. He suggested that he should go abroad again immediately in an effort to make it appear that he had had to flee to escape arrest. Since it was clear that no confession was to be wrung from him—and his stubbornness in resisting all accusations put doubts into the police chiefs' minds as to whether they might not have wronged him after all—it was agreed that he should return to western Europe.

Before he left Russia, however, Azeff went to Moscow and there met Gershuni at the house of the assistant director of the Moscow Electrical Station. They stayed together for three days, during which it is believed that Gershuni told Azeff for the first time that he had chosen him to succeed him as head of the Battle Organisation in the event of his own arrest. At the end of the meeting Azeff went abroad.

For his part Gershuni went to Ufa, in the foothills of the Urals, where a short time before the provincial governor, Bogdanovits, had ordered the shooting of a number of unarmed protesting workers. He had already arranged for a number of volunteers of the Battle Organisation to meet him there with the object of taking revenge on the governor. When he arrived at Ufa, however, he found that the local Social Revolutionaries led by V. V. Leonovich had been keeping an eye on Bogdanovich and had even found two members, Dulebov, a railway worker, and a still unidentified colleague known only as the Apostle, to act as his executioners.

Gershuni was told of their plan and approved, so sent his own men back to their homes while he stayed on until the assassination had been carried out. On 19th May 1903 as Bogdanovich was taking his customary noon-time walk in the cathedral gardens, Dulebov and the Apostle went up to him, thrust into his hand the sentence of the Battle Organisation and then pumped bullets into him. There were few people about, so the two men successfully made their escape by jumping over a low wall and disappearing into a ravine which led from the town. Many arrests were made, but those responsible were never caught.

Gershuni left Ufa at once and made for Saratov. Here he wrote a description of the assassination and sent it to Gotz in Switzerland. From Saratov he set off to follow Azeff abroad. Unfortunately he decided to break his journey in Kiev to see the local representative of the Party there, and sent a telegram announcing his arrival. By ill chance the telegram fell into the hands of a student called Rosenberg who was a petty police informer. Though Rosenberg had no idea who had sent the wire, the police decided to act upon it. So when the train carrying Gershuni drew into Kiev station in the evening of 26th May the station and its environs were alive with detectives.

When the train stopped there stepped down from it a neatly dressed man wearing an engineer's cap and carrying a brief-case. He went along the train glancing down at the wheels as though inspecting them. In fact it was Gershuni being extremely cautious, as he always was. What he observed did not please him.

Presently the train pulled out, and Gershuni went out into the street. Here he stopped, bent down and pretended to be re-tying a shoe-lace, under cover of which he saw a number of men whom he recognised as detectives. Believing that his only chance lay in his behaving naturally, since the police obviously did not know for whom they were looking otherwise they would have pounced before now, he crossed the street and went to a fruit stall where he asked for a glass of lemonade. Suddenly there was a shout from one of the detectives, "That's Gershuni!"[1] There was a rush, he was surrounded and in seconds seized. Returned to St Petersburg he was subsequently court-martialled and sentenced to death. This was commuted to penal servitude for life. We shall be hearing of him again later.

[1] After Grigoriev's arrest Gershuni's photograph had been circulated to all police forces in Russia.

Chapter Thirty

THE NEW CHIEF VERSUS PLEHVE

Before his arrest Gershuni had made his testamentary dispositions. He had left with his other intimate friend Gotz all the
information which would enable the Battle Organisation to
carry on without a break, and he had named Azeff as his
successor to the leadership of the Organisation. When Azeff
arrived in Geneva after the events in Kiev, therefore, he found
himself welcomed warmly by the other leaders and by their
unquestioning recognition of him as the new terrorist chief.

The next item on the Battle Organisation's agenda as drawn
up by Gershuni was the assassination of Plehve, and events had
taken place the previous month which made this choice of victim
quite acceptable to the new chief. For two days in April there
had been an anti-Jewish pogrom in Kishenev. Organised gangs
had plundered Jewish houses, looted shops, raped women and
murdered without regard for age or sex. As long as the Jews
made no attempt to resist the police remained passive; but as
soon as they showed signs of defending themselves, the police
had moved against them.

The Kishenev pogrom made a deep impression throughout all
western Europe, and an even deeper one throughout Russia. The
responsibility for the police behaviour was placed squarely upon
Plehve who had on more than one occasion expressed in public
the view that anti-Jewish pogroms were a good way of fighting
the revolutionary movement.

Though Azeff normally tended to ignore his Jewish background the Kishenev pogrom appears to have reminded him of it forcibly. He too blamed Plehve for what had happened and began to harbour for his former chief a truly burning hatred. These feelings he made no attempt to hide even from his chiefs in the Police Department. Zubatov has recorded that "he shook with fury and hate when speaking of Plehve, whom he considered responsible." And it was this hatred that enabled him to set about encompassing the Minister's death to the exclusion of all other considerations. A good case could be made out for the argument that the success of the Battle Organisation was essential if he was to remain its leader; and that this position alone attracted him because it gave him control of large sums of money for which he did not have to account, thus making it possible for him to transfer some of it secretly to his own use. Nevertheless there is no indication whatsoever of such an ulterior motive being present in his planning of Plehve's assassination.

At all events he lost no time in working out with Gotz, his right-hand man, a plan of campaign for killing Plehve based on the fact that the Minister went at regular intervals to report to the Tsar, travelling between Police headquarters and the Winter Palace in his carriage. All that was needed was that details should be discovered of the days and times at which Plehve paid these visits and the route he took.

Azeff's plan depended upon the concerted action of a fairly large group of people, and this may have been one of the reasons why, when it came to the point, it took several attempts, and the firm control of Azeff, to bring it to fruition. For, as we shall presently see, of all the men and women who were willingly available to take one part or another in it, only the leader himself had any experience of such work.

The original group chosen by Azeff consisted of six young students who had all been expelled from their university during the student demonstrations of 1899 to 1902. Their names were Sazunov, Savinkov, Schweitzer, Pokotilov and the two Matzevsky brothers. The group was divided into two sections; three were to observe Plehve's habits and on the appointed day give the necessary signals to the other three who were to throw the bomb or bombs, for Azeff was taking no chance of failure.

Before despatching them to St Petersburg Azeff had long talks with each member of the group, telling them how best to go about their tasks and exhorting them to let nothing deter them. He spoke always with a quiet assurance which, more than anything else, gave the young men confidence.

The watchers were sent off first, under the command of Savinkov. One of them was provided with money to buy a horse and cab and a cabby's uniform, another with funds to set himself up as a paper-seller, and the third as a pedlar. They set out in the middle of November 1903; Azeff was to arrive early in December.

The little group got down to their task with commendable speed and very soon had all the information necessary. Savinkov, however, was inclined to be a nervous young man and when Azeff had not appeared by the end of the first week of December, he wrote asking why, and when no reply came he called in his men, told them to disperse, and himself hurried back to find out what had happened to Azeff.

He first made contact with Gotz and Tchernov who told him that Azeff had not arrived because he had been engaged on very important Party business. They also pointed out that he could not really expect replies to letters sent to the wrong address. Finally they took him to task for breaking the discipline of the Battle Organisation by leaving his post without orders. These talks did a good deal to restore Savinkov's morale, and when he was instructed to go to Moscow to consult Azeff there about future plans, he readily set out taking with him his friend Kalayev, with Gotz's consent.

The explanation which they had given to Savinkov for Azeff's failure to arrive as planned was not quite so simple as Gotz and Tchernov made out. Though determined to kill Plehve, Azeff was not prepared to risk his own life in the attempt, and had, therefore, been busy laying down the foundations of an alibi.

First of all he had set about discovering whether the Police Department knew that anything was in the wind. In this he received a good deal of help from a new chief, a man called Ratayev, who had shortly before been appointed head of the Russian Political Police Abroad and who had his headquarters in Paris.

Though not at all devoid of intelligence, Ratayev was not the man for this position, especially as one of his duties was controlling Azeff. He was essentially a man-of-the-world who preferred the society of beautiful women and the pleasures of dining out

and theatre-going to police work. True, his twenty years with
the Police Department had given him a knowledge of police
routine, and if pushed to it he could equal any one of his colleagues in such matters, but a congenital laziness usually made
the effort too much for him. Plehve disapproved of him and for
this reason had removed him from the direction of the Political
Police and sent him abroad to this lesser appointment. Since
Ratayev realised that this move was demotion, he was less inclined than ever to exert himself in police matters.

Naturally Azeff found such a man easy to handle. He could
be fobbed off with excuses for not providing information of any
value, and his brains could be picked about police matters without his being aware that this was happening. From Ratayev
Azeff learned that the Police Department knew that Savinkov
had returned to St Petersburg and that he had told his friends
before he left that he was determined to kill Plehve. The Department had no suspicion, however, that a definite plot had been
hatched.

At the same time that he learned this in Paris Azeff also
received another piece of information which also played into his
hands. This was that a woman terrorist, S. Klitchoglu, who had
at one time worked with Gershuni in the Battle Organisation,
had set up her own independent terrorist organisation and
planned to assassinate Plehve. This did not suit Azeff's plans at
all, for it was essential to his reputation as leader of the Battle
Organisation that the Plehve assassination should be known as
the sole work of the Battle Organisation.

So he set out for St Petersburg intent upon destroying
Klitchoglu's group and in so doing turn it to his own personal
account. Information about the Klitchoglu group would put him
in a strong position with the Department.

He told Ratayev first about the independent plot and said that
he must hurry to St Petersburg to warn the Department. He
also persuaded Ratayev to accompany him, hinting that his
being there and taking part in the disclosures would raise his
own prestige officially. His motive for getting Ratayev to come
with him was that he believed his immediate chief's protection
would be valuable to him in this particular very delicate double
ploy.

The Klitchoglu group was not difficult to discover, and it was
rounded up with the effect on the Department that Azeff had

hoped it would have. He now felt able to proceed with his Battle Organisation plans with every confidence that he would not be implicated in them by the police at any stage.

In the middle of February 1904 the Savinkov group assembled in St Petersburg once more and resumed their duties in watching Plehve's movements. Within a short time they believed they had all the data they required, and began to press Azeff to set the day, which, after some consideration, he did, naming 31st March.

Two or three days before, he made further attempts to insure himself against detection by the Department by going to them with the story that he had discovered that an attempt was to be made shortly on the life of Lopukhin. He described all the details of the apocryphal attempt basing them on the actual details for his own plan against Plehve. He said that bombs were to be used, and that the place chosen was not far from the Department building on the Fontanka. This covered him completely with the Department, for his description was wrong in only one detail—the identity of the victim—and this he would be able to explain away quite satisfactorily he felt.

He had arranged to meet the group in Dvinsk on 4th April, after the attempt, but instead he went abroad, calling first on Gotz in Geneva to tell him that he was doubtful about the success of the operation because the group in his view had chosen a bad site, and then went on to Paris to see Ratayev. This was just one more insurance policy taken out against accusations by either side.

He had been in Paris a couple of days or so when he told Ratayev that his elderly mother had fallen ill and that he must go to see her in Vladikavkaz, intending in fact to go to Dvinsk. By this time 31st March had passed and there had been no news at all about the attempt on Plehve, and he presumed that either the attack had been carried out and had failed—though if this were the case he could not understand why word of it had not leaked out—or that it had been bungled.

On his arrival in Dvinsk he found that none of the group had come there, so he set out for St Petersburg. Quite by chance he encountered Pokotilov on the train, and from him learned what had happened.

On the appointed day the group had taken up their allotted positions. Savinkov had been in general command, Kalayev and the two Matzevskys had been look-outs, while the bomb-throwers had been Sazunov, Borishansky and Pokotilov himself. They had kept fairly close together between the Department building and the Neva. But this was their first attempt and they were all nervous. Whether the Okhrana were taking special precautions after the disclosure of the Klitchoglu plot or whether the group imagined that there were more detectives about than usual it is not possible to say. At all events Borishansky got the impression that he was being closely watched and decided to leave his post. This threw the other members of the group off balance and Savinkov had called off the attempt.

Savinkov and Pokotilov had then gone to Dvinsk to meet Azeff to tell him what had happened and seek his advice about what they should do now, but when he did not appear Savinkov became convinced that he had been arrested. Pokotilov maintained that this should make no difference to their plans, but Savinkov insisted that without Azeff the group was not strong enough to carry out the attack on Plehve, and suggested that they should try to kill the Governor of Kiev, Kleygels, instead. This, he said, would be a fairly easy matter because Kleygels habitually drove through the streets of the city quite openly. The main objection to the plan was, however, that the killing of Kleygels would have no political significance, for though he had repressed the St Petersburg students ruthlessly some years earlier, it had happened so long ago that scarcely anyone remembered him.

Savinkov's views were opposed by the rest of the group except Kalayev and Schweitzer, and as the result of some heated discussions a compromise was reached. The group split up into two parts; Sazunov, the Matzevskys, Borishansky and Pokotilov were to continue with the plan to kill Plehve, while Savinkov, Kalayev and Schweitzer were to assassinate Kleygels.

This division of strength was a disastrous decision, as Azeff saw at once. Pokotilov and Borishansky had already gone to St Petersburg to kill Plehve on 7th April, but the Minister had not appeared. They had fixed the next attempt for 14th April and Pokotilov was now on his way to the capital for this purpose. Azeff tried to persuade the young man that he was courting certain failure, but nothing he could say would make Pokotilov change his mind; his nerves were too taut; if he did not at least attempt to kill Plehve, he said, he would go out of his mind,

7. The conspirators of 1st March 1881 on the scaffold. Rysakov, Zhelyabov, Perovskaya, Mikhailov and Kibalchich.

8. (*Left*) Peter Stolypin, Prime Minister of Russia, was shot by a secret police agent in a Kiev theatre in 1911. Before this, in 1906, a bomb attempt had been made on his life.

(*Above*) The assassins' carriage was wrecked by the bomb and Stolypin's children injured.

Radio Times-Hulton Library

Azeff washed his hands of the whole affair. Pokotilov carried on to St Petersburg, and on the evening of 13th April, as he was checking one of his bombs, it exploded and killed him. His death had the effect of completing the demoralisation of the whole group. Borishansky returned to Kiev to consult with Savinkov and the others there, and it was decided to give up the attempt on Plehve and concentrate on Kleygels. Schweitzer was sent at once to St Petersburg to tell Sazunov and the Matzevskys to sell their cabmen's disguises and to go abroad.

Schweitzer had only just left when Azeff arrived in Kiev. He had been to Odessa and there he had learned that there was a good deal of mistrust of the Battle Organisation among the Social Revolutionaries in the port and they had called for an inquiry into its operation. They had said quite openly that if what they learned did not appear to them to be satisfactory they would consider themselves at liberty to form a terrorist organisation of their own. This was a clear threat to Azeff's authority in the Party, and he realised that an attempt on Plehve, and a successful one too, was the only way in which to silence these criticisms.

So when he met the group he was in his best sergeant-major mood. He spoke to them severely, reprimanded them for changing the decisions of the Central Committee, and declared that Plehve had to be killed, and that if the group did not kill him, nobody else would.

"Azeff's insistence, his coolness and assurance," Savinkov said later, "restored the group's spirits. It may be said without fear of exaggeration that Azeff recreated the organisation. We return to our task with a renewed determination to kill Plehve and with the faith that this time we would succeed."

The watching-group returned to St Petersburg at the beginning of May and there took an apartment in the centre of the city at 31 Zhukovsky-street, where Savinkov played the role of gentleman of the house, Dora Brilliant, the daughter of a wealthy Jewish merchant, that of his mistress, Sazunov that of butler and P. C. Ivanovskaya[1] that of cook.

By now the young men of the group were far more experi-

[1] Ivanovskaya was a revolutionary of long standing. She had been a member of the Executive Committee of *Narodnaya Volya*, and for her part in plots to assassinate Alexander II had been arrested and sentenced to forced labour for life. Some twenty-five years later she had escaped from Siberia, and had now joined the Social Revolutionaries.

enced and some of them, especially Kalayev, comported themselves like old hands. In mid-June they were joined by Azeff, who stayed at the apartment for a week during which he saw personally all the conspirators and arranged a meeting of the group for early July. At this meeting the date for Plehve's assassination was fixed for 21st July, and the bomb-throwers were chosen—Sazunov, Kalayev, Borishansky, and another worker from Bielostok called Sikorsky, whom Azeff had brought in on Borishansky's recommendation. It was also arranged that Azeff would wait in Vilno with Ivanovskaya for the results.

This time Azeff kept his promise. The appointed day came, and when the prearranged telegram did not arrive Azeff grew very agitated. According to Ivanovskaya he said, "This means either a complete failure or betrayal," and he was really put out because he had staked his future on the operation.

The fears and doubts were set at rest next day, however, when the bomb-throwers themselves arrived at Vilno and Sazunov somewhat shamefacedly explained that he had arrived late at his rendezvous and it had been necessary to call off the attempt. Azeff still showed signs of nerves nevertheless, and he spent hours with the group going over and over again every detail of the plan to see whether or not there ought to be changes made in it.

The new date was fixed for 28th July. This time there was no slip-up. On cue the four bomb-throwers moved into the Ismailovsky Prospekt. Borishansky was out ahead; he was to act only if the others failed. Some yards behind Borishansky came Sazunov, who was to make the main attempt. If he failed, Kalayev would try, and failing him, Sikorsky.

The 28th July was a beautiful summer's day, and exactly on the minute Plehve's carriage turned into the Ismailovsky. As the carriage drew level with Sazunov it had to slow down to avoid a *droshky*. Taking advantage of the incident, Sazunov ran forward and hurled his twelve-pound bomb through the carriage window. It exploded immediately, and all that remained of the carriage were a few scattered sticks and cushions.

Unfortunately Sazunov was himself seriously injured by the explosion and he was seized by the police. The rest of the group made good their escape.

The assassination made a tremendous impression throughout revolutionary circles everywhere. The Social Revolutionaries were holding a congress at Geneva and when the news reached them late the same evening, according to one delegate, "For several minutes pandemonium reigned. A number of men and women became hysterical, everyone embraced everybody else and on all sides there were shouts of joy. I can still see N. He was standing a little apart from the rest. He dashed a glass of water on the floor and through gritted teeth shouted, 'That's for Kishenev.'" Azeff's reputation had never stood higher, and his authority in the Party reached its zenith during the following weeks.

Though his position was now assured, Azeff did not appear quite so happy as he might justifiably have been. For this final attempt he and Ivanovskaya had arranged to wait for news in Warsaw and there receive Savinkov to discuss the future activities of the group. Almost immediately word of Sazunov's success reached him, however, without telling Ivanovskaya what he intended, he left for Vienna. It is clear that he was still anxious lest he should be connected in some way with the assassination, for immediately on arrival in Vienna he sent Ratayev a quite innocuous telegram which could be produced later if the need arose to prove that he had been in the Austrian capital when the crime was committed.

But for the fact that Plehve's murder took the Police Department completely by surprise and that the subsequent inquiry was carried out with almost criminal neglect, Azeff's position might have become very precarious indeed. Though Sazunov was delirious, in his delirium he kept repeating the names *Valentine* and *Auntie*, and some of the agents who sat by his bedside to take a note of the unhappy young man's babblings knew that *Valentine* was one of Azeff's Party cover-names. It was also established that one of Sazunov's companions, Sikorsky, had been in Vilno a few days before the assassination and that Azeff had been there at the same time. So it should not have been difficult to piece together enough evidence at least to warrant an investigation of Azeff's recent operations. But as Boris Nikolayevsky has said, "When perusing the documents connected with this case it is at times difficult not to feel that the investigators were pursuing their researches merely as a matter of form, and that in their hearts they were ready to condone the act. Hated in his lifetime, Plehve went to his grave deserted by all."

Chapter Thirty-one

AZEFF SUPREME

The assassination of Plehve was applauded not only by the revolutionaries; Liberals and even peaceable people who stood aloof from active politics saw in it a justifiable act which relieved the whole nation of the main architect of oppression. Probably no other single act had so great an effect on the general course of political development in this period, the culmination of which was the October Revolution of 1905.

As Azeff had hoped, and presently was to be convinced, his own position vis-à-vis the police was unaffected. Sazunov's references to people and events were disregarded by the authorities, and though Azeff was questioned about why he had not been in a position to warn the Department about the plot, his explanations were found acceptable.

On the other hand his prestige in the Party had reached new heights. He was now regarded by the leaders as the one man who could impart to the Social Revolutionary cause an influence which could make it felt in every corner of the empire. The fate of the man who, by his courage, had bestowed this power on the double-agent was to be far different.

Some time later Sazunov wrote his *Confessions*, and in them described what happened to him after he had thrown the bomb.

> I took my bomb (he wrote) and flung it at the window-pane. What happened next I neither saw nor heard. Everything disappeared.

216

But the next moment consciousness returned. I was lying on the pavement. My first thought was astonishment at being still alive. I tried to get up, but my body felt as if it were not there; I felt as if nothing were left but thought. I passionately wanted to know the result of my deed.

Somehow I managed to raise myself on my elbow and look around. Through the smoke I saw a red general's cloak lying on the ground, and something else, but neither carriage nor horses. According to an eye-witness, I shouted: "Long live freedom!"

Without knowing how badly I was wounded, I was filled with the wish not to be caught by my enemies. The thought, "I may get delirious," ran through my mind. "Rather commit *hara-kiri* in the Japanese fashion than die at the filthy hands of the gendarmes." I tried to take my revolver from my pocket, but my hands would not obey me.

In the meantime one of the police who always escorted Plehve's carriage on bicycles rushed up, attracted by my cry. He fell upon me and held me down with the weight of his body. And then there began the scenes that are usual in such cases.

The first man started hitting me. Then others turned up and began belabouring me in every possible way with their fists, with kicks, with the butts of their revolvers. Yet I felt no pain and no resentment. Everything was indifferent to me. In the blessedness of victory and the peace of approaching death everything faded into insignificance. I heard shouts of "Where's the other bomb?"

The revolver in my pocket might have gone off and wounded someone while they were flogging me, and I decided that this was unnecessary, so I said, "Leave me alone! I haven't got another bomb. Take the revolver from my pocket." Then they decided to remove me.

I was seized by the leg and dragged along, and my head bumped on the pavement. I was dragged up to the third floor of an hotel, flung on the bare floor, my clothes were torn off from my body, and they beat me again with gnashing of teeth.

I do not know how long I lay there naked; I was only semi-conscious. I saw as in a mist that the room was full of police and officials. Some one felt my head and said, "He'll live; but it's dangerous to hit him."

Sazunov was then taken to hospital and came round on the operating table at the moment that a tube was being inserted in his throat to pump poison, if there were any, from his stomach. He was then anaesthetised, and two pieces of the bomb were removed and two of his toes amputated. When he came round from this there was a man at his bedside who said he was the examining magistrate, and that he was being charged with Plehve's murder. He refused to give his name but did say that he belonged to the Battle Organisation. His account goes on:

> The interrogation lasted a long time and completely exhausted me. Next morning I was taken to the Kresty prison hospital. My eyes were bandaged. Some one bent over me and asked in a friendly tone how I felt. "I am the doctor," he explained. "We have been waiting for you to wake up, and now I can tell you that you've been delirious and mentioned several names. Your bomb killed and wounded many people. What is particularly dreadful is that a five-year-old girl was killed too."
> I cried out loud and seized the "doctor's" hand. This torture continued. It was beyond my strength. I had an attack of hysteria. I chased the "doctor" away; I implored him not to make me a traitor, and then lost consciousness again. When I came to my senses he appeared once more. I did not let him speak. "Go away or I'll shout. You're no doctor; you're an examining magistrate or a police agent."

The man went away but was replaced by the prison doctor's assistant. He assured Sazunov that they were alone in a cell, that he had been delirious and that the police had taken down everything he had said.

> My physical sufferings from the wounds were as nothing compared to the moral hell I was going through. Heaven knows what I might have said in my ravings. I cried aloud for death. . . .

What he feared most was that he might have betrayed the other members of the group and that they would be caught as a result. As it happened all escaped except Sikorsky, and he was not caught because of anything Sazunov had said. When he had heard the bomb explode, Sikorsky had rushed down to the Neva and there had hired a rowing boat, taken his bomb out into midstream and there dropped it over the side. But he had been seen behaving "suspiciously" and was later recognised by a police agent and arrested.

Sazunov lay helpless in bed for two and a half months. At the end of four months he was able to walk with the aid of crutches. On 30th November he and Sikorsky were tried and found guilty. They were not sentenced to death, however, for the impression made on the nation by Plehve's murder was not lost on the government. Sazunov was given life imprisonment, Sikorsky fifteen years forced labour. They spent the first year in the Schlüsselburg and were then transferred to Akatui, where Gershuni was. On 8th November 1910 he committed suicide along with six other prisoners as a protest against the floggings inflicted on political prisoners by a sadistic prison governor, Vissotsky.

Shortly after Plehve's assassination the members of the Battle Organisation met in Geneva, and reviewed their past work and laid plans for the future. Here they heard for the first time of differences which had sprung up in the Central Committee of the Party regarding the future of the Battle Organisation, some members proposing that the Organisation should be placed under the Committee's control. This was the last thing Azeff wanted since it would mean that he would no longer have his hands on the considerable funds provided for the Organisation's activities. Most of the other members of the group were against such an arrangement also, and Azeff skilfully used their irritation against the Committee to incite them to draw up for the Organisation a constitution of its own which would make it completely independent of the Committee.

Under this constitution a committee of three, composed of Azeff, Savinkov and Schweitzer, was set up to direct and control the affairs of the Organisation. In practice Savinkov and Schweitzer were content to leave everything to Azeff and he thus became, in effect, the Organisation.

In the late autumn of 1904 the Battle Organisation, whose membership had greatly increased, began to draw up a specific plan for the future. The new campaign, which received the approbation of the Central Committee, was aimed at the reactionary party at the Imperial Court. The Tsar's two eldest uncles, the Grand Dukes Sergey and Vladimir Alexandrovich, who were Nicholas's most influential counsellors, were to be the first targets, while Kleygels, the Governor-General of Kiev, was also added to the list.

Azeff proposed that the three men should be assassinated simultaneously, since a mass attempt, if it succeeded, would be bound to create a tremendous impression. This was agreed, so three groups of terrorists were selected. One, under the leadership of Schweitzer, and consisting of fifteen members, was sent to St Petersburg to arrange the assassination of the Grand Duke Vladimir and to explore the possibilities of killing Durnov, the Under Secretary of the Interior, and Trepov, the notorious Governor-General of the capital. The second, comprised of four men under Savinkov, was sent to Moscow to remove the Grand Duke Sergey, while the third—three men led by Borishansky—were to kill Kleygels in Kiev.

Azeff worked out the details of the plan, selected the men and gave each his task. He produced passports for all, and he arranged to have the dynamite needed made in a Paris laboratory and undertook to see that it was safely smuggled into Russia. In the second half of November the three groups left for Russia.

At the same time Azeff sent to the Police Department a series of reports giving details of the delegates to the Congress of Social Revolutionary Organisations Abroad, of the International Socialist Congress in Amsterdam, of the negotiations taking place between the Social Revolutionaries and the Finnish Activist Party, and of the Paris conference of the Revolutionary and Opposition Parties. None of these reports gave complete information, however, and not once did he make any mention of the Battle Organisation.

At this time events in the Far East were taking a very serious turn for the Tsar. Ever since his tour of Asia as a young man Nicholas seemed to have been especially attracted to the East, and as Tsar his foreign policy had been distinguished by an eastern slant. Under this policy there had taken place a peaceful penetration of the Far East which had provided Russia with legitimate commercial and other interests there which might have continued and expanded indefinitely had not Nicholas become somewhat alarmed at the increasing influence which other European countries and the Americans were gaining in China and Japan. To prevent Russia from being, as he thought she might, deprived of her share of the benefits which such influence brought with it, when the Germans acquired a ninety-nine year lease of Kiao-chow in 1897, Nicholas demanded and obtained a twenty-five year lease of the southern part of the Liaotung peninsula with Port Arthur. From this base the Russians rapidly developed interests in southern Manchuria.

Following on the Boxer Rebellion, which was directed by an exasperated China against the exploitation of foreigners, which Russian troops in 1900 and 1901 helped to suppress, tsarist troops remained in Manchuria on the pretext that local conditions represented a threat to the Trans-Siberian Railway which had been constructed from Moscow to Vladivostok between 1891 and 1903. South Manchuria was under Japanese domination and the presence of Russian troops to the north stood in their way to acquiring the whole of the country. After a few rather half-hearted attempts to initiate negotiations for the withdrawal of Russian troops, the Japanese decided to take the bull by the horns and launched a surprise attack at Port Arthur, where they caught the unsuspecting Russian fleet absolutely unawares and completely disabled it. Nicholas had immediately declared war on Japan and after ten months' fighting, by the close of 1904 saw defeat staring him in the face. Obstinately he continued to fight until fortunately Japanese resources began to run out and as a result of their secret representations to him President Theodore Roosevelt arranged a peace conference in August 1905. While it has to be admitted that Russia came out of this adventure rather better than she had any right to expect, the war had been a costly one in men and materials, and the defeats inflicted by the Japanese had shattered her prestige as a military power. This was keenly felt by the Russian people, and by the autumn of 1904 serious rumblings of discontent such as had never been heard before in Russia were beginning to manifest themselves.

The actual direct cause of this discontent was the increase in unemployment which had been taking place among the industrial population over the past two or three years. By the beginning of 1905 the atmosphere had become really explosive, and only a single spark was needed to set off a conflagration. Inevitably, or so it seems, the spark flew. Five men were dismissed from a St Petersburg factory for some trivial offence. The men working on the same shift struck in protest, and the other shift came out in support. The news soon ran throughout the industrial regions of the city and the workers in other factories also laid down their tools. Within two or three days the whole city was at a standstill.

On the following Sunday, 22nd January 1905, a large crowd carrying icons and portraits of the Tsar marched slowly and in an orderly manner towards the Winter Palace with the intention of presenting to the Tsar a petition setting out the workers' grievances signed by many thousands. At their head was a priest, Father Gapon, who, having first joined the Social Demo-

crats and abandoned them when he saw that he could never
play a leading role in their movement, had then joined the Social
Revolutionaries and withdrawn from them for the same reasons,
had eventually decided to form his own party.

As the procession neared the Winter Palace the authorities,
who had no policy for meeting a mass demonstration of this
sort, opened fire on the defenceless crowd and many hundreds
were killed. In a single instant the relationship between the Tsar
and his people was changed, and the mood of the people became
such that even Nicholas saw that new policies would have to be
introduced.

"Bloody Sunday", as the day has become known in history,
roused the whole nation, and General Trepov exacerbated an
already delicate situation by the measures he took against those
who had taken part in the procession; he ordered their expulsion
from the capital. At once an epidemic of strikes broke out over
the whole country, in which, as the weeks passed, practically
every profession and trade participated. "This general movement," says Sir Bernard Pares, "of wholesale opposition to the
government, when it extended to the non-Russian provinces of
the empire, particularly Poland, assumed a threatening character
not far removed from open separation. Thirteen railway lines
stopped work; isolated police officials were murdered all over the
country, the assailants almost invariably escaping."

These events could not help but inspire the Battle Organisation to wish to expand their programme. The times were ripe for
action on the widest possible scale, the younger members proclaimed. Now was the time to strike everywhere, even at the
Tsar. But when they put these plans to Azeff he refused to
countenance them. In fact, according to Ivanovskaya, he was at
this time in such a state of nerves that he was seriously considering fleeing to America.

Left to themselves, deprived of the coolness and resource of
their admired leader and receiving no help from the other
leaders abroad, the groups in St Petersburg, Moscow and Kiev
hesitated. All their plans might have proved to have been in
vain but for the action of Kalayev.

Taking a bomb from the armoury on 17th February, he went
out by himself in search of Grand Duke Sergey and came upon
him as he was walking in the Kremlin. Drawing the bomb from
under his coat he tossed it at the Grand Duke's feet. He made no

attempt to escape and at his subsequent interrogations betrayed nothing and no one. Even when the Grand Duchess Elizabeth offered to appeal to the Tsar for his life, he refused her offer.

Kalayev's action spurred the others to new activity. Since it was apparent that they could hope for no assistance from Azeff, Marc Schweitzer took over the leadership of the Organisation. He ordered Borishansky to abandon the attempt on Kleygel's life in Kiev and to come to St Petersburg. For the Petersburg group he drew up a new plan. On 14th March the leading members of the government were to attend a memorial service for Alexander II in the Peter and Paul cathedral. All routes to the cathedral were to be watched by his men and each of them would attempt to kill any leading official who happened along, concentrating on the Grand Duke Vladimir, Trepov and Bulygin, the Minister of the Interior, and his assistant Durnovo.

Schweitzer was a young, daring and fearless young man, a sincere Socialist. If he had a fault it was too much confidence in himself. Unfortunately the task which he had now undertaken was to prove beyond his limits. Apparently unable to delegate, he not only assumed leadership of the group and chief organiser, but because he was a trained chemist he insisted on preparing the bombs. It was clear to his companions when they last saw him on 10th March that he had over-tired himself, though they were not prepared for what was to happen. The following evening, as he was working on the bombs in his hotel bedroom, one of them exploded and he was blown to pieces.

The death of their leader led to yet another demoralisation of the rest of the group. They decided that the mass attempt planned for 14th March had to be abandoned, but they still hoped, rather half-heartedly, that they might carry out separate attempts on Trepov and Bulygin, if only Savinkov, who might bring Azeff with him, would arrive to help them.

But they were already doomed. A certain Tatarov, who had been arrested and imprisoned, had been seduced by the Governor-General of Eastern Siberia, Count Kutaisov, into becoming a police informer. He had been allowed to "escape" from Siberia and had penetrated the ranks of the Battle Organisation. As a result of his information the police struck on 29th and 30th March and all the St Petersburg group, with the exception of Dora Brilliant, were arrested.

The arrests not only spelled the doom of the Battle Organisation, but represented a defeat for the Social Revolutionary Party in the political sphere. The Organisation had never been so strong as it had been immediately after Plehve's murder; now it was put completely out of action at the very moment when most revolutionaries believed decisive action to be essential.

The role of the Battle Organisation, as conceived by Gershuni, had been that of blazing the trail for the revolutionary movement and to attract sympathy and support to the movement. The mass movement was regarded merely as the background for the Battle Organisation's terror and the sacrifice of life and liberty of its members. On the morrow of each act of terror mammoth popular demonstrations were to manifest the support of the masses for the blows struck against reaction and oppression.

Bloody Sunday had done what the Battle Organisation had failed to do so far; it had produced the mass demonstrations. Once these had become a mode of expression which was understood by large numbers of people everywhere in the country, terrorism and demonstration ought to have henceforward gone hand in hand, and the cumulative effect should have been tremendous. Now the people understood what they could achieve by strikes, demonstrations and other forms of mass protest, the Battle Organisation was no longer in a position to play its part. As Boris Nikolayevsky puts it, "The heroic period of the Battle Organisation was over."

For different reasons both Azeff and Gotz came to this conclusion. After the assassination of the Grand Duke Sergey, Nicholas, under pressure from some of his ministers, had made a series of pronouncements. In a manifesto he had secured his own position by declaring his intention to maintain the autocracy, but he had then proceeded, in a rescript to the Minister of the Interior, to order a scheme to be drawn up under which "the worthiest persons should be elected to share in the drafting and discussing of laws," while in an edict to the Ministry he had instructed it to take note of all such suggestions submitted by whoever should take the trouble to do so. In addition certain reforms were announced; religious teaching was declared to be free, some of the restrictions were lifted from the Jews, and measures were introduced to relieve the distress of the peasants.

The people took the edict to the Ministry of the Interior to be an invitation to organise parties and draw up political programmes, but even in this new climate, the reformers tended to split into various factions instead of presenting a united front. The Zemstvo Liberals, for example, drew up an advanced programme, while the moderates put forward a programme not so sweeping in its changes, and a number of professional unions came out with a radical platform.

On 27th and 28th May, however, the Russian fleet was annihilated by the Japanese at Tsushima. The effect of the news was to draw all factions closer together again. A demand was made for the war to be stopped. Fortunately there were influences already working towards this end. On 19th June the Tsar received a joint deputation of the zemstva and town councils, led by a distinguished non-party man, Prince Sergey Trubetskoy. To the Prince's representatives the Tsar quite unexpectedly replied with a definite promise to summon the Duma, the national assembly, as soon as possible, and expressed the hope that the people would co-operate in initiating the new regime.

At last it seemed as if the powers of reaction had realised they were defeated. A great surge of encouragement went through the reformers, and at a congress held in Moscow in the middle of July a draft constitution was drawn up. Hopes were dashed on 19th August, however, when the law for the summoning the Duma was promulgated, and it was seen to be wholly unacceptable since it produced a body which was to have consultative powers only and one besides chosen by an electorate from which country teachers and doctors, the professional men in the towns and the workers were excluded.

A fresh outbreak of disorders now erupted all over Russia. Late in the summer the crew of the battleship *Potemkin*, under the auspices of the revolutionaries, mutinied and seized their ship. The mutineers withdrew the battleship from the fleet and in it "terrorised the Black Sea until necessity compelled (them) to seek internment in Rumania." On 25th September another zemstvo congress met and decided to accept the proposed Duma so that it could be turned into something better once it had been formed.

Now for the first time the general excitement had penetrated even the peasants. This was largely the doing of the Social Revolutionaries who were practically the only party to concern themselves with the peasants. Their battle-cry "All the land for the peasants" met with a response that was immediate and successful, and a Peasants' Union was formed with this programme. Told by the agitators that the matter of land-ownership, which had been a continuing problem since the Great Reforms, would now be decided by the Duma, the peasants grew restless and everywhere began to invade private estates and to ransack them.

This restlessness was mirrored also in the towns. Because of their outspokenness, on 20th October the whole congress of the Railwaymen's Union, the strongest of all the new professional unions, were arrested. At once nearly all the railways came out on strike and were followed by most of the factories. The main demand of the strikers was for a constituent assembly based on universal suffrage. Soon the strike movement became general, and now for the first time the soviets, councils of elected delegates, made their appearance. The factory unions took the lead in this, and were followed by the Union of Unions, a body representing all the professional unions.

While this had been going on Count Witte had been in America negotiating peace terms with the Japanese. He returned now, and on seeing the situation, he sent Nicholas a strongly worded memorandum in which he said that he was now convinced that some kind of constitution must be granted. In this Witte had the strong support of the Grand Duke Nicholas, and it was the latter's advice that at last persuaded the Tsar to retreat. The Committee of Ministers was transformed into a Council of Ministers with a responsibility for general policy. Witte was appointed President of this first form of cabinet ever to be introduced in Russia. On 30th October an imperial manifesto was promulgated which undertook to introduce all the reforms put forward by the Zemstvo Congress in November 1904, while a promise was made to expand the Duma franchise.

While Witte was trying to overcome the opposition of the reactionaries to the changes, strikes and other demonstrations continued all over the country, chief of which was the mutiny at the Kronstadt naval base. It was put down with the most barbarous cruelty and for a moment the population wavered. Strikes called by the St Petersburg Soviet fizzled out. But it was only a temporary hesitation and riots and disturbances broke out in a new wave.

But two men had seen the weakness of the St Petersburg Soviet—Durnovo, the Under Secretary of the Interior, and

Trepov, now commandant of all the Imperial Police; and both were Witte's enemies. They set about undermining his influence with the Tsar. The result of their labours was the Tsar's declaration of martial law in St Petersburg on 12th December. This led the St Petersburg Soviet to call a third general strike. It failed but it had repercussions in Moscow where there was a rising of a number of revolutionaries which attempted an attack on the authorities. Following on this disturbances broke out at all the chief centres in the south. However, the failure of the St Petersburg Soviet to show that it was capable of controlling and directing revolution was beginning to take effect. The more peaceable elements in the population were gradually withdrawing their moral support from the activists, and by the end of the year the movement of revolution came definitely to an end.

It was against the background of these events that the Central Committee of the Social Revolutionary Party met early in November 1905 to discuss the situation and particularly the role that terror ought to play in it. Gotz believed that terror was not only superfluous, but might at this stage undermine the influence of the Party. Azeff supported him, but, as I have already said, for quite different reasons. The arrests in St Petersburg which had shattered the Battle Organisation had really frightened him and he was against terror because he feared that his continued involvement in its activities might be fatal for him.

Already there had been some very shrewd digs at him by Lopukhin and others, and to appease the Police Department he had arranged to betray Savinkov to them. For the time being then, Azeff, as supreme head of the Battle Organisation, called a halt to terror.

His relations with it were never to be the same again, for though it did renew its activities, Azeff had decided that it would be more beneficial for him to concentrate on his relations with his other providers—the police.

Chapter Thirty-two

AZEFF AND RATCHKOVSKY

The Central Committee's deliberations which decided the abandonment of terror and the dissolution of the Battle Organisation was also a milestone in the development of the Social Revolutionary Party for another reason: all the exiled members of the Committee, with the exception of Gotz who by now was a very sick man, announced their intention of returning to Russia so that they might make a direct contribution to the events which all believed must inevitably be enacted there. This was important in itself, but it had an even deeper significance, for though there was no apportionment of roles, the stand-point taken in the discussions which led to this decision defined the future position of each outstanding figure in the movement towards and during the Revolution. Azeff was no exception.

The assassination of the Grand Duke Sergey had led to great changes in the personnel of the Police Department. The outspokenly blunt Trepov had held Lopukhin personally responsible for the Grand Duke's death and had publicly and in his presence called him a murderer. Because of Trepov's influence over the Tsar the latter was also persuaded to express his dissatisfaction with the recent record of the Department, and this left Lopukhin no alternative but resignation. Appointed in his stead was his greatest enemy Ratchkovsky.

Ratchkovsky had begun his career in the government service as a minor official in Kiev, Odessa and Warsaw, during which time he formed a relationship with the police which in 1879 led to his becoming a secret agent in the Third Division. He did not sustain this role for long, however, for the revolutionaries quickly discovered his connection with the Third Division, whereupon he openly joined the police and became one of the keen promoters of the *agent provocateur* system. His subsequent rise was rapid; by 1884 he had been appointed chief of the Russian police abroad. He scored a considerable success in this post by infiltrating many of his agents into the ranks of the exiled revolutionaries.

His headquarters were in Paris where he made it one of his chief aims to establish close links with the French police. This in turn gave him contact with the Press and thence with those French politicians who were advocating an alliance between their country and Russia. It is not an exaggeration to say that he played an important part in laying the foundations of the eventual secret Franco-Russian pact of 1893. At the same time he speculated on the Bourse with extraordinary success, and amassed a large private fortune, not always by using strictly legal methods.

He fell foul of Alexander III because he pried too deeply into the affairs of the widow of Alexander II who had settled in France, and though he made a good start with Nicholas II he soon alienated him by a scathing report on Philippe of Lyons, the notorious crystal-gazer whom the Tsarina had invited to the Court for consultations about the birth of an heir. Plehve, who disliked Ratchkovsky intensely, took advantage of this to engineer his removal with Lopukhin's aid. The latter drew up the notice of dismissal in extraordinarily offensive terms and Ratchkovsky never forgave him.

Trepov, who had been given dictatorial powers on his appointment as Governor-General of St Petersburg, had determined from the first days to replace Lopukhin, and the day after the assassination of the Grand Duke Sergey he had made the first move by appointing Ratchkovsky Special Commissioner to the Ministry of the Interior with the task of controlling the activities of the St Petersburg Okhrana. In July Trepov was made assistant to the Minister of the Interior and he acquired promotion for Ratchkovsky also, appointing him Vice-Director of the Police Department with special responsibility for the political section.

Ratchkovsky at once set about levelling scores with Lopukhin by dismissing many of the men appointed by the latter, among whom was Ratayef, Azeff's main police contact. Ratayef's removal created an extremely difficult situation for Azeff, for he now came under Ratchkovsky's direct orders. He knew Ratchkovsky's method of prying more deeply than anyone else, and he realised that he must supply more genuine information if his treachery were to remain concealed from his new chief.

Unhappily for Azeff this was not his only problem at this time. One of the most trusted officials in the Police Department, L. P. Menshikov, took it into his head to tell the Central Committee about Azeff's police connections. Menshikov later explained his motives, which serve as a very good example of the complexity of the whole police and revolutionary set-ups.

Menshikov had been arrested in Moscow in 1887 for being connected with a small and unimportant revolutionary group. Convinced that he was surrounded by treachery on all sides, he had decided to enter police employment with the long-term aim of handing over their secrets to the revolutionaries. He applied for admission to the Moscow Okhrana and was not long in drawing attention to himself by the clarity of his reports, and this had led, by the time Ratchkovsky came upon the scene, to his being promoted to a position of some responsibility. Believing himself a likely victim of Ratchkovsky's axe he reckoned that the time had come for which he had been planning over all these years and for which he had secretly collected a great mass of information.

On 8th September 1905 Rostkovsky, a member of the St Petersburg Social Revolutionary Committee received a visit from an unknown heavily veiled lady who thrust a sealed envelope into his hand and immediately disappeared. The letter warned the revolutionaries that the Party was being betrayed by two police spies, and specifically named the renegade Tatarov, whom I have briefly mentioned earlier, and "the engineer Azeff, a Jew, who has recently arrived from abroad," and it backed this statement by giving details of the betrayals made by each.

That same day Azeff happened to call on a very perturbed Rostkovsky, who showed him the letter. On reading it Azeff turned pale and commented, "The engineer Azeff, that must be me. My name is Azeff." Whereupon he threw down the letter and the cigarette he was smoking and stalked out of the room without another word. This upset Rostkovsky more than ever.

In the evening Azeff saw Ratchkovsky and told him what had happened, and expressed in no uncertain terms exactly what he thought of a Police Department which could not keep its secrets. Ratchkovsky was impressed by his apparent *sang froid*. Azeff, however, appreciated the damage which the letter could do him and immediately left for Moscow where he told Potapov, a member of the Central Committee, about it.

The letter did, in fact, make a tremendous impression both in Moscow and in emigré revolutionary circles. Fortunately for Azeff he was at the very crest of his reputation within the Party and no one would believe that the organiser of Plehve's assassination could be guilty of such treachery, and it was decided to forget about the incident as quickly as possible.

At the same time a thorough investigation of Tatarov was instituted by the Party, and his showing at his interrogation spelled his end. For since Rostkovsky had deliberately withheld the news of the letter from him, he was taken unawares and condemned himself out of his own mouth. However, the Party was unable to pin anything specific on him, and though there had been a suggestion that he should be liquidated, it was not acted upon and he was allowed to return to Russia on undertaking to keep the Central Committee informed of all his movements, a decision which made Azeff very angry.

Tatarov's days were numbered in any event, for when those arrested at the end of March were freed in October, a number of them gave evidence of Tatarov's part in identifying them. Savinkov was then given the task of organising his "execution", and on 4th April 1906 the traitor was stabbed to death in his father's house in Warsaw.

Though Azeff had emerged unscathed from the incident, it had been a great shock and a warning to him. He realised, perhaps for the first time really seriously, the danger he ran from both sides; and he saw that once suspicions were aroused he would have to make a firm decision either to withdraw altogether or to give his support only to one side. It would seem from the fact that he called on Ratayef, who had retired to Paris, and told him he could continue working for the police no longer, that in the autumn of 1905, when strikes, disturbances and uprisings were keeping most of Russia in a ferment of revolutionary unrest, he was more in favour of giving his whole attention to the revolutionaries. However, on his return to Moscow from this visit to the west, he lost something of his confidence in the immediate success of the Revolution.

During these days revolutionaries of all parties were deeply immersed in ideological discussions, and all the differences which were later to leave their stamp on the movement as a whole began to manifest themselves. This was particularly true of the Social Revolutionary Party which, before many months were out, was to split into various factions which included the moderates (who called themselves National Socialists and were shortly to form a separate party) and an extreme left wing who called themselves the Social Revolutionary Maximalist Party.

Within a brief time of taking over the control of the Police Department Ratchkovsky had introduced an innovation into the police battle with the revolutionaries. He formed an organisation known as the Black Band, which attacked revolutionaries wherever they could be found with a counter-terror. One evening early in December as he was taking a short cut through a dark alley Azeff was attacked by two members of the Black Band. Fortunately for him he was wearing a thick fur-lined coat which the dagger did not succeed in piercing. He was very upset by the actual attack, but what worried him much more was: How much had Ratchkovsky had to do with it? Had the police chief intended it as a warning of what would happen if he should ever double-cross him? Apparently deciding that it would be wise to ingratiate himself with Ratchkovsky he betrayed all the plans of Savinkov who, despite the dissolution of the Battle Organisation continued to preach terror to a number of kindred spirits. For some reason, though he acted on the information and caused Savinkov to complain, "We had to call all off for the places selected were so closely guarded as to suggest that the police had been warned," Ratchkovsky cold-shouldered Azeff, and did not even acknowledge his letters.

When, in January 1906, it became quite clear that the government forces were gaining control of the situation and that the revolutionary movement had lost its impetus, the Central Committee once more decided to reopen the terror. The Battle Organisation was resuscitated and Azeff was again put in control of it. The response to Azeff's call was gratifying. Most of the former members had been released from imprisonment and without exception rallied to the Organisation, while volunteers came forward in considerable numbers.

But even under Azeff's leadership and the impact of Savinkov's keenness the new Organisation's members were no longer Zubatov's "artists in terror". The reason for this was undoubtedly Azeff's less-than-full-commitment to terror. He put forward a plan of campaign—approved by the Central Committee—which was a mere repetition of the old, while the methods he proposed using were exactly the same as those which had been employed in Plehve's assassination. There was neither inspiration nor invention. Indeed, it seems only too clear that Azeff's involvement was the result of one consideration only— that it gave him control of a very full and large money-bag. I doubt whether the new Organisation would have achieved any success even if it had been unhampered by treachery.

Chapter Thirty-three

THE END OF A PRIEST

The traitor was none other than Father Gapon, who had led the procession of workers to the Winter Palace on Bloody Sunday.

From his subsequent behaviour it is quite obvious that even if he had become involved with the workers from the best of motives, any altruism there was was not deep-rooted and quickly withered. He had emerged from the events of Bloody Sunday the hero of the day, and his character was so basically shallow that the adulation went to his head. Everywhere he was feted and money for his "workers' movement"—of which he was really the only member—was showered upon him. He went abroad, where the same treatment was meted out to him and his real weaknesses rapidly began to show themselves. He was a gourmandiser and a womaniser on no mean scale, he squandered his funds on gambling at Monte Carlo and on riotous living in Paris. Inevitably he sickened his erstwhile supporters; equally inevitably his money ran out; and when it did he returned to St Petersburg where he was an easy prey for anyone who could pay well and wished to make use of his services.

Among those who sought his acquaintance was a popular journalist called Manasevich-Monoilov, who was also an agent in Prime Minister Witte's private secret service. Manasevich-Monoilov immediately appreciated that Gapon was ready to do anything for money, and introduced him to Ratchkovsky.

Ratchkovsky saw the possibility of transforming the priest

into a second Azeff, and very cleverly began to win him over by flattery. The government, Ratchkovsky said, were sorry about what had happened on Bloody Sunday, that the shooting had been the result of a sad misunderstanding and that it would like to obtain the Father's valuable services because of his relations with the workers. Specifically they would like him to organise a labour movement on peaceful lines which would educate the workers along paths that the government sincerely believed would in the long run serve all their aspirations.

Gapon fell for it all with an ease which surprised even Ratchkovsky who believed that he had summed up his man's purely mercenary character correctly. There were several meetings in exclusive, expensive restaurants—always in private rooms—and by degrees and very skilfully Ratchkovsky drew the priest into his net. Ratchkovsky, referring to his own advancing years, told Gapon that Russia stood in great need of men like him. Soon he, Ratchkovsky, would be retiring and if Father Gapon would agree to help the police now by revealing what he knew of revolutionary activities and especially of the Battle Organisation's intentions, who knew, perhaps he might succeed him as chief of the Police Department?

For his part, Gapon, while responding favourably, let Ratchkovsky know that the cost of his services would be very high indeed. They were in fact so high that Ratchkovsky had to apply to the new Minister of the Interior, P. Durnovo, for authorisation to spend such sums on the project. But despite the fact that Ratchkovsky was able to tell the Minister that Gapon was a close friend of an engineer called Rutenberg, who had close connections with the Battle Organisation, Durnovo decided to seek the advice of the chief of the Moscow Okhrana, a Colonel Gerassimov.

Gerassimov did not at all share Ratchkovsky's enthusiasm for the scheme. For one thing his information was that Rutenberg was a sincere revolutionary and not at all the type of man who would be prepared to betray his comrades for money. Because of this Durnovo suggested that Gerassimov should meet Gapon and have a chat with him, and a meeting was arranged which only served to strengthen the Colonel's doubts. In the end, however, Ratchkovsky had his way and Gapon was authorised to approach Rutenberg, who at the time was in hiding from the police.

Despite the fact that on 22nd January 1905 "he had lain by Gapon's side in the snow as the bullets of the Tsar's soldiers rained over them", and had helped to draw up the famous petition, Rutenberg was at once made suspicious of the priest's motives by his ham-fisted presentation of his cover-story. This, concocted with Ratchkovsky's aid, was that he, Gapon, had made contact with Ratchkovsky whom he intended to use for his own revolutionary aims. But Gapon had not assimilated the details of his story, and there were so many contradictions in it that Rutenberg at once believed that Gapon was in contact with the police for reasons very different from those he had put forward. If he were right, Rutenberg argued, then his comrades would be in danger, and to protect them by finding out all he could about the priest's real aims, he pretended to go along with him. He played his part much more convincingly than Gapon played his. In no time at all he had succeeded in extracting from Gapon the information that Ratchkovsky was prepared to pay a very high price indeed for news of the Battle Organisation's proposed campaign of terror.

Having told the Party chief of Gapon's planned treachery, Rutenberg went to Helsinki where, since Finland had recently been granted independence, Azeff had established the head-quarters of the Battle Organisation. Azeff's response was un-equivocal: "Gapon ought to be killed like a snake." He suggested that Rutenberg should invite him to a certain restaurant for dinner and as they were driving back through the forest in a sleigh provided by the Battle Organisation he should stab the priest and throw his body out.

Unfortunately this simple solution was not feasible. Though he had lost the respect of the revolutionaries Gapon was still worshipped by the workers. This being so, the Central Committee decided that his death had to be arranged in such a way that the extent of his treachery was made clear to the masses. At the same time Ratchkovsky was also to be liquidated.

So, Rutenberg, acting on the Committee's instructions to continue to "co-operate" with Gapon, returned to St Petersberg and told the priest that he had finally decided to work with him. Gapon's next concern was for Rutenberg to meet Ratchkovsky, and indeed the latter was impatient for the meeting to take place. After some hesitations it was fixed for 17th March in a restaurant.

However, Gerassimov had been keeping an eye on Rutenberg and had become very suspicious of his recent movements; so in the afternoon of the 17th the Colonel telephoned Ratchkovsky and advised him not to keep the appointment. Ratchkovsky's first reaction was to believe that Gerassimov was being too suspicious and ultra-careful, but he did at length agree to take his advice. Not long afterwards it began to be clear that he had somewhat inexplicably changed his mind about the whole affair, for it was evident that he had lost interest in both Gapon and Rutenberg.

This change was no mere accident. It would have been in the interests of Azeff's continuing safety for Ratchkovsky to die, because, of all the members of the Police Department, its chief was the only one to regard Azeff with suspicion. Tatarov had told him of Azeff's real role in the Battle Organisation, and now he heard the same thing from Gapon. He had doubted Tatarov, and just when he was beginning to wonder whether Gapon's apparent confirmation might not contain an element of truth, he received a letter from Azeff warning him of a plot to kill him. This, combined with Gerassimov's warning, cooled his ardour for the project though he shrank from taking action against Rutenberg. Azeff's change of front, on the other hand, was typical of him. He never missed an opportunity of warning one of his police chiefs of danger threatening them for he had learned that ruthless though they might be they were always less inclined to believe the worst if they had been personally saved. At the same time Azeff was fully determined that Gapon should be removed, so to overcome the complication of the Central Committee's decision to kill both the priest and the policeman, he undertook the responsibility for the whole operation.

By this time, too, Rutenberg was beginning to lose his nerve. He had no stomach for the double killing, and seizing on this Azeff urged him to lose no time in bringing Gapon to justice.

In order that the workers should be disillusioned about their favourite priest, Azeff planned that Gapon should be "executed" after a trial. An empty villa on the outskirts of St Petersburg was taken and there in the early evening of 10th April 1906 the workers chosen to act as judges were concealed in a room divided from its neighbour by only a thin partition. Shortly afterwards Rutenberg arrived and was presently joined by Gapon. The latter had been inveigled there in the belief that they were to settle the terms on which Rutenberg would be prepared to betray the Battle Organisation. The two men went into the room adjoining that where the judges were hidden.

Gapon was in an angry mood already on account of Rutenberg's inability to bring himself to a decision, and when the engineer still showed signs of uncertainty he spoke harshly and loudly.

"Twenty thousand roubles isn't bad money," he cajoled. "I really can't think why you're behaving like such a fool."

"What I can't quite stomach," Rutenberg explained, "is that if they're arrested these men will hang."

"Supposing they do!" Gapon replied. "It's bad luck, but we can't afford to think of that. You can't cut down a tree without some splinters flying. And I promise you, you've nothing to fear. Ratchkovsky is very clever. He'll arrange everything so that no one will ever know you've had anything to do with it."

Rutenberg could stand no more of it, and striding to the door between the two rooms, he flung it open and called in the judges. They had heard every word through the thin dividing wall, and had hardly been able to contain themselves. Now they burst in and threw themselves upon the priest who, recognising some of his former friends among them, fell on his knees and begged for mercy.

"Forgive me, brothers, for the past's sake!" he urged them.

"Ratchkovsky is your brother. We are not," they told him, slipping a noose of rope round Gapon's neck.

Rutenberg hurried away sobbing, unable to wait to see the task completed.

The riding end of the rope was flung over a hook which they had fixed near the rail for drying clothes, and a few seconds later the priest's body was jerking spasmodically, high in the air. They waited until he was dead, and then quietly left the villa.

Rutenberg hurried at once to Helsinki to tell the Battle Organisation and was puzzled and pained by Azeff's denial that he had given permission for Gapon alone to be executed, or that he had been informed in advance that this was to happen. He told the Central Committee quite firmly that if anyone accepted Rutenberg's word and rejected his, he would regard it as an insult. No one did, and Rutenberg found himself accused of flouting Party discipline and slandering one of the most respected members of the Central Committee. The Party also denied all responsibility for Gapon's death and Rutenberg was so overwhelmed by this desertion that he left the revolutionary movement for good.

Chapter Thirty-four

THE CASE OF THE THIRD MAN

While Rutenberg had been making his preparations for the liquidation of Gapon the Battle Organisation had been similarly employed on a plan for assassinating Durnovo, the Minister of the Interior. Unfortunately they were careless, and the police not only got wind of the proposed attempt but obtained the additional most useful information that Durnovo's movements were being watched by terrorists disguised as cabbies.

As a result of information acquired during the interrogations following the arrests in March 1905, the police had organised a permanent mass watch on cabbies. As soon as news came in of the attempt to be made against Durnovo this watch was intensified and presently it was learned from the owner of some cabbies' quarters, who was in police pay, that he believed one of his tenants was one of the disguised terrorists. A detective was set on to keep this "cabby" permanently under surveillance and this led to the further discovery that their quarry was in touch with two other cabbies and with a third man who was obviously in charge of them.

In his reports of this surveillance the detective referred to this third man as "our Philipovsky", and this attracted the attention of Gerassimov, who by this time had been promoted chief of the St Petersburg Okhrana. So he called the detective to him and asked him to explain what he meant by "our Philipovsky". The detective said that five or six years before the chief of the

Investigation Department, Mednikov, had pointed a man out to him one day in the Philipov café, and had said that he was one of the Police Department's best secret agents and had to be protected against arrest. Not knowing the man's real identity he had always thought of him since as "our Philipovsky", from the name of the café.

Gerassimov on being told of this had to go carefully. He dared not arrest the third man, but he was determined all the same to make no mistake, so asked the Police Department to tell him "Philipovsky's" true identity and the nature of his relationship with the police. The Department firmly denied all knowledge of Philipovsky, whereupon Gerassimov asked them to check again very carefully as "he might be some agent whom the Department usually knew under another name." This time Ratchkovsky himself assured the Okhrana chief that there was no police agent in contact with the Battle Organisation.

Gerassimov believed that he could not afford to ignore the detective's evidence so he decided to ask Philipovsky himself to explain what his role was and gave instructions for his arrest. So one evening in the middle of April 1906 Philipovsky was arrested as he was returning at dusk from interviewing one of the cabbies.

Philipovsky protested vehemently against being treated in this way and at Okhrana he produced papers in the name of Engineer Cherkass and demanded immediate release, threatening that if he were not set free he would tell the newspapers about what had happened.

Gerassimov was quite unmoved by these threats and told Philipovsky-Cherkass that he could wait indefinitely for him to make up his mind to talk. "When you do," said Gerassimov, "tell the warder." So Philipovsky was put in an Okhrana cell where he spent two days before finally deciding to co-operate.

"But," he said to Gerassimov, "before I speak I would like my former chief Pyotr Ivanovich to be here."

Gerassimov was to identify Pyotr Ivanovich at once as Ratchkovsky and telephoned him, announcing, "You remember Philipovsky about whom we consulted you? Well, we've arrested him, and just think, he says he knows you very well, that he once served under you and that he wishes you to be present when he speaks."

As Gerassimov had expected it might, this news rather

embarrassed Ratchkovsky and he tried to pass it off by suggesting that the man might be Azeff. This was the first time the Okhrana chief had heard Azeff's name.

Ratchkovsky came to Gerassimov's private office in the Okhrana building at once.

"Ah, my dear Azeff!" he exclaimed with his "sweet smile" as he came into the room. "We haven't seen each other for a long time, have we?"

But Azeff was in no mood for pleasantries and he let loose at Ratchkovsky a searing flow of invective which, even to the experienced Gerassimov, was in a large part quite novel. Ratchkovsky, however, was unperturbed by it and still smiling he urged Azeff to keep calm and not get so excited.

When Azeff had cooled off a little and the conversation had become slightly more rational, Gerassimov learned that the two men had not seen one another since the day the Menshikov letter compromising Azeff and Tatarov had arrived at the St Petersburg Social Revolutionary Committee six months earlier. To begin with Azeff had judged it wiser to have no contact with Ratchkovsky for fear he might be compromised further, but when all had passed off satisfactorily with the revolutionaries he began to contact the Department and Ratchkovsky had chosen to ignore his letters. It was because Ratchkovsky had abandoned him in this way that Azeff had abused him. He reminded Ratchkovsky more than once about his warning of the Rutenberg plot against his life and pointed out that Gapon's death proved how serious the danger had been, while for his part Ratchkovsky could put up no coherent defence of his behaviour.

"Even I felt a pang of conscience over Ratchkovsky's treatment of Azeff," Gerassimov says in his memoirs. "I was quite amazed that such incompetents were running the Political Department. Azeff read Ratchkovsky a well-deserved and timely lecture."

Eventually the two men patched it up and Ratchkovsky apologised for behaving so badly, and asked Azeff to take up his police work again. After a face-saving show of reluctance Azeff agreed on condition that his back pay for the last six months plus a sum for expenses should be paid to him. He got his way.

Gerassimov, while an interested spectator of this scene between master and agent, nevertheless felt constrained to ask Azeff how he came to be involved in a plot against the life of a

Minister. Azeff replied that since Ratchkovsky had abandoned him he felt at liberty to engage in his "professional Party work," an explanation which Gerassimov found quite acceptable.

Before they parted Azeff passed on a certain amount of information about the Battle Organisation's plans and activities, but he was careful to give no lead on which the Okhrana might act. For example, the Battle Organisation was simultaneously engaged in preparations for attempts against the lives of two Ministers. The group of cabbies with whom he had been connected—A. R. Gotz, Pavlov and Treyanov—and a second group led by Savinkov were both planning the death of Durnovo. Azeff said nothing at all about Savinkov's group and nothing at all about a third group conspiring against the life of Dubassov, Governor-General of St Petersburg. In effect, he told the police nothing they did not already know.

He did tell them about a group led by Zenzinov who with Azeff's aid had drawn up a plan to "execute" two officers of the Semeonovsky Regiment, General Min and Colonel Riman. Though he mentioned no names the police were able to arrange to protect the two officers.

It was at this first meeting that Gerassimov and Ratchkovsky heard for the first time that Gapon was really dead. Even so Azeff did not—perhaps could not—tell them the address of the empty villa, and only a thorough police search came upon the body a month later.

Finally it was agreed that Azeff's cabbies should not be arrested. Azeff argued that to do so would be to discredit him in revolutionary eyes. Instead they were to be frightened off by Azeff warning them that the police were on their trail.

Gerassimov believed that Azeff's usefulness was now at an end. He had reached this conclusion not because Azeff had no contacts left, but because, as police chief he felt he could not guarantee Azeff's security from betrayal owing to the fact that by this time the agent was known to so many detectives. Another betrayal must mean Azeff's certain liquidation by the revolutionaries.

Gerassimov explained all this to Durnovo who said at once that he could not accept this point of view. The police needed all the secret agents they could muster at this time, the Minister said, and as Azeff was prepared to carry on, he must know the risks, and if anything happened to him that was his responsibility. So he signed the authorisation for five thousand roubles and Azeff was reprieved once more.

His first task after his re-emergence was to explain to the Battle Organisation the reason for his absence, and the story he put about was that he had discovered that the police were on his track, so he had gone into hiding for a while. Gerassimov then frightened off the cabbies by instructing his detectives to make their presence so obvious that they could not be missed. The police also put into circulation rumours of the impending arrest of three cab-drivers who were watching Durnovo. This was picked up by the wife of a member of the Central Committee, who reported it to her husband, who reported it to Azeff, who hurried at once to warn Savinkov. They decided that the cabbies should be disbanded without delay.

This decision, which in any normal circumstances would have been a wise one, caused a crisis within the Battle Organisation. The Central Committee had approved the Organisation's programme provided that it was carried out before the Duma met, because it was felt that any terrorist acts performed while the Duma was sitting might make its deliberations difficult. The day for the opening of the Duma was 10th May (1906) and was only a week or two away. Elections were in full swing throughout the country and it was clear that they were going in favour of the progressive parties who were making their appearance on the Russian political scene for the first time.

All this meant that the end of the Battle Organisation was already in sight, and not a single item in its programme had been realised. In fact failure doggedly clung to its heels and there seemed nothing anyone could do to shake it off. This was not due entirely to Azeff's pact with Ratchkovsky and Gerassimov. He had not revealed the smallest detail of the plot on Dubassov's life but somehow the Moscow police got wind of it. Consequently, on the heels of the frightening-off of the St Petersburg cabbies, the group responsible escaped arrest only by the skin of their teeth. Savinkov probably came closer to disaster than he had ever been.

This catastrophe was, in its turn, closely followed by the failure of the attempt on Min and Riman. This was Azeff's doing. As a result of his information the police put a special guard at the houses of the officers who allowed admittance to no one who could not produce satisfactory credentials. So when

Samoylov calling himself Prince Vadbolsky, and Yakovlev, calling himself Prince Drutzky-Sokolensky, presented themselves at Min's and Riman's homes respectively, not even their splendid guards uniforms nor their assumed titles would admit them because they carried no identification papers. Yakovlev went away, acquired some false papers and returned three or four hours later, and was arrested because in the meantime the police had consulted the records and discovered that Yakovlev was far too young to be the real currently surviving Prince Drutzky-Sokolensky.

Azeff's young men felt all these set-backs very keenly as reflections on the honour of the Battle Organisation, and in order to retrieve the Organisation's good name they were prepared to consider the most fantastic suggestions. A measure of their desperation can be seen in their consideration of a plan put forward by the usually level-headed Gotz for the assassination of Durnovo. A number of young men were to force their way into his house wearing coats lined with dynamite and were to blow up themselves, the house and everyone in it. Azeff vetoed the proposal as being far too wasteful of human material.

Azeff then proposed new plans for the liquidation of Durnovo and Dubassov. The attempt on Durnovo was entrusted to Savinkov, while he made himself responsible for the one on Dubassov. Savinkov's luck was entirely out, for while the police got no wind of his preparations they guarded the Minister so carefully that none of Savinkov's band caught even a fleeting glimpse of him. Azeff had better luck.

He chose for his attempt the day of the Tsarina's birthday, 6th May, because on that day Dubassov, as Governor-General of Moscow, would have to attend a thanksgiving service in the Kremlin. He would be killed on his way back from this service.

Azeff made his plans very carefully. While he remained in Helsinki until the very last moment, he sent his assistants to Moscow. A week before the chosen day the explosive expert blew himself up and nearly all the supply of dynamite went with him. This set-back provided an excellent excuse to abandon the whole project had Azeff wanted one; but it is quite obvious that he wished to succeed at all costs. He sent another man to take the dead man's place, and provided more dynamite.

On 3rd May he told Gerassimov and Ratchkovsky that he was

going to Moscow on private business and arrived there on 5th May. He made no mention at all of the forthcoming attack on Dubassov and on the face of it it looks as if he were running a considerable risk not only in going to Moscow at all, but in telling the police chiefs of his intention. Certainly it was entirely contrary to all his past practice, because he had always made certain that he was miles from the scene of the crime with a good alibi.

The young man selected to throw the bomb was called Vronovsky. He placed himself near Dubassov's house at the corner of Chernishevsky Street and Tverskoy Square and waited for the Governor's return from the Kremlin. Dubassov was riding in an open carriage and was accompanied by his aide-de-camp, Count Konovnitzin. As the carriage approached Vronovsky broke through the crowd and the troops lining the streets and lobbed the bomb under the carriage. It exploded immediately, shattered the carriage, killed Konovnitzin and Vronovsky, and though Dubassov survived he was so badly injured that he could never resume his duties.

As soon as the Moscow Okhrana heard of the attempt they rushed a large detachment to the Philipov café which they knew to be a favourite rendezvous of the revolutionaries, and arrested everyone they found there, including Azeff who happened to be nearby. A senior detective recognised him as a secret agent, however, and ordered his release.

It now becomes clear why Azeff had departed from his usual custom and gone to Moscow. The Moscow Okhrana had in its employ a revolutionary informer called Zinaida Zhutchenkova who kept it *au courant* with all terrorist plots being hatched in the city. Besides this, though she was not a member of the Battle Organisation somehow or other she was able to keep her finger on its pulse too, and had only recently betrayed Savinkov's group. Azeff had given strict instructions to his Dubassov group to have no contact whatsoever with the local group, but on the day of the attempt one of the leaders of the local group caught sight of Azeff in the street and assumed that he had been responsible for the attempt on the Governor-General. He mentioned this to Zhutchenkova who immediately informed her Okhrana masters, who, in their turn, telegraphed St Petersburg.

On 7th May Azeff left Moscow and returned to St Petersburg where he was summoned to the Police Department and confronted by Gerassimov and a really furious Ratchkovsky who shouted at him, "This affair in Moscow is your doing!"

According to Gerassimov who was expecting an outburst from Azeff in reply, the latter merely shrugged his shoulders and replied calmly, "All right, if you think that, arrest me! But you'll be making a bad mistake. The person who organised the whole thing was a terrorist called Zinaida Zhutchenkova."

"Impossible," shouted Ratchkovsky and went on to tell Azeff what he already knew, "Zhutchenkova is an Okhrana secret agent."

"So am I," Azeff replied. "Why should you think me capable of doing such a thing and not she? Anyway my information is that she organised the business."

This, of course, placed the police in a quandary. If they arrested either of their secret agents there would be a great scandal, for it would inevitably become known that the police were employing *agents provocateurs*. With the Duma meeting in a few days from now, this was quite the wrong time for such a revelation to be made, for the system was regarded with abhorrence even by some members of the government. All they could do was to leave things well alone.

The Dubassov incident affected Azeff in two ways. He was realist enough to know that when mud is thrown some of it is bound to stick, and this he was sure had happened as the result of the Menshikov letter. Though the leadership of the Party were satisfied that the accusations in the letter were lies so far as Azeff was concerned, there were some who nursed seeds of doubt. The Dubassov affair and Azeff's role in it helped to dispel these doubts.

The other effect it had on Azeff bore on his relations with Gerassimov and Ratchkovsky. He realised that they were not convinced that he had nothing to do with the attempt, and in trying to overcome their doubts for some months afterwards he dropped his double role and set about proving to them that he was genuinely on the side of authority. Gerassimov took advantage of this and once more demanded the betrayal of Savinkov. Azeff was this time fully prepared to hand the younger man over; but as happened on the first occasion, Savinkov again escaped through no fault of Azeff's.

In the Duma elections the Socialist and Liberal opposition parties were returned with a very large majority, and in accordance with their avowed intention the Central Committee announced the suspension of terror so long as the Duma remained in session. But the Central Committee was no longer the supreme policy-making body of the Party; its resolutions now had to receive the approval of the Party soviet.

A few days before the soviet was to meet, although he was aware of the Central Committee's resolution, Azeff sent Savinkov and his group to Sevastopol to assassinate Admiral Chuknin who had quelled the uprising in the Black Sea fleet in 1905 with great ruthlessness. Azeff had planned all this with Gerassimov's full knowledge and when the group left for the south they were followed by Okhrana agents who were going to arrest them as soon as it was certain they were in possession of evidence which would inevitably lead to the imposition of the death sentence.

Two days after Savinkov's arrival in Sevastopol the local Social Revolutionaries, who for some time past had been organising terror on their own initiative, as we shall presently see, attempted to assassinate the city commandant, General Nepluyev. Though the Okhrana was perfectly well aware that Savinkov's men had had no part in the affair they arrested them and charged them before a court-martial with attempted murder.

As soon as the news of the arrests arrived in St Petersburg, a number of Savinkov's young friends of the Battle Organisation without saying a word to anyone, rushed south, where they organised a daring plan to rescue Savinkov. The plan succeeded, Savinkov walked out of the prison one day disguised as a soldier and escaped abroad. Without the leader of the terrorists in the dock, the trial of the group lost much of its significance and the authorities were content to pass sentences of exile and forced labour.

Chapter Thirty-five

CHANGES

A number of changes were now at hand, not only in the Battle
Organisation but in the government and Police Department as
well.

Count Witte, despite the great services he had rendered to
Russia as Finance Minister, and more latterly as Prime Minister,
had long since disgusted the Tsar both by his personal character
—he was a coarse man of little refinement and had little time
for the manners of the Court—and by his reforming concessions
in the last months of 1905, was replaced, as soon as he had got
the armies safely home from the Far East, by the colourless
Goremykin. Goremykin at once made changes in his ministry
and replaced Durnovo at the Ministry of the Interior by Peter
Stolypin.

This was the first appearance of Stolypin on the St Petersburg
scene. He had never previously held a ministerial appointment
of any kind and he owed his promotion now to the fact that
during the winter troubles of 1905 he was almost the only
provincial governor who had retained perfect control of his
province. He had risked his life unhesitatingly in restraining
mobs of reactionary hooligans, and had often secured without
bloodshed the submission of a village taken over by the revolutionaries. In his approach to these difficult problems he had won
the admiration of friend and foe alike.

Stolypin came to his important post with a good many per-

sonal doubts as to his ability to cope with the exigencies of high
office. Naturally he was ambitious to succeed, so he surrounded
himself with knowledgeable men whom he felt he could trust
and removed those he could not. As a result, one of his first
victims was Ratchkovsky about whose exploits he had learned
from his close friend Lopukhin, Ratchkovsky's sworn enemy.

Ratchkovsky's post was filled by Trussevich, but the man who
now came to the fore was the chief of the St Petersburg Okhrana,
promoted General Gerassimov. The leadership of the St Petersburg Okhrana was already one of the major police posts in the
empire; Gerassimov was soon to make it more important still, a
process which he had initiated when he had demanded the arrest
of the St Petersburg Workers' Soviet and had won his point
against the opposition of the Department chiefs, and Durnovo.

Stolypin very quickly recognised Gerassimov's qualities and
his talents as a policeman and he had not been in office long
when he granted Gerassimov privileges and influence enjoyed
by no former police chief. He made the Okhrana quite independent of the Police Department and it did not take Gerassimov
long to subordinate the Department to the Okhrana, though in
theory the Department remained predominant. The only man
who controlled Gerassimov was Stolypin.

Stolypin was particularly interested in all the activities of the
revolutionary parties and it was Gerassimov's first charge to
organise a secret agency within the revolutionaries to provide
all the information his Minister required. In meeting this charge
Gerassimov adopted a policy that ran counter to all the previous
official conceptions of the role that the agents of such an
organisation should adopt. He required his agents to become
actual members of Party organisations and to achieve as high a
position in the Party as they could. In return Gerassimov introduced a system whereby he shielded his agents from arrest.

Somewhat naturally Gerassimov received a good deal of
opposition to these innovations from the older officials in the
Department who tried to win the support of Stolypin. The latter,
however, fully appreciated the advantages of Gerassimov's
system and gave him his official backing, unlimited funds and
independence of action.

In Gerassimov's organisation the leading role was played by
Azeff who came under the Okhrana chief's exclusive control.
Gerassimov had entertained doubts of Azeff's loyalty to the

police, but they were based purely on suspicion, and since such
doubts were not a sound basis for the relationship he felt it
necessary to have with his agent, realistically he put them away,
and was later to write, "I assumed full responsibility for any
provocative act Azeff might commit and I am quite certain that
in return Azeff never deceived me."

Gerassimov, as we have seen, highly disapproved of Ratchkovsky's treatment of Azeff, and himself set about to establish
a relationship between them based on mutual trust. To this end
he doubled Azeff's salary, making it a thousand roubles a
month and persuaded him to save the whole of it—since he
received sufficient from his Party activities to live on—and
invest it against a rainy day. He also defined very carefully
Azeff's duties as a secret agent. He was to obtain information
about events and people only of the highest importance, and
even if he had information of lesser importance he need only
pass it on if he personally decided to. For his part Gerassimov
undertook never to arrest any of the revolutionaries without
first consulting Azeff.

One of Azeff's specific tasks was to collect information relating to questions posed by Stolypin from time to time. No doubt
he was honoured by the high recognition implicit in the requests
addressed directly to him—though he received them through
Gerassimov—by the Minister.

It is quite certain that Azeff found this regime far more to
his liking than any of the treatment he had received from his
former chiefs, and one could perhaps have understood had he
decided there and then to devote his main activities to supplying
the requirements of his chief. He did, in fact, go quite a long
way towards doing so, but the double role he had been playing
for so long must have got too strong a hold over him for him
ever to give his loyalty to one side. As we shall see, Gerassimov
was deceived.

High on Gerassimov's list of requirements of Azeff was the
fullest details concerning the activities of the Battle Organisation. The soviet of the Social Revolutionary Party had met a few
days after the opening of the Duma and had approved the
Central Committee's resolution to suspend terrorism while the
Duma was sitting. Azeff participated in the meetings of the
soviet and though to the members of the Battle Organisation
he expressed the belief that the decision was a wrong one, he

nevertheless obeyed it and set about temporarily dissolving the Organisation, work in which he was helped by Savinkov who had been unhappy abroad and had soon returned to Russia, despite the risks this entailed.

Within a few months of the Duma's first meeting it became evident to everyone that it and the government would never agree on the reforms, and particularly on the details of a constitution, which had been the ostensible reason for the summoning of the Duma. In consequence, within a short time of disbanding the Battle Organisation the Party Leaders were once more considering reopening the terror.

The leaders were split on the issue. It was not a clear-cut split, for there were renewal-waverers and no-terror-waverers, and they might have gone on arguing for a long time had not their hand been forced by the arrival of the leader of the independent terrorist group in the south to demand permission to assassinate Admiral Chukin. The Sevastopol leader put forward some very cogent arguments in favour of Chukin's death, particularly that it would greatly help the Party in their efforts, already begun, to stir up mutiny in the armed services. The Central Committee saw the force of this argument and gave the permission requested and the Admiral was assassinated a week or two later by a sailor called Akimov who made good his escape.

The effects of the assassination were as the Sevastopol leader had forecast and the Central Committee now swung round to the view that terrorist activities were most unlikely to prevent progress towards revolution. So it was decided to reconstitute the Battle Organisation under the leadership of Azeff. For the time being it was allotted only one task—the assassination of Stolypin.

The choice of Stolypin at this juncture in my view indicates that the Social Revolutionaries had somewhat changed their policy for selecting their victims. In the past all those who were either assassinated or who had attempts made on their lives had been guilty of harsh repressive measures against the revolutionaries; the fact that they were Ministers of the Interior or city governors or police chiefs was incidental. That Stolypin was chosen because he was Minister of the Interior seems clear since he had not a record of counter-terrorism, either as a provincial governor or as Minister, of sufficient ruthlessness to warrant his sentence of death.

Since his appointment as Minister of the Interior, despite his obvious personal feelings of insecurity in the performance of his high office, Stolypin had made surprising progress. The government had envisaged the functions of the Duma as being similar to those of the Prussian Reichstag, a consultative and ratifying body rather than a legislating body like the British Parliament. When the First Duma met, therefore, the Speech from the Throne contained no political programme. The Duma, on the other hand, was determined to be something more than a talking-shop, so in its Humble Address in reply to the Speech, it outlined a political programme of its own. Thus from the very outset the ground was prepared for the creation of deadlock between Duma and government; and soon this happened.

When Goremykin, the Prime Minister, and the members of his government attended the Duma to announce that the introduction of a political programme was inadmissable, Nabokov, the leader of the Cadets, as the Constitutional Democrat Party was colloquially known, rose to propose a vote of censure on the government which, after a long debate unmasking every government abuse, was carried unanimously. This was a hollow victory for the Duma since it had no means at its command to force the government's resignation. For two months the two sides were locked in an impasse, neither being prepared to move from its position, until on 21st July the Duma was dissolved.

For the dissolution the colourless Prime Minister, Goremykin, was removed and replaced by Stolypin. Few politicians anywhere have had such a meteoric rise. While decreeing the dissolution of the First Duma he gave the necessary notice for calling the second, which was to assemble in March 1907, just inside the legal time-limit. Only now, while preparing to introduce some moderate reforms, did he undertake to crush revolution wherever it might be found. Though within another two months he set up field courts-martial empowered and required to deal drastically with revolutionaries—the usual sentence of these courts was death, and while they were effective six hundred people were executed—at the time that the Central Committee made him the Battle Organisation's target he had not shown his hand in this respect.

Stolypin as Prime Minister revealed himself as a man of purpose, possessing a good deal of moral courage. Naturally the revolutionaries regarded him as their enemy, but he was opposed

also by the reactionary parties, and particularly by those reactionary circles close to and influential at the Court. But he
applied himself to remedying Russia's problems as he interpreted
them and in so doing acted fearlessly and honestly. As I have
said earlier, he is regarded by some Russian historians as Russia's
last great minister.

Commissioned to assassinate the very man whose personal
adviser on revolutionary affairs he had become, Azeff began
reconstituting the Battle Organisation. Without exception, all
former members came forward, while volunteers offered themselves, as always, in impressive numbers. Old and new alike were
fired with a firm belief in the inevitable success of their undertaking, a view which Azeff not only did not share but made
plain he did not share.

True to his new arrangements with Gerassimov, Azeff kept
his chief informed of all the Battle Organisation's affairs and the
details of its plans. At any given moment Gerassimov could
have arrested all the members of the Organisation; that he fore-
bore to do so was due to the danger such a move would have
represented to his prize agent. Instead, for the time being,
Gerassimov and Azeff combined to nullify all the Organisation's
activities by every means short of arrest.

Personally seeing the success of his methods in neutralising
the effectiveness of the Organisation's effort, Azeff devised a
scheme which he believed would eventually compel the Central
Committee to accept the contention that organised terror on a
grand scale was impossible to achieve. His plan was to bring the
Battle Organisation to running at full pressure while at the same
time the results it achieved would be so negligible as to be almost
despicable. When this had been the situation for some time
Azeff would then draw the Central Committee's attention to it
and suggest that the Battle Organisation should be permanently
dissolved, pointing out that it was costing a very great deal of
money while achieving nothing, and in addition, by its ineffec-
tualness was bringing the Party politically into disrepute.

Gerassimov fully approved this scheme and the specific plan
which Azeff was to follow to make it successful—no less than
an attempt on Stolypin's life. Stolypin, somewhat naturally, was
not so enthusiastic. Though he did not say so, it is clear that he
feared there might be some slip-up on Azeff's part and that he
might be killed. However, when both Gerassimov and Azeff

virtually guaranteed that there would be no accidents, he gave his approval.

Azeff immediately put the Battle Organisation on to making the preparations to kill the Prime Minister, bringing into use all the old methods. The terrorists themselves worked as usual with exemplary zeal, but as time went by it began to become apparent that absolutely no results were being obtained. Azeff played a prominent, though clandestine, part in frustrating his men's efforts by misdirecting them, while Gerassimov used every security device to protect Stolypin, which served to increase the Organisation's sense of futility.

For a time the terrorists grew despondent, but there were one or two among them with initiative and presently these began to put forward plans of their own. When they began to be too insistent that they should be allowed to try out their schemes Azeff agreed though he carefully pointed out where he believed they were wrong, and made sure that his belief in their failure was understood by all.

So the plotters were given their heads, but as soon as they were all keyed up and ready to strike, Gerassimov went into action. The Okhrana employed a number of detectives specifically for the purpose of frightening people, no more. They were men who were, it seems, congenitally incapable of following a man without betraying their presence. They even had a special appellation—*branders*.

At the crucial moment Gerassimov let loose his *branders* on the cabbies, hawkers and others who were watching Stolypin's movements. They could not possibly remain unaware that they were being followed, for the *branders* literally breathed down their necks. They would report at once to Azeff, who occasionally pretended not to believe them, but when they "persuaded" him to examine the evidence he had to agree that they were right. He would then tell them what they must do to escape, which invariably included the abandonment of apartments, disguises and all the other paraphanalia they had been using, so that the next attempt had to be started absolutely from scratch.

After each "escape" the plotters would meet in Finland to hold a post mortem. The verdict arrived at was always the same —that the police had got on their trail purely by chance and that they had escaped because the police had not had time to discover their identities.

Each incident of this kind had two effects, both cumulative. One, since Azeff had foretold failure his reputation as an expert increased; two, since the police appeared just at the moment when the terrorists seemed to have made contact with Stolypin it began to appear to them that he had surrounded himself with an impenetrable protective police barrier. As for Azeff, he lost no opportunity to ram home to both Battle Organisation and Central Committee the uselessness of the old methods of working.

As the background to this deception of the Battle Organisation there were uprisings in many of the provinces, especially Estonia, and a mutiny at Kronstadt, the naval base at the mouth of the Neva. There had also been widespread acts of terror by independent groups and individuals directed against police and gendarmerie officials, governors-general and provincial government officials and bureaucrats. On the other hand there was no great explosion as there had been in the autumn and winter of the previous year. It was to deal with this situation that Stolypin introduced the field courts-martial which by their ruthless suppression of all revolutionary activities earned for the Prime Minister in next to no time, a reputation for being the inspirer of cruelty and the leader of reaction, though the latter was not true.

This brought Stolypin within the orbit of one other party at least, the Maximalists, the left-wing of the Social Revolutionaries who had broken away and formed their own party. The Maximalists now entered into direct competition with the Battle Organisation, and had organised a terror-section for the liquidation of Stolypin.

It would seem that the Okhrana had not penetrated the Maximalist terror-section, for no news of their preparations reached Gerassimov. They prepared their attempt on very different lines from the Battle Organisation. There were no watching cabbies or hawkers; they chose a time when access to their victim was more likely to be possible than not; and they were ready to take considerably greater risks either of blowing themselves up with their own bombs or of being caught.

Stolypin lived with his family in a fairly commodious villa on Apothecary Island on which Gerassimov kept a permanently heavy guard. The guard, however, was somewhat hampered in carrying out its duties by the fact that though the Prime Minister knew he was a target for terrorists, he insisted on entertaining on the lavish scale which was customary among high-ranking officials of the government as it was among the aristocracy. At least once a week he and Madame Stolypin were At Home to all visitors and for one reason or another quite large numbers found it politic to call. On these occasions it was well-nigh impossible for the guard to check the credentials or recognise the identities of all the guests, so when, one day in August 1906 three Maximalists suitably dressed drove up to the villa in a carriage at the hour of reception they were granted admission. However, the detectives in the hall of the villa seemed to sense that these guests were not of the usual run of those who called on the Stolypins and stopped them from going further into the villa; whereupon all three produced their bombs and tossed them into the middle of the hall.

The explosion killed all those who were passing through the hall at the time, the guards and the three terrorists themselves, while the greater part of the villa was wrecked. Stolypin's small children were severely injured, but Stolypin himself happened to be in his study on the other side of the house, where the explosion was scarcely felt, and he escaped with a few scratches. The Tsar, who lived more or less permanently at the Peterhoff at this time, insisted that the Stolypins should move into the Winter Palace, and for the remainder of his ministry the Prime Minister emerged from the palace only when it was strictly necessary, a move which made any attempt on his life even more difficult than it had been before.

Azeff was in Finland when the incident occurred and he became extremely perturbed when the news of it reached him. He feared that Gerassimov and Stolypin would believe that the Battle Organisation was responsible for the attempt. After an hour or two's hesitation he decided to go to St Petersburg to explain to the Okhrana chief that he honestly had had no inkling that the attempt was to be made. Gerassimov accepted the assurance without difficulty but both agreed that Stolypin would not be so easily convinced. The best way of overcoming this difficulty, Azeff believed, would be to persuade the Central Committee to issue a manifesto denying all responsibility for the incident. The members of the Committee were reluctant to take this step but gave way before his insistence, and he was delegated to draft the manifesto himself. In the event it proved unnecessary for a day or two after the manifesto was issued the Maximalists published one of their own claiming full responsibility.

Azeff never forgave the Maximalists for—quite unconsciously —placing him in such jeopardy. From this time he made it one of his chief concerns to gather all the information he could about their leaders which he passed at once to Gerassimov.

Chapter Thirty-six

"THE HEART OF THE BATTLE ORGANISATION"

There was a passage in the manifesto which led to a good deal of disquiet among the rank and file Social Revolutionaries, and even among the members of the Battle Organisation. It had escaped deletion, in any event, only because of Azeff's insistence that it must be included.

The passage amounted to a forthright condemnation on moral and political grounds of the methods used by the Maximalists on Apothecary Island and it prompted the questions, "Why does the Central Committee condemn any method of promoting terror, since terror in any case is an ultimate? Can this be one of the reasons why the Battle Organisation is being so ineffective?"

In these circumstances these questions were natural, for it was apparent to all that while the Battle Organisation had not let off a single bomb for months past, an almost tyro organisation had nearly succeeded in killing the Prime Minister at its first attempt. Soon the Battle Organisation was being subjected to a campaign of criticism, and when it was at its height a group of revolutionaries not inexperienced in terror decided to take over the control of the Organisation's activities. They kept Azeff in ignorance of their intention and had not been long at their investigations into the Organisation's methods of preparation, before they discovered that these were on entirely wrong lines.

Azeff was still the hero of the members of the Battle Organisation and in their view criticisms of their methods of working were criticisms of their adored leader. In consequence battle was joined between critics and members, the latter concentrating on defending Azeff rather than their record.

Azeff's chief supporter was Boris Savinkov who was the recognised senior member of the Organisation next after Azeff. To the younger members he was the personification of the Organisation. An intimate friend of past heroes Sazunov, Kalayev and Schweitzer, who were already legends, his own record of uninterrupted endeavour on the Organisation's behalf could be equalled by none but the leader. But besides this his character made him beloved by all for himself alone, and all in all, he was, as Zenzinov, a later member of the organisation dubbed him, "The heart of the Battle Organisation."

He could not have reached this position of trust, admiration and affection had he not possessed strong positive qualities. But there was another side to him which permanently prevented him from becoming the great man he might otherwise have been.

He had no qualities of leadership. He was equipped to be a first-class second-in-command only, for he lacked the three vital talents which make the leader—independence of thought, the courage of independent decision and the courage of initiative. This lack automatically led him into making one great mistake in so far as the Battle Organisation was concerned—he placed too much reliance on Azeff. What attracted him to Azeff was the latter's lack of any scruples or doubts concerning the use of terror, scruples and doubts which greatly exercised the minds of so many intellectual revolutionaries at this period and which, more than any other factor, tended to weaken The Cause as a whole. While being convinced that the men who wielded sway over millions upon millions of ordinary men were the representatives of an authority which wrought the greatest harm for those millions, the great majority of revolutionaries nevertheless hesitated when it came to the question of taking human life however much the owner of that life might be detested for his deeds or what he represented.

In my view the hesitations of conscience exhibited by so many of the revolutionaries belie Maxim Gorky's contention that cruelty is "the most prominent feature of the Russian national character" and that "to whatever party Russians may belong,

in their cruelty they are all alike". How widespread were
doubts of the moral justification of terrorism is well indicated
by the fact that each debate on practical questions in the Second
Duma was whenever possible diverted into a discussion of revolutionary terrorism. This evidence in its turn is further
heightened by the full-dress debate on terrorism which occupied
the Duma on 30th May 1907. Jealousy between the Cadets and
the Poles prevented the adoption of the only formula that might
have been acceptable to the majority—it was put forward by
the Poles—that "terrorism is incompatible with parliamentary
institutions", a formula which reveals an uncertainty which
tends towards the rejection of moral justification for terrorism,
but which at the same time implicitly acknowledges that terror
was the only weapon that all revolutionaries and reactionaries
alike in their respective ambitions could wield against their
enemies. The reactionaries, that is those who opposed political
progress, were in a far stronger position because they did not
hesitate to use terror and sincerely believed its use to be justifiable in countering terror; while the revolutionaries, unable to
find a formula on such a burning question that would be
acceptable to all, ultimately rendered their use of terror ineffective. Had all the Russians, to whatever party they belonged,
been alike in their cruelty, then the conflict over the Battle
Organisation within the Social Revolutionary Party could not
have arisen except over personalities, and since Savinkov had
all his life been convinced of the justification for terrorism, he
would not, taking into consideration his standing in the
Organisation and in the Party, have had to spring to the defence
of the Organisation, even though its leader was Azeff.

For his part, Azeff had not the convictions which motivated
Savinkov. It is safe to say that Azeff never once paused to consider "the rightness" of what he proposed to do or was doing.
Yet while Savinkov admired Azeff for his single-mindedness in
preaching terror—that is, his lack of scruples—and was always
the first to support him, even at this juncture he devoted a great
deal of private thought to the question; for he was basically one
of those revolutionaries, of whom there were very many, who
gave more thought about how they would *die* for The Cause
than about how they would *kill* for it. We can see this in all his
work for the Battle Organisation up to this point. In other
circumstances it seems quite certain that he would have eventu-

ally, joyously given his life; as it was, as a result of the conflict within the Party over the Battle Organisation, his future role in it was to be more than a good second-in-command. For, under a leader, Savinkov had demonstrated that he was an organiser, and an organiser was what the Battle Organisation was soon desperately to need.

After his four months abroad, following upon his escape from Sevastopol, Savinkov had returned to the Battle Organisation eager for action, and perhaps more than any other member of the Organisation, was depressed as well as confounded by the failure upon failure which attended all their efforts. Naturally he tried to discover the causes for the failures, and unfortunately listened first to Azeff who told him that the terrorists' methods were out of date while Gerassimov had improved police counter-methods out of all recognition. By playing skilfully upon Savinkov's devotion to the Battle Organisation and all it stood for, and his inclination to be contemptuous of all revolutionaries who were not terrorists, Azeff was able to provide himself with a mouthpiece, for he maintained his policy of taking no part in the public argument.

If there were not to be complete stagnation there had to be a climax and it came at a conference of the Central Committee held in Finland in September 1906. The discussion was long, and at times very heated, but Savinkov was so effective that no mention was made of the Battle Organisation's failure, and a vote of confidence in the Organisation was unanimously passed, while Savinkov was elected to membership of the Central Committee.

Behind the scenes, when the conference was over, Azeff did quite a lot of private lobbying. He approached those members of the Committee who had been the strongest critics of the Organisation—among them were Chernov and Sletov—and told them that Savinkov's arguments had not really represented what was wrong with the Organisation. He emphasised that the old methods were out of date and that new techniques must be found. While the search was being made for these he suggested that the Organisation ought to be temporarily dissolved.

Strangely, and to his surprise, Azeff discovered that his suggestion had scarcely any support at all in the Committee. On the other hand, it was favourably received by the Battle Organisation, except Savinkov. The latter countered his suggestion by putting forward a plan of his own, and eventually Azeff agreed that Savinkov should try it out.

The plan was based on the fact that Stolypin was now installed in the Winter Palace, which he rarely left except for occasional visits to the Tsar. Even when he made these visits he travelled by river, and Savinkov proposed dropping a bomb on the launch carrying him as it passed under one of the Neva bridges. The plan was doomed to failure because the launch shot the bridges very quickly, and in any case the bridges were so closely guarded that no suspicious-looking person could have got near them, for the police seemed to have become very proficient at detecting young men with bombs in their pockets or bulging inside their coats. Savinkov soon realised that his plan would never work, so proposed instead that Stolypin should be attacked at the moment that he was boarding the launch. But this, too, had to be abandoned because of the strong guard at the jetty.

Savinkov now had to agree that Azeff had been right. At another meeting of the Central Committee in October, both proposed the temporary dissolution of the Battle Organisation. When this was rejected, both resigned.

Azeff still believed that he could put an end to terror for a time—as he had promised Gerassimov and Stolypin to do—so he summoned all the St Petersburg members of the Organisation to the Finnish headquarters in the Tourist Hotel at Imatra Falls. Again Savinkov was the spokesman and he asked the twenty members present whether they would be prepared to carry on the terror under other leaders. The majority indicated that they would not, and armed with this decision Azeff and Savinkov went to the next meeting of the Central Committee, which was also to be held at the Tourist Hotel.

The Central Committee, though aware that something of this sort was in the wind, were taken aback by the laconic but firm statement made by Savinkov. A discussion followed which ended in the decision to call *all* the terrorists together and put the question to the vote of the entire Battle Organisation. When this was done, it soon became clear that the majority of members supported the Committee, and nothing Savinkov could say could change this. Azeff and Savinkov were asked to withdraw their resignations in view of this, and when they refused the Committee appointed a new leader, a former student of mathematics, a brilliant organiser and a committed terrorist called Zilberberg.

Azeff had been unable to take part in the later discussions because he had been taken seriously ill with an abscess in the throat. For a time it was thought that he might die. When he was sufficiently recovered he went to Alassio on the Italian Riviera to convalesce. This was the first real rest he had taken. He quickly began to regain his strength, but for the time being the terror went forward without the benefit of his advice and double-crossing.

Chapter Thirty-seven

THE END OF THE MONOPOLY IN TERROR

Up to now, with the exceptions of the attempts of the Sevastopol revolutionaries on Admiral Chukin and the Maximalists on Stolypin, the Battle Organisation had had the monopoly in organised terror. Now it was decided that this monopoly should be broken and although each group still had to be approved by the Central Committee, approval was rarely withheld. The effect of this new policy was a diversification of terrorist activity, an increase in specific acts of terror by groups, and the introduction of terrorist attempts by individuals.

In so far as groups were concerned, in the St Petersburg area alone three distinct organisations for terror came into being. First, there were the former members of the Battle Organisation under the leadership of Zilberberg; second, a group formed for the specific purpose of liquidating the city commandant of St Petersburg, General von Launitz, made up again of Battle Organisation members, led by Lapina, known in the Party as Comrade Bella; and third, a small independent group which had no connections with the Organisation and which was led by a Lett called Prauberg, whose cover-name was Karl.

Approval was granted to this last group after a long and heated discussion in the Central Committee. Most of the opposition to Karl came from Savinkov whose chief objection was that Karl's aims and methods were not at all like those of the Battle Organisation. Chernov and Argunov, by now veterans, supported him, but Savinkov suffered yet another defeat. The group became known as *The Flying Terrorist Detachment of the Northern Region*.

With Azeff no longer there to help him Gerassimov's battle against the terrorists became much more difficult. He had hoped at first that he would be able to keep control of the terrorists by following the same policy that he had adopted when Azeff was there. Soon, however, he found this to be impossible since the links he had with the organised groups were tenuous, the agents unreliable; while, in addition, all the groups changed their tactics and methods and no longer employed cabbies and hawkers whom the police could identify.

Within a comparatively short time Gerassimov found himself quite ignorant of the terrorists' intentions and the results of this ignorance soon became only too painfully apparent. On 15th December 1906 Karl's Flying Detachment made a second attempt on Dubassov, on 8th January 1907 killed General Pavlov, chief military prosecutor, and three weeks later liquidated General Gudima, governor of the temporary prison in St Petersburg established to house political prisoners.

Zilberberg's group had also not dallied in making their preparations for the attempt on General von Launitz, but when the attempt was made it was an entirely impromptu affair, and demonstrates very clearly the change which had come over the terrorists' methods of working. Shortly before 3rd January 1907 news reached Zilberberg that the ceremonial opening of the new Institute of Experimental Medicine had been planned for that day and that Stolypin was proposing to make one of his very rare public appearances in order to be present.

This seemed to all to be far too good an opportunity to be missed not only to get at the Prime Minister but to liquidate von Launitz, who was also to be present. The effect of a double assassination, it was felt, would be tremendous.

The men chosen for the two jobs were Sulyatitsky, the soldier who had rescued Savinkov from prison and whose target was to be Stolypin; and a former student, Kudryavtzev, who was to kill von Launitz, who had earned his death sentence when as Governor of Tambov he had crushed peasant risings with outstanding ruthlessness. Kudryavtzev had been engaged in revolutionary work in Tambov at the time of the uprisings and had made a vow that one day he would kill von Launitz.

News of the intended attempts reached Gerassimov only the day before they were due to take place. Even so, the information was extremely vague; all that he was told was that they would be made "in the next day or two". Gerassimov immediately warned both Stolypin and von Launitz not to leave their houses until the Okhrana had learned more. Stolypin wisely took this advice, but von Launitz disregarded the warning and attended the opening of the Institute.

Sulyatitsky and Kudryavtzev arrived for the ceremony resplendent in faultless white-tie-and-tails. After the dedication service the guests were entertained to luncheon. As Stolypin had not appeared by this time, the two men rightly assumed that he had changed his mind, so, as Zilberberg had instructed him Sulyatitsky left. Kudryavtzev, however, gradually worked his way towards von Launitz and coming close to him on a half-landing on the staircase, drew his pistol and fired three shots at him at point-blank range, then turned the weapon on himself.

The Okhrana had no idea who the dead terrorist was, so Gerassimov ordered his head to be removed, preserved in spirit in a glass jar and put on public exhibition, with the request that anyone who recognised the features should inform the police of the man's identity.

Confronted by this failure, Gerassimov got in touch with Azeff and asked for his help. Azeff responded by telling Gerassimov that Zilberberg had taken over the old headquarters of the Battle Organisation in Finland at the Tourist Hotel for his own base. Though there was no evidence that this group had been responsible for von Launitz's death, Gerassimov decided to suppress it since it was the only group on which he had a lead. He had not long been making plans for doing so when the porter and a maid at the Tourist Hotel came forward to say that though they did not know his name, the man whose head was preserved in spirit had often stayed at the hotel with other men whom Gerassimov was able to identify as two terrorists called Gronsky and Shtiftar, members of Zilberberg's group. (In fact Gronsky was Sulyatitsky, and Shtiftar was Zilberberg.) This evidence made the suppression of the group all the more necessary.

The Tourist Hotel was owned by a Finn sympathetic towards the revolutionaries and he had placed it at their exclusive disposal. All the servants were Finnish and no one who did not belong to the group was admitted to the hotel, would-be guests always being turned away on one excuse or another.

Late one evening towards the end of January, however, a young man and woman who said they were students, arrived and begged for beds. As the weather was very bad and a renewal of blizzards was expected, the manager decided that it was impossible to turn them away, and admitted them.

On the following day the two students revealed themselves as young people of very varied talents. They could sing and dance, they had a large store of anecdotes and their conversation was cheeringly witty. Soon they were accepted by all the other "guests" and as they were not asked to leave they stayed on for a day or two. When they eventually left no one was aware that they were carrying with them photographs of everyone present which the young man had secretly taken.

Gerassimov's task was now easy. He could not seize the group on independent Finnish soil without creating an incident, but he knew that sooner or later they would return to St Petersburg. He could afford to be patient.

The first to fall into his net were Sulyatitsky and Zilberberg who were arrested in St Petersburg at the railway station a week or two later. On the porter's and maid's evidence that they had often been in the company of von Launitz's assassin, they were brought before a court-martial charged with being concerned in the crime, found guilty and hanged on 29th July. They cheated Gerassimov at the end, however, for they never revealed their true identities and were executed as Gronsky and Shtiftar.

If Gerassimov felt powerless where organised groups were concerned he could sometimes by the betrayals of perverted informers, go into action against them; but he had no remedy at all against individuals who made up their minds to perform an act of terror, told no one of their intentions and carried out their purpose.

Such a one was Maria Spiridonova. Her personal act of terror allied her to Zilberberg and his group, though neither knew the other, for the man she killed deserved death as much as von Launitz whose minion he had been.

Chapter Thirty-eight

THE ACT OF MARIA SPIRIDONOVA

Maria Spiridonova lived with her elderly mother and three younger sisters in the town of Tambov, capital of the Government of Tambov, whose governor was General von Launitz. The Spiridonovs were a reasonably well-to-do family and the girls received an education in keeping with their social circumstances. In 1905 at the age of nineteen Maria embarked on a course of nursing and her future seemed assured.

The year is significant. Undercurrents of revolution ran everywhere; they even reached Tambov. Maria and her friends felt the effects of them for there was not one who had not read Tolstoy, Gorky and Andreyev and believed that they saw in the events of these days the fulfilment of the dreams inspired by these great Liberal writers.

On 18th October 1905 demonstrations were held in the streets of Tambov. Maria Spiridonova joined them. She had already decided which camp she would enter, for rejecting Marxism because it based its conclusions exclusively on the point of view of the proletariat she chose as her spiritual guide the Social Revolutionary doctrine of land and liberty. But her allegiance to this party was based on reasons other than purely doctrinal attraction. This was the party which, as the heir of *Narodnaya Volya*, could claim among its heroes the outstanding heroines of the whole revolutionary movement, such women as Sofie Perovskaya, Vera Figner and the Grandmother of the

Revolution, Yekaterina Breshko-Breshkovskaya, whose life had already become a legend.

Meanwhile the reactionaries, receiving their orders from St Petersburg, went from excess to excess. In the year ending April 1906 more than 14,000 people lost their lives. A thousand died on the scaffolds, while 7000 were imprisoned or exiled. Some of these victims were in her own region, whence every day came the stories of atrocities—of peasant huts and granaries burned, of men and women smashed to pulp by the knout.

A Social Democrat, Alexander Dubrovin, went to a village to try to persuade the peasants not to burn the landlords' property because he believed that one day the buildings would be turned into hospitals and schools. But the soldiers, not knowing who he was, seized him and for four days beat him, so that—

> When his relatives went to see him, in the guise of chance travellers, they did not recognise him. Instead of the tall handsome young man, they found a heap of torn flesh, bones and blood. He gasped for breath, and when he asked for water it was refused him. When he crept to the open door for a little fresh air the Cossack shouted: "Get back, you dog!" and beat him back into the corner with his whip.
>
> *(Spiridonova's statement at her trial)*

Behind these atrocities in the Tambov region was General Luzhenovsky, appointed by the governor, General von Launitz, to be special military commandant of the Borissoglebsk district. Luzhenovsky, a Tambov landowner, led punitive expeditions to eighteen villages in person. At his arrival the drums were beaten to call all the villagers together. The immediate surrender of the ringleaders was demanded, and at the same time a wholesale flogging would be begun. When the heavily armed company rode into a village, the peasants received them on their knees. At the entrance to every peasant home men and women knelt with propitiary offerings of bread and salt. But, said Spiridonova, "after his departure the invariable appearance of the villages was that which we generally associate with Bulgarian villages after they have been devastated by the Turks."

Each day Luzhenovsky sent a telegram to von Launitz to acquaint him of his progress. On 6th November 1905, for example, he telegraphed

> Peasants at Beresovka received me on bended knee. They

promised to hand over the ringleaders and surrender stolen property. Explained they were led away by students. Two killed, wounded unknown. Tomorrow I bring Semyonovka to hell.

To which von Launitz replied

Unable to express the extent of my thanks for your energetic action. May God help you! Do not concern yourself with the law. Shoot first, inquire afterwards. Arrest on the slightest suspicion. Sending you presents by special messenger: from my wife two swords and four torches. My thanks to the brave soldiers and to each a present of one rouble. May God protect you.

To Maria Spiridonova, von Launitz the governor was remote; Luzhenovsky, on the other hand, was real and near, and a monster. If the Social Revolutionaries put him on their list of those who should pay the penalty for their cruelty, she would kill him herself.

As soon as Luzhenovsky was listed, Spiridonova acquired a revolver and went in search of him. Like so many of the revolutionaries she believed that she could make no greater contribution to The Cause than the sacrifice of her own life. She fully expected to be seized and hanged for what she was going to do; that was the high privilege which support of the Revolution bestowed on her. So she made no preparations for escape; all she wanted was to be able to get so near to Luzhenovsky that her bullets could not miss.

But this she found more difficult than she had expected. Day after day she dogged his footsteps, spending cold nights in station waiting-rooms, changing from train to train, following him from city to village, from village to city. But he was surrounded always by his Cossacks who seemed deliberately to shield him with their bodies.

Then on 16th January he came to Borissoglebsk. As the train pulled into the station Spiridonova stepped down on to the running-board of her carriage which was next to Luzhenovsky's. With an upsurge of elation she saw him doing something he had never done before—he was leaving the carriage first and was unprotected by the Cossacks who were busy pushing back the press of silent peasants who crowded the platform.

Still clinging to the running-board with one hand, with her muff-hand she aimed at Luzhenovsky and fired. Then she jumped down and ran towards him so as to vary her aim and fired again, several shots. The shots followed one another so quickly that it was impossible to tell how many people were firing. Luzhenovsky staggered and fell to the platform, mortally wounded, though still breathing.

The firing had taken everyone, Cossacks and spectators alike, by surprise. For a moment there was complete silence before pandemonium broke out. Then above the noise could be heard a high shrill voice shouting, "Shoot me! Shoot me!" On turning to see who was shouting the crowd saw a young woman dressed like a school-girl pointing a revolver at her temple.

The Cossack nearest her hit her across the head with his knout and she fell to the ground, dropping the revolver. Avramov, the officer in charge of the Cossacks, sprang forward and seizing a plait of her hair, wound it round his arm and jerked her to her feet with such force that she seemed to leap through the air, at the same time hitting her several blows across the head with his club. Then throwing her back on the ground he ordered his men to whip her and show no mercy.

Avramov had been Luzhenovsky's personal bodyguard. He seemed to have gone quite mad. While he took over the beating and kicking of Spiridonova he commanded the Cossacks to flog everyone present. As the Cossacks began to lay about them everybody tried to run. They caught one old man and beat him till the blood flowed; in their lust they even beat the train guard and a corporal of the gendarmerie.

The beating of Spiridonova, according to some eye-witnesses, was stopped by the station gendarme officer Belanovsky, who pointed out that if she died before she could be questioned they would never be able to trace her accomplices. So they placed her, unconscious, in a cab and drove her to district headquarters. By the time they arrived there she had come round. She was so weak and dazed that she could scarcely move, and she stood leaning against the wall gasping for breath.

"Where is your revolver?" Avramov asked her.

"I dropped it when I was struck at the station," she told him.

"What is your name?" he asked.

"I don't live in this town," she replied.

He repeated the question and she said, "I don't live here. I come from Tambov."

The officer struck her several times about the face.

"Why do you hit me?" she asked. "Take me before the court. Shoot me, but don't hit me."

Presently it was decided to take her to the police-station. Avramov sat beside her in the sleigh. Her head was flung back and her face was cut and bleeding. She was obviously unconscious for Avramov had to support her. It was snowing and the wind streamed out her hair behind her.

At the police-station she was taken into a room and stripped naked. A few days later a police warder who was there was dismissed from his job because he told a friend, "I was freezing in my overcoat and there she was naked. Avramov seized her by the hair and held her up by it with her feet off the ground striking her with the knout while he did so. And she didn't make a sound."

Avramov and the police officer in charge of the station, Zhdanov, were instructed to carry out her preliminary examination. After a time Avramov who had been drinking went away to see Luzhenovsky. The general had been taken to the house of the district chief. He died a few hours later, having been conscious all the time. Once he whispered, "I really did go too far!"

At eleven o'clock that night it was decided to take Spiridonova to Tambov, but she was in such a state that a doctor was detailed to go with her as far as Ternovka. Her escort was Avramov and his Cossacks. He was still very drunk and seemed to have lost his reason, for he kept up a flow of obscene insults and threats. Presently, however, as the train neared Ternovka he calmed down and his manner towards Spiridonova changed. Later Spiridonova complained that after the doctor had left he had unbuttoned her dress and begun to caress her whispering, "Your breasts are as soft as silk. You have a beautiful body," and had tried to rape her.

Zhdanov had also tortured her during Avramov's absence. He kicked her into a corner of the room towards a Cossack, who stamped on her back and then threw her back towards Zhdanov, who put his boot on her throat. Again and again, under this treatment, she became delirious, but she did not betray any of her friends in the Tambov Social Revolutionary Party. No wonder that by the time she reached Tambov prison she was very ill. Nevertheless she was interrogated and confessed that she had killed Luzhenovsky and why.

From Tambov prison she was able to smuggle out a letter to

her revolutionary friends in, which she described everything that had happened to her. The St Petersburg Liberal newspaper *Russ* printed it and soon the name of Spiridonova was known throughout all Russia.

By the beginning of March she had recovered sufficiently to face trial and on 12th March she was arraigned before a court-martial. After the reading of the indictment, since she pleaded guilty, Spiridonova began to read her prepared statement. In it she gave a lucid exposition of her political beliefs and her reasons for killing Luzhenovsky. At the end of three and a half hours she was sentenced to death by hanging, but because there were certain extenuating circumstances this was commuted to penal servitude for life. From now until her death at some unknown date during the Second World War she was to know only sixteen months of freedom, for she fell foul of the Bolshevik regime, was arrested at the Fifth Soviet Congress in 1918 and imprisoned until in 1930 she was banished for life to a remote town in the Urals.

It was against such individual attempts as these that Gerassimov had no antidote. Soon, however, Azeff was to grow tired of inactivity and returned to St Petersburg.

Chapter Thirty-nine

THE PLOT AGAINST THE TSAR

In October 1906 Gershuni, the founder and first leader of the Battle Organisation, who had been caught in the spring of 1903 and had his death sentence commuted to forced labour for life in Siberia, escaped from the convict settlement at Akatui hidden in a barrel of sauerkraut.[1] Making his way via Japan and the United States he returned to Russia early in 1907. Azeff himself had returned a short time before, and at the earliest opportunity Gershuni arranged a meeting with the man whom he had designated his successor to the leadership of the Battle Organisation and whose role in the assassinations of Plehve and the Grand Duke Sergey had greatly impressed him. Gershuni could not envisage the Battle Organisation without Azeff and begged him to take up the leadership of it once again. Azeff responded by saying that if he did not go back to the Organisation he would at least take up active work on behalf of the Party.

Together the two men went to the second Congress of the Social Revolutionary Party which was held at Tammerfors, in Finland, at the end of February 1907. Though Gershuni had adopted the cover-name of Kapustin—from the Russian word *kapusta* meaning *cabbage*—everyone knew who he was and on account of his record and of his recent escape he became the current idol of the Party. Since Azeff was Gershuni's disciple,

[1] A full account of this exciting incident may be found in *Spiridonova* by L. Steinberg (London: Methuen, 1935.)

some of the glory heaped upon the man who had been one of the most active members of the Party brushed off onto him, and he was re-elected to the Central Committee, greatly to Gerassimov's delight.

Now, though the executions of Sulyatitsky and Zilberberg had been a disaster of the first order, their group did not break up. It had, in fact, built up a very influential connection; so influential that they felt justified in planning attempts on the Grand Duke Nicholas by blowing up his train, and on Stolypin, by a mass attack on the Winter Palace. From such plans as these it was but a short step towards plotting an attempt against the Tsar himself.

In 1902, it will be recalled, the Central Committee had laid a ban on the Battle Organisation forbidding it to make any attempt on the Tsar's life. This decision had been taken because at that time the Tsar's role had not been properly understood; to all outward appearances he seemed to be holding himself aloof from politics. From the slogans which had been carried in the processions on Bloody Sunday, it was clear that he was regarded affectionately by the masses as the Little Father of all his Peoples. This was particularly true of the peasants. Since the October uprising of 1905, however, his real involvement had become plain and the feelings of the people towards him had changed. The Central Committee ban, however, was still in force.

An attempt against the Tsar had first been mooted by Zilberberg, who had consulted Kraft, the Battle Organisation's representative on the Central Committee, and he in turn had discussed it with Chernov and Natanson, who, while concluding that an attempt should be made, decided that the right moment for it had not yet arrived. This had been the situation when, after Zilberberg's death, the leadership of the group had been taken over by Nikitenko, a retired naval lieutenant, who had been converted to Socialism as a result of his experiences during the mutiny in the Black Sea Fleet. He had helped Savinkov to escape from Sevastopol, and in 1906 had offered his services to the Battle Organisation. He was only twenty-two or -three, a factor which doubtless played a part in subsequent events.

When Zilberberg had designed his plan for killing the Tsar he had made contact with Naumov, the son of the manager of the palace telephone exchange in New Peterhoff, where the Tsar seemed to have decided to live permanently. Zilberberg's motive in forming this friendship was to try to discover from Naumov the times at which Stolypin and the Grand Duke Nicholas visited the Tsar. In the course of their talks Naumov had told Zilberberg that he knew an officer in the Tsar's guard who was sympathetic towards the revolutionaries. This had first put the idea of an attempt against the Tsar into Zilberberg's head, and he and Naumov had discussed one or two possible plans of campaign.

Nikitenko was at Tammerfors for the congress and there was introduced to Azeff. He was finding collecting information about Stolypin's and the Grand Duke's movements, as well as exploring the possibilities of an attack on the Tsar rather beyond his capabilities. Somewhat naturally he sought the advice of the former leader of the Battle Organisation and revealed to Azeff all the group's plans, including the attempt on the Tsar's life. He pressed Azeff to take over the leadership of the group, but this Azeff refused to do on the grounds that he knew none of the members of the group and could not be sure that there was not an Okhrana agent among them, though his real motive was that he had decided to betray the plan to Gerassimov.

This turned out to be one of the wisest decisions he ever made, for as it happened the group had been penetrated. The guards officer Ratimov, was, in fact, acting as a secret agent on the instructions of General Spiridovich, commander of the Palace Police. He was not a revolutionary fellow-traveller, but a hard-drinker and spender, and he was playing the role purely for money.

As soon as he returned from Tammerfors, Azeff told Gerassimov all he had learned from Nikitenko, including the information that the group had "established some sort of relations with the Tsar's guards." He also said that the Central Committee had lifted the ban on attempts against the Tsar, so Gerassimov ought to be particularly on his guard.

Gerassimov at once set his men on watching the Nikitenko group, but he failed to discover Ratimov. However, when he was on the point of arresting the group, Spiridovich revealed his part in trying to detect the plotters and Ratimov's role, and together they pooled their evidence and placed it before Stolypin.

Stolypin recognised immediately what a political weapon the two policemen had put into his hands. The Second Duma, in which the Left predominated, was on the point of meeting, and the Prime Minister was determined to dissolve it as soon as he could find a suitable excuse. What better excuse, he argued, than a sensational trial of terrorists for plotting to kill the Tsar?

So Gerassimov was instructed to collect as much evidence as possible as quickly as possible. This was not difficult and on 14th April he arrested twenty-eight members of the Battle Organisation. This was practically the whole of the group. At the preliminary investigation Naumov, a new-comer to terror and psychologically unprepared for the inevitable end of all trapped terrorists, offered to turn informer in return for his life. This clinched the case for the prosecution.

Immediately the arrests had been made, Stolypin launched his attack in the Duma. The attempt on the Tsar's life, he said, had been planned on the direct orders of the Central Committee of the Social Revolutionary Party. As he knew it would, this claim greatly embarrassed the Social Revolutionary deputies who, as the political representatives of the Party, would shoulder the whole responsibility before the people. They were not directly in touch with the Battle Organisation and knew nothing of its plans, and when they approached Chernov he denied that the Central Committee had lifted the ban. The speech in which Deputy Shirsky made this assertion did not, however, carry conviction. This led to the confusion that Stolypin had hoped to create among the moderates and progressives in the Duma, which greatly weakened them and automatically strengthened the reactionary parties.

Eighteen of the twenty-eight arrested men were brought before a court-martial at the end of August. The denial of the Central Committee that they had approved the plot naturally made it impossible for the accused to put their case forcibly since they could not claim the backing of the whole Party.

Though Naumov retracted part of his confession this did not help them either. It also proved fatal to him, for it gave the authorities an excuse for withdrawing their promise not to sentence him to death. Fifteen of the prisoners received life sentences; Nikitenko, and a former student called Sinyavsky were sentenced to death and executed on 3rd September 1907.

Gerassimov gave his full protection to Azeff, who, a few days before the arrests were made, went down to the Crimea "for reasons of health." His name was not mentioned at the trial, Ratimov's part alone being disclosed.

Chapter Forty

KARL'S FLYING DETACHMENTS

The outcome of the *Plot against the Tsar* once more destroyed the Battle Organisation, and of the three groups in the St Petersburg area only Karl's Flying Detachment remained intact. Despite their denial that they had not approved Nikitenko's plan, the Central Committee now decided that the Tsar must be killed and to this end ordered the reconstitution of the Battle Organisation. So that the latter could concentrate on the Tsar's assassination all other acts of terror were confided to Karl's group.

The outlook for the Russian people in the weeks and months following upon the trial of the Nikitenko group was a bleak one. The mass movement had been stamped out and in every sphere of life reaction was triumphant. The proletariat were silent and morose, the peasants writhed dispiritedly under the lash of repression. There were no strikes, no demonstrations of any sort. The Tsar and autocracy had emerged successful after all.

In these conditions it would have been a miracle indeed had the revolutionaries not reflected the common mood of despair. This mood was revealed in a withdrawal of men and women from participation in revolutionary activities. Where previously there had been a glad acceptance of self-denial so that the movement might have life, now people began to think of themselves. The search for pleasure replaced the old revolutionary discipline; the rights of the individual took the place of the rights of society.

Though it seemed as if the revolutionary movement might be moribund, if not actually dead, there were still one or two who resisted the general mood. They possessed stronger wills than the rest and were more sincere in their convictions, but since they could not count any more on the masses they decided that they would carry on as best they could, deciding for themselves the course along which they would conduct their private struggles. Those who made up their minds to continue the terror did so in a desire for revenge rather than with any hope of victory. As Boris Nikolayevsky has put it, "In the days when the masses were still inactive individual terrorists had begun the struggle in the vanguard, now, when the masses had already ceased to be active, these individual terrorists were the last to leave the field of battle, covering the retreat of the revolutionary army by a rearguard action."

Karl's Flying Detachment, though a closely knit group, presented the paradox of being composed of individual terrorists of the type just described. The very antithesis of the Battle Organisation who conceived things on a grand scale and never stopped to count the cost, Karl's men lived entirely independently of Party funds, and not only financed their own activities but actually subscribed as well to the Party coffers.

Nominally the affairs of the group were directed by Karl from the group's headquarters in Finland, but the basis of all its activities was so democratic that if any member wished to take a personal initiative, he was encouraged to do so. Furthermore, Karl's men never made their own preparations, which were all done for them by sympathisers. When the preparations were complete those chosen would arrive in St Petersburg, make their attempt and immediately retreat into Finland, where the Russian police were unable to touch them.

The assassination of General Pavlov, the chief military prosecutor, provides a good example of Karl's method of working. Fully alive to the fact that he was a natural target for the terrorists, Pavlov rarely left his private apartment in the military building. But even there he was not safe, for Karl's men found sympathisers among the clerks who worked for the tribunal. One of these supplied the information that every day at a certain hour the general took a constitutional in the grounds of the building. There one day, Igorov, one of the leaders of the

Kronstadt mutiny, disguised as a courier, got into the grounds and shot Pavlov dead.

The chief interest of the Detachment was those prison administrators who, in the triumph of reaction embarked upon a campaign of cruelty towards political prisoners in their charge. This so-called Prison Terror characterised the years following upon Stolypin's victory over the Duma in 1907 and succeeding Dumas. But the free revolutionaries kept a protective eye on their imprisoned comrades and did not hesitate to take reprisals against the worst official offenders. One of Karl's earliest victims of this type was Borodulin, governor of Algachi prison in Siberia, and the first governor to order the flogging of political prisoners. They caught him in Pskov, as he was returning from the house of the prison governor there. While one man seized the horses' reins, another jumped on to the carriage running-board and shot him dead. Unfortunately the actual executioner was caught, taken before a court-martial the same day, condemned to death and hanged the next.

Not long afterwards a young twenty-one-year-old woman called Tolya Ragosinikova went into the reception-room at the headquarters of the prison department in St Petersburg and asked to see Maximovsky, head of the department. She was elegantly dressed and perfumed, and the attendant was impressed. So, apparently, was Maximovsky, for he consented to see her. Immediately she was shown in to him she pulled a revolver and shot him dead.

She could have escaped in the confusion that followed, but chose instead to stand her ground. She was taken into a room and matrons were called to search her. As they approached her she cried out, "Be careful, you'll all be blown up!" The women backed away and the officers hurriedly consulted. They decided to send for an artillery officer and when he arrived she protested vehemently against being searched, for she had hoped and expected to be taken to Okhrana headquarters.

The officer seems to have been shrewd, determined and foolhardy. He walked straight up to her without comment, pinioned her arms and tripped her up so that she lay on her back on the ground. While he held her down the matrons stripped her and discovered that she had been uttering no idle threat. In her corsets they found three pounds of dynamite complete with detonators and fuse.

On the following day she was court-martialled. She refused to say a word throughout the whole proceedings. Two days later she was hanged.

Karl's Detachment was planning other attempts similar to these when Azeff and Gershuni received orders from the Central Committee to take over the direction of the group's activities. These plans included attempts on the lives of Shcheglovitov, the Minister of Justice, Dratchevsky, the military commander of the St Petersburg region and Gershelman, military commander of the Moscow region, while Karl himself was supervising preparations for a scheme to blow up the Cabinet while it was in session with the State Council. All the details of this programme were submitted to the two controllers, who gave their approval. Azeff, though in a position to frustrate all the plans, had decided once more to operate on the side of the revolutionaries, but though attempts were made on Shcheglovitov, Dratchevsky and Gershelman, all were unsuccessful.

The man who had put up the plan for wiping out the Cabinet was an intellectual called Lebedintzev. He was a brilliant linguist, a specialist in astronomy and mathematics, a gifted artist and musician. He had lived in Italy for some years on an Italian passport in the name of Mario Calvino, and as Calvino had obtained the post of correspondent in St Petersburg for an important Italian newspaper. This had given him the entree to the press gallery of the State Council and the Duma, and it was while he sat listening to the proceedings of the former that he conceived his plan for blowing it up. It was too extensive a scheme for him to undertake on his own, so he had asked Karl's Detachment to help him.

Now, though Azeff had not interfered with Karl's lesser plans he seems to have become afraid that the success of this major project would damage his prestige with the police. On the other hand if he betrayed the plan directly this held equally grave risks from the other side. So, while not mentioning anything to Gerassimov he began a systematic obstruction of Karl's preparations. This latter led to very strained relations between the members of the Detachment and Azeff, and soon there was talk of disobeying the Central Committee and making the attempt at their own risk.

By this they appear to have frightened Azeff into betraying them directly to Gerassimov, though he gave the latter little

information which would have justified a move against Karl.
Azeff pressed, however, for the arrest of Karl, saying to the
Okhrana chief, "You will have little peace until he is behind
bars."

A little later he told Gerassimov of the plot to blow up the
State Council, but again he gave few useful details, maintaining
that the project was being considered by the Central Committee.
He himself, he said, had spoken against the plan in the Committee, but there was a possibility of the Detachment defying
the Committee and he urged that precautionary steps should be
taken at once.

Gerassimov needed no second warning. Knowing that the
Detachment's headquarters were "somewhere in Finland" he
put every available detective on to watch all Finnish railway
stations. Presently two mysterious apartments were found near
Kelomyak station, and on 5th December 1907 with Stolypin's
blessing Gerassimov violated Finnish territory, raided the apartments and arrested two unidentified women and a man found
there.

Much more important than this, however, was the discovery
made in one flat of full details of the plan to blow up the State
Council, a discovery which at once destroyed all hopes of carrying the scheme out. Since the man arrested with the women was
Karl himself, the rest of the group appointed Lebedintzev as
their leader, and he at once set about devising plans for the
assassination of the Grand Duke Nicholas and the Minister of
Justice as they drove to the Tsar's New Year's Day levée.

This scheme was betrayed to Gerassimov by another agent on
New Year's Eve and he immediately advised the Minister and
the Grand Duke not to leave their homes until he gave the all-
clear, a move which successfully thwarted the attempts. During
the next six weeks, however, the Detachment intensified their
efforts. With nerves at breaking point they went out daily with
bombs hoping to encounter the Grand Duke or the Minister,
both of whom remained house-bound on Gerassimov's advice.

Gerassimov has written that during this time he asked Azeff
for information which would make it possible for him to act
against the terrorists, but Azeff insisted that he knew no more
than he had told him. In fact, he was in almost daily contact
with the Detachment. Presently, however, he seems to have
taken pity on Gerassimov and gave him a clue. He understood,

he said, that a former political prisoner called Anna Rasputina was connected with the Detachment.

This was enough for Gerassimov. He put out a drag-net for Rasputina and quickly found her. She was kept under constant surveillance and all her contacts noted.

On 20th February 1908 Gerassimov went into action. Nine terrorists were arrested, three of them in possession of bombs and three of firearms, while in the rooms of the others explosives were found. They were immediately court-martialled, and seven, including three women, were sentenced to death and executed the same day. A short time later Karl and other members of the Detachment already in custody were brought to trial and executed.

The Flying Detachment had been wiped from the face of the earth.

Chapter Forty-one

THE BEGINNING OF AZEFF'S END

The events of the autumn and winter of 1905–6, besides shaking the regime to its foundations, also had a deleterious effect on the Political Police, which was revealed most glaringly in the number of police officials who went to the revolutionaries with betrayals of the Department's secrets. Among such officers was one Bakay, who a few years previously had been arrested for having revolutionary connections, had recanted and became a secret police agent.

Most of the officers sought out the Central Committee for their betrayals. Bakay did not. Instead he went to V. L. Burtzev, editor of an historical review, *Byloye (The Past)*.

At first Burtzev was not inclined to accept his stories, but when careful investigation began to prove that he was invariably speaking the truth, Burtzev had to change his opinion. On his advice, Bakay resigned from the police and devoted his time to compiling his memoirs. Azeff got wind of what was happening and put in a report to Gerassimov, who immediately had Bakay arrested and sent to Siberia by administrative process. Bakay escaped almost at once and fled abroad, from where he supplied Burtzev with yet more exposures.

Now, among the information that Bakay gave to Burtzev was an item which claimed that a police agent known as Raskin had penetrated the Central Committee of the Social Revolutionary Party. He could say very little about Raskin personally, but he did know some of the details of the man's activities, and from these Burtzev had to conclude that the traitor was to be found among the leaders of the Party.

Burtzev knew all the Party leaders including Azeff, very well and there was not one of them whom he could believe filled the role described by Bakay. Yet Bakay's information could not be disregarded.

Then quite fortuitously one day he was given a kind of indirect clue. It was the late autumn of 1906 and the police were making widespread arrests, which made it necessary for the revolutionary leaders to comport themselves with the greatest discretion. Yet as he passed down the street he saw Azeff riding by quite calmly in an open cab!

This struck him as very odd, and at first he could not believe that the director of terror was a police agent; yet only if he was sure of immunity from arrest would he dare to appear as openly as this. However, as he went over all he knew about Azeff's terrorist activities, "Unexpectedly to myself even, I asked myself whether Raskin and Azeff were not one and the same person. It seemed a monstrous idea yet I was forced to admit that the more I weighed the suggestion the more plausible did it become."

From this moment Burtzev embarked on his long fight to expose Azeff. For Azeff it was the beginning of the end.

Azeff, aware of Burtzev's suspicions, arranged for the elimination of his source of information. From this moment his relationship with Gerassimov underwent a change, and he began to withhold a good deal of information from him.

On his return to revolutionary activity in February 1907 Azeff had engaged only in general organisational tasks, such as the setting up of printing presses and so on. But Gershuni soon began to agitate for the revival of terror and despite, or because of, the failure of Nikitenko's plot against the Tsar, urged the Central Committee, immediately after the dissolution of the Second Duma, to make the Tsar's death the main target of the Party. The Central Committee were persuaded and orders were given for the Battle Organisation to be revived once more. Naturally the leadership was offered to Azeff; surprisingly he accepted it—but did not tell Gerassimov. After some preliminary skirmishing with Savinkov over the methods to be adopted Azeff found his control of the Organisation as complete as it had ever been.

He was given unlimited funds and a free hand in choosing the Organisation's personnel. He chose for his second-in-command Karpovich, who, besides the assassination of Bogolepov, Minister of Education, in February 1901, had a number of terrorist acts to his credit.

Azeff went about the preparatory work very carefully, and there was not one who did not believe that he was doing everything he could to assure the success of the attempt. Contrary to his usual practice he spoke of his plans at some length in the Central Committee, giving his reason for doing so the complexity of the task and his own isolation caused by the death of Gershuni towards the end of 1907.

He explained that two alternatives seemed to offer themselves. The first was to kill the Tsar when he was out hunting; the second when he went to Reval (Tallinn) for a meeting with King Edward VII of England. He made preparations for both.

But he had no intention of allowing either to come to fruition, and he gave Gerassimov most of the details. Gerassimov still had the greatest confidence in Azeff and did everything he could to safeguard him. He undertook to make no arrests, and if any took place without his prior knowledge he skilfully arranged "escapes".

Up to now Azeff had always managed to keep his family affairs well in the background. Very early on in his double career he had married a young and very sincere revolutionary by whom he had three children. The Party knew of this family and looked upon him as a devoted husband and father.

But in his private life he had been playing a double role, too. He had a passion for casual love-making, and whenever he was abroad he gave full rein to it, spending night after night in brothels.

In the winter of 1907-8 Azeff was approaching forty, the age when men of this kind usually tend to begin to become a little more staid. But he realised, too, that if he were ever exposed it would mean the break-up of his marriage, since his wife would never have anything more to do with him if she ever discovered the double role he had been playing. So as an insurance, it would seem, against loneliness, he now took a permanent mistress, a cabaret-singer known as La Bella Heddy de Hero, or Madame N.

Mme N was quite a beautiful woman, and if not much of a

singer possessed other talents which made her very popular in
the very highest circles of gay society. On the face of it, it is a
mystery how such a woman could take such an unprepossessing
man as Azeff as her lover. But he represented himself as a
prosperous merchant, was kind, considerate and generous, and
perhaps for the first time brought into Mme N's life an element
of stability. At all events, they set up an establishment together.

All this might have been accepted in due course by both the
Party and the police, had it not been for the fact that Azeff's
lavish presents of jewellery to Mme N began to raise suspicions
about where he got the money to pay for them. Gerassimov was
moved to have a private word with his prize agent, to which
Azeff responded that if his love for Mme N was to be held to be
an impediment to his work, he had better resign. Gerassimov
agreed that he deserved a rest after fifteen years of constant risk
to his life; all he asked was that Azeff should defer his retirement
until the plot against the Tsar had been frustrated; to which
Azeff consented.

About this time Karpovich was accidentally arrested. The
incident upset Azeff inordinately. Gerassimov has recorded that
he called on him and launched at once into an hysterical scene.
Gerassimov agreed that the arrest could seriously compromise
Azeff with the Party, and promised to arrange Karpovich's
"escape".

Azeff now hurried forward his preparations for the plot
against the Tsar. He abandoned the plan for killing while hunting and concentrated on the visit to Reval. He made several
alternative plans with the Battle Organisation, but in the event,
all were thwarted, and the Tsar's visit passed off without a hitch.

Azeff had believed that the revolutionaries must connect the
failure of the plan with him and had definitely decided to retire
and go abroad and settle down with Mme N. To his relief, however, the Party gave no sign of such suspicions. He nevertheless
carried out his plan for retiring from the police service and going
abroad, but at the same time undertook to investigate on behalf
of the Party the possibilities for carrying out yet another attempt
on Nicholas's life.

Leaving Mme N in Germany in June 1908 he hurried to
Glasgow where a new cruiser for the Russian fleet, the *Rurik*,
was being built by Vickers. With the help of a naval engineer,
Rostenko, he went aboard the cruiser with the aim of exploring

the possibilities for assassinating the Tsar when the latter inspected the cruiser on her arrival at Kronstadt. He looked especially for places in which two assassins might be concealed, but he had to report that no such spots existed.

So the Party had to abandon this idea, and it concentrated instead on finding two volunteers among the crew prepared to die for killing the Tsar. They found them in a sailor, Gerassim Avdeyev, and a signaller Kaptelovich. They were to shoot the Tsar while he was inspecting the *Rurik*.

The Tsar carried out his inspection on 7th October. Both the intended assassins had excellent opportunities for killing him. But neither made any attempt. The explanation they subsequently gave was that their intention had been discovered by the other members of the crew who were themselves planning to mutiny and seize Kronstadt. These conspirators persuaded the two men not to carry out their plan since subsequent police investigations would be bound to uncover the plans to mutiny.

So this last attempt of Azeff failed through no fault of his. That it was his last undertaking for either side was due to the indefatigable Burtzev.

Chapter Forty-two

EXPOSURE

While all this had been going on Burtzev had been desperately trying to collect irrefutable evidence to prove that Raskin and Azeff were the same person. Though he had no documentary proof or other certain evidence, he was so convinced by this time that Azeff was the traitor that he no longer bothered to keep his suspicions to himself, and he found that he was not alone in thinking as he did.

The continued failures of the Battle Organisation had at last forced some to consider seriously the possibility of treachery, and investigations proved that this must be so and that the traitor was Azeff. Like Burtzev, however, these men had no definite proof, and they were very few in number.

Burtzev learned of this, and decided to take drastic action. Learning that Azeff would be attending the Party conference to be held in London in August 1908, Burtzev wrote to his old friend Teplov and made a direct accusation of treachery against Azeff. Teplov put the letter before the Central Committee, which to a man refused to believe the accusations and proposed putting Burtzev on trial for libelling Azeff.

Still Burtzev could not bring himself to give up the struggle and now suddenly he had an idea. There was one man who might be able to provide the evidence he was looking for—Lopuhin, the former police chief. The problem that now faced him was how to draw Lopuhin, whom he knew well, into conversation and persuade him to divulge the truth.

With considerable skill Burtzev set about doing just this. He learned that on a certain day Lopukhin would be travelling in the Eastern Express from Cologne to Berlin. Burtzev went to Cologne and boarded the train. When it was some miles out of the city, he went along the corridor and finding Lopukhin alone in a compartment went in, expressed surprise at seeing him there and asked if he might join him.

Lopukhin was agreeable and after a few preliminary inconsequentialities Burtzev announced that in the coming number of *Byloye* he was proposing to expose the activities of a very important police agent who was also the leader of the Battle Organisation. At first Lopukhin seemed uninterested, and to gain his attention Burtzev asked if he might tell him all he had discovered about this agent. Lopukhin was willing, but again made little response until Burtzev came to the assassination of Plehve.

Plehve had played a major role in the development of Lopukhin's own career, and his death had been the first step in Lopukhin's decline. He had sentiments of a special kind for the murdered man, and on hearing Burtzev claim that the double-agent had actually planned the assassination he said, "You are quite sure of this, Vladimir Lvovich?"

"Quite sure, Alexey Alexandrovich," Burtzev assured him.

Lopukhin was silent for some moments then he said, "I have not heard of Raskin, but I have seen the engineer Yevno Azeff several times."

"Of course," Burtzev recounted later, "this name was no surprise to me. For over a year it had been running through my head at every moment. But when I heard it from Lopukhin's lips, it struck me like a thunderbolt."

The two men continued their conversation until Berlin was reached, but it was now Lopukhin who did most of the talking. Immediately on arriving in St Petersburg Burtzev sat down and wrote an open letter to the members of the Social Revolutionary Party in which he renewed his accusations against Azeff. This time the Central Committee decided to bring Burtzev before a court of honour and such a court was convened in Paris. Among the judges were three veteran revolutionaries, Vera Figner, Lopatin and Krapotkin. Chernov, Natanson and Savinkov represented the Central Committee.

At first Burtzev put forward his evidence without mentioning Lopukhin's name, but when he found that none of his judges would believe him, he decided to break his promise to Lopukhin. He related the meeting in the train, and "When I repeated Lopukhin's words...everybody jumped up and began talking at once." The situation was completely changed, and after a brief consultation the judges announced that they would have to verify Lopukhin's story. At the same time, for the first time, orders were given for a full investigation into Azeff's activities.

Azeff had been fully aware of Burtzev's accusations and had actually taken part in drawing up the procedure the court of honour was to follow. He had then left Paris, having refused to appear before the court as he was "too disgusted to wallow in the mud Burtzev was stirring up." He entrusted his defence to his close friends in the Party.

At first Azeff had not been particularly worried about the trial, but when he heard about the Lopukhin conversation with Burtzev he became alarmed and hurried to Paris to try to defend himself. On arrival there, however, he found that the situation was much worse than he had expected.

Really frightened, unknown to his comrades, he went post haste to St Petersburg to try to persuade Lopukhin to retract before Argunov came to question him. Gerassimov accompanied him on his visits to Lopukhin, but they could do nothing to make him change his mind. In fact, their efforts persuaded him to go the whole way, and when Argunov arrived he told him all he knew of Azeff's connection with the police and offered to go to London to repeat the story to Savinkov and Chernov.

On 5th January 1909 the Central Committee called a meeting of the Party leaders to decide what should be done. The death sentence was voted but this was not unanimous and it was agreed that some quiet way of disposing of Azeff must be found to avoid causing a split in the Party, for many would still not believe in Azeff's guilt.

When the news of this decision reached him, Azeff prepared at once to flee. At half-past three in the morning of 6th January 1909 he slipped out of his apartment, and took the train for Vienna. The next several months he spent on a "honeymoon" with Mme N in Italy, Greece, Egypt, Sweden, Norway and Denmark. Then he disappeared from public view.

Chapter Forty-three

AFTER AZEFF

The Azeff affair had a devastating effect on the whole Social Revolutionary movement, and particularly on its attitude towards terror.

When the first sensation had worn off, Savinkov had proposed that the honour of the Battle Organisation must be vindicated. He knew only one way in which this could be done—by resurrecting the Organisation itself. He made an appeal and chose twelve from those who came forward to form his group. All of them were veterans and it seemed that if anyone could succeed in their appointed task, they must.

In fact it all turned into a fiasco. Savinkov, the leader, lost his courage and wandered aimlessly abroad, while three of the twelve were eventually revealed as traitors.

In one of his articles on the Azeff affair, Chernov wrote, "The terror was not begun by Azeff and will not end with him." Only the first half of this statement proved to be true. Some time later, Sletov, while travelling secretly in Russia, felt constrained to report that everywhere there was either indifference to or prejudice against terror. "My impression is that even if the Party succeeded in killing the Tsar himself most of its members would suspect it to be the result of provocation."

From now until the Revolution, there were only isolated acts of terror mostly performed by individuals. The outstanding among them was that carried out by Bagrov in the summer of 1911.

The Tsar was paying a visit to Kiev. In his suite was the Prime Minister, Stolypin. A few days after the arrival of the Court in Kiev a former secret police agent, Bagrov, called on the local Okhrana and reported that he knew the details of a plot against the Tsar which the Kievan revolutionaries had prepared. His story was convincing, and the already stringent security arrangements were strengthened even further.

The royal programme included a gala performance at the Kiev Theatre. General Kurlov, chief of the Special Police, intensified his protective measures. No one who was not at once identifiable as safe was to be allowed near the theatre.

Shortly after the performance had begun Bagrov came to the theatre saying he had some important information for Lieutenant Kulyabko, chief of the Kiev Special Police. Kulyabko saw him, told him he was exaggerating and ordered him to go home. Unfortunately Kulyabko did not make sure that Bagrov obeyed his last order.

A few minutes later several shots rang out across the auditorium, and Stolypin was seen to collapse. He was severely wounded and died two days later.

Postscript

On 12th June 1915 a German detective inspector approached a Herr Alexander Neumayer, a stockbroker, and his wife as they made their way home after dining out.

"I have reason to believe that you are Eugen Azeff, a Russian," said the detective. "Will you please come with me?"

Neumayer submissively did as he was bid, and at the police station admitted that his real name was Azeff. He believed that he had been arrested because of his former connection with the Russian police, but soon learned that he was being held as a dangerous revolutionary and terrorist, who, according to international police conventions, was to be handed to the Russian authorities at the end of the war. Despite his energetic denials, he was held in custody. After a short time he fell ill and was transferred to the hospital of the Moabit prison where he was kept in solitary confinement until his release at the end of 1917, after the collapse of the tsarist regime and Russia's withdrawal from the war.

His imprisonment had seriously affected his health and about the middle of April 1918 he entered hospital with kidney trouble. His condition quickly deteriorated and at four o'clock in the afternoon of 24th April he died. He was buried in the Wilmersdorf cemetery two days later, his only mourner—Madame N.

Bibliography

Sir Bernard Pares, A History of Russia. (London, 1926.)
F. Venturi, Roots of Revolution. (London, 1960.)
E. Lampert, Studies in Rebellion. (London, 1957.)
A. Yarmolinsky, Road to Revolution. (London, 1957.)
B. Wolfe, Three Who Made a Revolution. (London, 1956.)
D. Footman, Red Prelude. (London, 1944.)
B. Nikolaeevsky, Azeff: the Russian Judas. (London, 1934.)
A. T. Vasilyev, The Okhrana. (London, 1930.)
A. I. Spiridovich, Histoire du térrorisme russe. (Paris, 1926.)
I. N. Steinberg, Spiridonova. (London, 1935.)
I. Deutscher, The Prophet Armed. (London, 1954.)
E. H. Carr, The Romantic Exiles. (London, 1933.)
P. Krapotkin, Memoirs of a Revolutionary. (London, 1899.)
V. Figner, Mémoires d'une révolutionnaire. (Paris, 1930.)
B. Savinkov, Memoirs of a Terrorist. (New York, 1931.)
S. Hargreave, First Blood. (New York, 1964.)
N. V. Riasanovsky, A History of Russia. (New York, 1963.)
General Gerassimov, Mémoires. (Paris, 1934.)
Theodore Dan, The Origins of Bolshevism. (London, 1964.)

INDEX

23, 000, 000

100, 000

31. JAN. 1967